THE MAKING OF THE MIDDLE AGES

Crucifixion from the Gospels of Countess Judith (English, prob. 1050–65)

THE MAKING OF THE
MIDDLE AGES

R. W. SOUTHERN

NEW HAVEN & LONDON
YALE UNIVERSITY PRESS

First published, August 1953.
Twenty-seventh printing, 1980.

Printed in the United States of America by
BookCrafters, Inc., Fredericksburg, Virginia.

Published in Canada and the Philippines by
Yale University Press and elsewhere by
Hutchinson & Co., Ltd., London.

ISBN: 0–300–00967–4 (cloth), 0–300–00230–0 (paper)

CONTENTS

ILLUSTRATIONS

Pierpont Morgan Library, New York, Morgan M.S. 709, f. 16. *frontispiece*

The Gospel Book of which this picture forms part belonged to Judith of Flanders, wife of Earl Tostig of Northumbria, who is probably depicted in the female figure clinging to the Cross. All the evidence of style (as Professor Wormald kindly tells me) is compatible with a date in the third quarter of the eleventh century, and it is probable that the manuscript was made for the Countess Judith while she was in England, between about 1051 and 1065. The manuscript is certainly of English origin. It was taken abroad by the Countess in 1065, and (her husband having been killed at the battle of Stamford Bridge in the following year) she never returned to England. She later married Welf IV, Duke of Bavaria, and on her death she left the manuscript with several others to the monastery of Weingarten in southern Germany. Here it remained until the Napoleonic Wars, when it began the journeys which brought it back to England for nearly a century, and finally took it across the Atlantic to the Pierpont Morgan Library in New York. For a history of the manuscript, see M. Harrsen, *The Countess Judith of Flanders and the Library of Weingarten Abbey*, Papers of the Bibliographical Society of America, 1930, XXIV, 1-13; and for its place in eleventh-century English Illumination, F. Wormald, *The Survival of Anglo-Saxon Illumination after the Norman Conquest* (British Academy Hertz Lecture, 1944).

Tree of Jesse (Cîteaux, 1110–1120). Dijon, Bibliothèque Municipal, MS. 641, f. 40 verso. (Photograph: Remy, Dijon.) *facing page* 240

For the bibliography of this manuscript, see below p. 239.

The Aaby Crucifix (Copenhagen, National Museum, II, No. D. 629). *between pages* 240 and 241

The Tirstrup Crucifix (Copenhagen, National Museum, II, No. D. 5100). *between pages* 240 and 241

These two Danish crucifixes are discussed in relation to the other works of the period in P. Nörlund, *Gyldne Altre* (Copenhagen, 1926), pp. 61-8, figs. 40 and 42; and pp. 99-106, figs. 77-81, 84-6.

ABBREVIATIONS

D.H.G.E.	*Dictionnaire d'histoire et de géographie ecclésiastiques*, ed. A. Baudrillart, A. Vogt, U. Rouziès, etc. (1912–).
E.H.R.	*English Historical Review.*
M.G.H.	*Monumenta Germaniae Historica.*
P.L.	*Patrologiae Cursus Completus, series latina*, ed. J. P. Migne.
R.S.	Rolls Series
Schmitt	*Sancti Anselmi Opera Omnia*, ed. F. S. Schmitt, O.S.B., (vols. 1–5, 1938–51).

PREFACE

THIS book owes its existence in the first place to Sir Maurice Powicke who suggested that I should write it. His influence pervades it in many ways which I should find it difficult to describe, but which will be discernible to all those who know his work. The same may be said of the many conversations with Professor V. H. Galbraith, which over now more than twenty years have helped to form my attitude to the subjects discussed in this book. To both these scholars I owe a great and abiding debt which is only partially reflected in the pages which follow. My obligations to Dr. R. W. Hunt are almost equally extensive. I have turned to him in every difficulty, and there is perhaps no section of this book which does not owe something to his wide and generous learning. My wife has read the book at every stage, and I have relied on her judgement at innumerable points. Mrs. R. F. I. Bunn has put me deeply in her debt by reading the proofs with a searching eye and by making the index. Miss M. J. Crook eased my labour by the care and skill which she devoted to the typing of the manuscript; and the forbearance of Sister M. H. Barker and the nurses of the Osler Pavilion, Oxford, made it possible to use some months of illness in writing a large part of the text which follows. To all these, and to others who have helped me, I offer my warmest thanks.

I have also to thank the following scholars and institutions for permission to reproduce the illustrations in this book: Professor F. Wormald, the Oxford University Press, the British Academy and the Pierpont Morgan Library for permission to reproduce the frontispiece, and to use the block prepared for Professor Wormald's lecture on "The Survival of Anglo-Saxon Illumination after the Norman Conquest"; the National Museum, Copenhagen, for Plates II and III; the Librarian of the Bibliothèque Municipale at Dijon for Plate I, and the Director of the Archives Centrales Iconographiques d'Art National at Brussels for Plate IV.

Finally, it is a pleasure to acknowledge with gratitude the patience and long-suffering of my publishers, and the help of

Mrs. John Klauber of Messrs. Hutchinson, during the period of
protracted labour, which the making of this book had as a
common characteristic with the making of the Middle Ages
themselves.

BALLIOL   COLLEGE,   R. W. SOUTHERN.
OXFORD.
30th November, 1952

INTRODUCTION

THE formation of western Europe from the late tenth to the early thirteenth century is the subject of this book. The two dates within which it could most conveniently be framed are 972 and 1204. In these years there occurred two events, of very unequal importance in the public eye but not so unequally matched in their suggestion of new opportunities in thought and politics. It was in the first of these years in all probability that the scholar Gerbert, a young man at the height of his powers and bursting with intellectual life, having absorbed the scientific learning of Italy and the Spanish March, felt himself called to the study of logic and moved from Rome to Rheims for that purpose. The works which he wrote, the methods of teaching he devised and the pupils he taught at Rheims became the most important factor in the advancement of learning in northern Europe during the next two generations—particularly in enlarging the scope of the study of logic and in forwarding that reconquest of Greek thought which was the foundation of the medieval intellectual achievement. The later date, 1204, the year of the physical conquest of the Greek Empire of Constantinople, discloses through all the confusion of events the trend and limitations of western political thinking, and throws a dramatic light on the commercial domination of the Mediterranean, which had seemed so infinitely remote from the land-locked Europe of the tenth century and was now an accomplished fact. The restoration of the Mediterranean in European politics—its partial restoration as Europe's centre of gravity after a long decline—is one of the main influences in later medieval civilization. The intellectual conquest of Greek thought was much less complete by 1204 than most contemporaries would have believed: scholars were only on the edge of the natural science and metaphysics which so profoundly affected the thinking of the thirteenth century, and they were mostly quite ignorant of the Greek language and literature which only made their influence felt much later. Yet it may be questioned whether any of these later developments could compete in permanent importance with the embracing of Aristotelian logic in the eleventh and twelfth centuries.

It would, however, be absurd to allow much more than a symbolic importance to the dates 972 and 1204, and we shall frequently overstep these limits. Sometimes, when the words of later writers seem in some significant way to look back to developments which took place during this period, we shall overstep these limits by a large margin. The excuse for this must be that the importance of these centuries in the development of Europe can only be understood by taking a wide view. For a thousand years Europe has been the chief centre of political experiment, economic expansion and intellectual discovery in the world. It gained this position during the period with which we are concerned: it is only losing it in our own day. The position was achieved slowly and silently, unheralded by any great military events or clear-cut political or social revolution. The battle of the Lech in 955, for example, will never be as famous as the battle of Marathon—it left no memories behind it, it took its place in the Chronicles for a generation and then disappeared from the popular imagination for ever. Yet the battle on the Lech had a place in ensuring the territorial stability of the European nations perhaps not less important than Marathon in the formation of Greece. Both battles are only incidents in the course of a long effort and if the one held the imagination and the other did not, it is partly because the society which was slowly coming into existence in the tenth century was something bigger, more subtle and more complicated than the imagination could embrace. The deliverances which are celebrated in history are those which affect relatively small or closely knit communities, but medieval Europe was never anything but a sprawling and much divided community. The battle of Roncevaux in 778 which *did* retain a place in the popular memory was a defeat with no military significance, but it appealed to those qualities which held men together throughout Europe: personal valour, faithfulness to lord and companions, and confidence in the Christian religion and in the aid of the saints. Other loyalties were to be added in due course, but these were the basis of all else.

This silence in the great changes of history is something which meets us everywhere as we go through these centuries. The slow emergence of a knightly aristocracy which set the social tone of Europe for hundreds of years contains no dramatic events or clearly decisive moments such as those which have marked the course of

other great social revolutions. The economic face of Europe and
its position in the world was transformed in this period, but this
revolution was occasioned by no conspicuous discoveries or
inventions which focus our attention. There were of course re-
sounding events: the capture of Jerusalem by the Crusaders in 1099,
and of Constantinople by their successors in 1204, are great moments
for good or ill, but their greatness lies less in their practical consequences than in their indication of the forces at work in the world.
Indeed it is characteristic of the period that the importance of events
is to be measured less by the decisions which they enforce than
by their symbolic value as revelations of change or as portents of
things to come. The significant events are often the obscure ones,
and the significant utterances are often those of men withdrawn
from the world and speaking to a very few. The truly formative
work of the period was often hidden from the eyes of contemporaries and it is doubtless often hidden from ours. The stabilization
of the boundaries of Europe, the slow recovery of political order,
and the unprecedented acceleration of economic activity were not
only in themselves silent reversals of previous tendencies: they were
the conditions which made possible even more secret and momentous changes in thought and feeling, and in the direction of society
for both secular and spiritual ends. The results of all this are still
with us. In England we can perhaps feel the impact of these changes
more immediately, and discern their effects in the make-up of our
daily life more dramatically than anywhere else. The pattern of
monarchy and aristocracy, at least in their more formal manifestations, of law and law-courts, of parishes and parish churches
are too clearly the work of these centuries for the point to require emphasis. What the spiritual inheritance is, must be left to
everyone to judge for himself, but it can scarcely be doubted that
the questions which were raised and often apparently solved in
this period are as living and insistent now as they ever have
been.

The secret revolution of these centuries did not pass unnoticed
by contemporaries. By the second half of the twelfth century, the
consciousness of new achievement was widespread, especially
among those who practised the art of poetry. The form in which
the new historical perspective expressed itself was as a movement
of 'chivalry and learning'—all that we comprehend in the word

'civilization'—from Greece to Rome, and from Rome after a long interval to France, the mainstay of western Christendom:

> Our books have informed us that the pre-eminence in chivalry and learning once belonged to Greece. Then chivalry passed to Rome, together with that highest learning which now has come to France. God grant that it may be cherished here, that the honour which has taken refuge with us may never depart from France. God had awarded it as another's share, but of Greeks and Romans no more is heard; their fame is passed, and their glowing ash is dead.

These words were written by a poet, Chrétien of Troyes, about the year 1170: they would have been idle boasts at the beginning of our period. Now they could be spoken with the modesty of achievement and insight. How had this become possible?

CHAPTER I

LATIN CHRISTENDOM AND ITS NEIGHBOURS

I

THE DIVISIONS OF LATIN CHRISTENDOM

IT is easy to forget that the idea of the unity of Western civiliza-tion with which we are familiar arises from a radical simplification of the past. This simplification is justified, and we shall often have to make it in the following pages; but it is well to begin by remem-bering that Europe has always been the scene of more or less deep disunity and of conditions which, to a close observer, must appear chaotic.

The area of sheer chaos certainly diminished during the course of our period, but in the third quarter of the tenth century when our story begins, the outlook was not encouraging. Although some parts of Europe, notably Germany and southern England, exhibited a high degree of governmental skill and authority, yet over a great part of Europe there was no régime which promised a settled political order. Behind the façade of strong or weak rulers, there was an incoherent jumble of laws and customs, difficult to adjust to each other and hard even to understand. The survivals of barbaric codes of law jostled with varying mixtures of Roman law, local custom, and violence, and besides all this there was a maze of Church law, through which every bishop had to find his way as best he could. The widespread destruction caused by the persistent ravages of Scandinavian pirates during the previous century had not yet been made good. There was indeed a gleam of hope here: in Anjou, in the middle of the tenth century, we read of the unexpected discovery that the long depopulation of wide stretches of country had produced an unparalleled fertility in the soil. This was an encouragement to renewed activity, but the fact that the discovery could be made, shows how much damage there was to be made good.

Intellectually, the men and women who understood Latin were the inheritors of a rich and varied tradition, but, as we shall see, there were many obstacles which stood in the way of their entering into their inheritance. The most serious obstacle was the isolation of those men of learning and religion whose work held the promise of better things. It is hard for us—who are able to take a wide view of work which is being done in many parts of Europe—to remember how little the men of the tenth century knew of what was going on around them. If a man wanted to study mathematics or logic he might have to wait for a chance encounter which sent him to a distant corner of Europe to do so: and, in most cases, it is probable that the chance never came. We know of men with an ardent desire for a life of strict monastic observance, who wandered from one end of Europe to the other without apparently being able to find a community of sufficient austerity, though it would be easy now to name half a dozen famous places where all they sought was to be found.

Apart from the divisions which arose from lack of communications and social disorder, there was one clear division which retained its importance and even acquired a growing importance throughout and beyond the limits of our period. This is the division of Europe into two main language groups. The artificial divisions of political organization were too fluid to count for much. Areas of authority shaded into each other and overlaid each other with little relation either to geography or history. No political boundaries survived in their entirety the death of a ruler; they were all subject to the chances of domestic change, marriage, dowry, partition, death and forfeiture. But the line which separated the speakers of the various vernacular forms of Latin from the speakers of Germanic dialects, having become stabilized before the beginning of our period, remained almost unaltered through centuries of war, conquest and social upheaval. It ran, as with minor variations it still runs, from the neighbourhood of Boulogne, which in the eleventh century was known as a border town, eastwards to cross the Meuse above Maastricht, described in 1050 as "almost the last outpost of German soil";[1] thence southwards over the Ardennes, crossing the Moselle half-way between Trier and Metz; then up into the Vosges to the west of the line of the River Saar, across the Belfort gap into present-day Switzerland;

[1] The description occurs in the mortuary roll of Count Wifred of Cerdaña, which is discussed below.

here it turned sharply eastwards along the Alps and was lost in a maze of mountain and valley.

To the west and south of this line the Romance languages were, by the end of the eleventh century, everywhere dominant except in Ireland and the highlands of Wales and Scotland. As a result of the Norman Conquest England had effectively been added to the French-speaking world, and continued to be a part of this world throughout our period. This broad similarity of language from the lowlands of Scotland to Sicily was a real bond between men. Religious unity and family and political ties might provide common ground with the German world, but the language boundary formed a dividing line in many activities which might at first sight appear to be unrelated to it.

It is one of the fatalities of our period that the chief creations of the time, the bonds which drew western Europe most closely together, helped to underline the distinction between the lands of Germanic and Romance speech. The monastic families of Cluny and Cîteaux, the Crusades, the new schools of learning and the growing universities were all creations of the French-speaking world, and contemporaries were not slow to notice the widening of the gulf between the eastern and western halves of the Latin world. Already in the eleventh century it was noticeable that the drift of monastic reform was towards the West—away from the border country in the valleys of the Meuse and Moselle where it had flourished in the tenth century and into the purely French country of Burgundy and Champagne. A German Cluniac writer of the eleventh century drew attention to the difference between the French eagerness and the German reluctance to open hearts and purses in the cause of monastic reform. His words have the more weight because he had no tendency to exaggerate the natural virtue of the French: "What shall I say about the Franks, but this—that though they are an unsteady people, given to plunder and having no covering of righteousness, yet they have those among them who will give so much to a faithful servant of God that he can pay for whatever he needs."[1]

With the growing consciousness of the separation between

[1] The quotation comes from a description of the customs of Cluny written by Udalric, a monk of that house who died in or about 1093. (P. L. vol. 149, 635-778). He had had a varied career in France and Germany, and was in a position to speak with authority about the difference between the French and the Germans.

Frank and Teuton, the division of Europe into two main language groups became a matter of more importance in every way. In literature, there survived into the twelfth century the memory of a time when *Francia* and the *Franks* had included not only inhabitants of present-day France but also Rhinelanders and Bavarians: but, practically, this connotation had long ceased to have any significance. The Germanic origin of the Franks was forgotten and French noblemen spoke the language, and identified themselves with the fortunes of their subject people.

It was the Crusade which did more than anything else to widen the gap between the two halves of Latin Christendom. The appeal of the First Crusade was so wide, so surprisingly and unmistakably non-local in a highly localized world, that abstentions were all the more conspicuous. Men from unknown nations landed on the coast of France, speaking no recognizable language and only able to communicate their purpose by crossing their fingers in the sign of the Cross. Even the Scots were there, a race of men who had been believed to keep all their ferocity for domestic enemies: the French were amazed to see them, "drawn from their native swamps, with their bare legs, rough cloaks, purses hanging from their shoulders, hung about with arms, ridiculous enough in our eyes but offering the aid of their faith and devotion to our cause."[1] But where were the Germans? They were immobilized by the state of war between the German Emperor and the Pope who had set the Crusade in motion. A conversation which took place soon after the First Crusade between the French abbot of Nogent, near Paris, and a German archdeacon illustrates the atmosphere of hostility which was engendered by this defection:

Last year (wrote the abbot) I was talking to the archdeacon of Mainz and I reproached him with the rebelliousness of his people. He replied that they so despised our king and people because we gladly accepted Pope Paschal, that they refused any longer to allow us the name of Franks or free men. To which I replied, 'If you think us so torpid and lethargic that you foully abuse our name, which is famous as far as the Indian Ocean, tell

[1]Guibert, Abbot of Nogent, *Gesta Dei per Francos* Book I, i (P. L. vol. 156, 686). Mr. A. A. M. Duncan has studied the significance of this passage as the earliest known account of Scottish dress in the *Scottish Historical Review*, 1950, XXIX, 211-12.

me—did not Pope Urban seek our help against the Turks? Unless we had gone forth and stemmed the tide of barbarian invasion, there would have been no help from you Germans, whose name was not even heard in that expedition.' I believe (added the abbot) that God has preserved our people for this business.[1]

The passage of time did nothing to weaken this conviction. The Germans later made amends for their coolness towards the First Crusade; but, having missed the glories of the First, they succeeded only in sharing the futility of the Second and the disasters of the Third Crusade. They were not wanted in Palestine, and the history of German crusading really begins with the exploits of the Teutonic Knights in Prussia in the thirteenth century—but that was a purely German and not a European enterprise.

This misfiring of German leadership in Europe is one of the most puzzling and important facts with which we are confronted at the turn of the eleventh and twelfth centuries. If there was one thing about which a critical and well-informed observer at the beginning of our period might have felt confident in making a prediction, it was that the future of Latin Christendom lay in the hands of the rulers and people of the German-speaking lands. The transformation of Germany during the fifty years before the death of the Emperor Otto I in 973 was the one conspicuously hopeful feature of the European situation. Beyond all doubt the late Emperor had been the greatest ruler in Europe. It was not only that the extent of his authority, from the Baltic to the Tiber, was very great, but he had able men to serve him, and a tradition of service such as existed nowhere else in Europe. Despite all the tensions of family feud, there appeared to be a solidarity of effort in Germany which could be paralleled only in the tiny kingdom of Wessex. It was on the Eastern and North-Eastern frontiers of Germany alone that Christendom was expanding: elsewhere there was, to all appearances, only an uneasy lull in the contraction.

In these circumstances, the future of Europe might reasonably have appeared to lie in the hands of the kings of Germany, the Emperors of the West. This prediction would not have been greatly disturbed by the appearance of a series of remarkable native Christian rulers in the late tenth and early eleventh centuries, in Norway,

[1]Guibert of Nogent, *op. cit.*, II, i. (P. L. 156, 697).

Denmark, Poland, Bohemia and Hungary. Their appearance simply emphasized the success of the German initiative and underlined the importance of the co-operation of Popes, German Emperors and the new Christian rulers in the consolidation of Christendom. Here if anywhere appeared to be the key to the rebirth of civilization in Europe. But any such prediction was destined to be falsified by events. For the renovating activities of the eleventh and twelfth centuries we shall have to look away from Germany towards the West, to the lands of Romance speech, to France in the first place, to Norman England and to Italy.

It would be a mistake to see in this contrast any evidence of the backwardness of German civilization. The contrary is probably truer. Renovation was less needed because the destruction of the old order was less serious. The Germany of the eleventh and even of the twelfth century continued to present the most solid political structure in Europe. For two hundred and fifty years there was a series of emperors who, whatever their lapses and failures, had no rivals among the secular rulers of Europe for largeness of designs, personal grandeur and the respect paid them by their contemporaries. The failure, if it was one, lay in the fact that, having too much to hold on to, they slowly lost what they had. On the whole, it was those who had least who were able to move most freely to the new world which was coming into existence.

To the west of Germany lay the lands of Romance speech. The likenesses of language over this broad area were sufficiently pronounced to facilitate ease of movement both of men and of ideas: it took relatively few alterations to make a Provençal song intelligible in England, and a member of the English baronage could, without much difficulty, make himself at home in Italy. Yet the unity of the Romance world must not be pressed too far. Within the broad unity of common linguistic origins, there was room for every kind of diversity of social organization, political allegiance and condition of life.

The main division was between North and South: between the lands which felt the pull of the Mediterranean, which had formed the core of the Roman Empire, and on which the character of the South is impressed by olive groves and cypress trees; and those lands which were separated from the Mediterranean by the heights of Auvergne or a journey through the appalling Alps.

Broadly speaking, the farther North one goes, the fainter becomes the evidence for the continuous and involuntary persistence of classical Roman influence. It is quite natural that this should be so, and the fact is very conspicuous in many fields of activity. In architecture for instance the features of the late classical style were familiar in Italy long after they had been abandoned in Northern France. In law, written codes, which to a greater or less extent were based on Roman models, were the foundation of legal practice as far North as a line from the mouth of the Gironde to the Jura mountains: beyond this line was the land of custom in which any Roman influence was an importation of the twelfth and thirteenth centuries. Most conspicuous of all were the variations in language. When Dante wrote his treatise on the vulgar tongue he distinguished three main types of Romance speech according to the way in which the speaker said 'yes': in Italy the word was *si; from* the Italian frontier to a line between the Gironde and the Jura (almost the same as the legal division already mentioned) the word was *oc;* North of this line it was the modern French *oui.* The political unification of France has almost ironed out the distinction between the land of *oc* and *oui,* and has given the victory to the speech of the North; but the first of Dante's lines of demarcation still exists. These variations of speech provide a good illustration of the gradual shading away of Roman influence. The *si* (Latin: *sic*) of Italy descends from good classical usage; the *oc* (*hoc*) of southern France is in this context barbarous Latin, but still recognizable as a survival of late classical popular speech; but in the *oui* (*hoc illud*) of the North we have a language which, by classical standards, is all at sea.

These distinctions have more than a purely formal significance, as a single example will suffice to show.

It happens that we are fortunate enough to be able to follow the footsteps of a highly informative but nameless traveller, who in the year 1051 journeyed from the neighbourhood of Barcelona as far North as Maastricht, and back again to the monastery of Canigou in the Pyrenees. He thus traversed the length and breadth of the lands of *oc* and *oui,* and he visited well over a hundred monasteries and collegiate churches on the way. We have the names of the places he visited, we can follow his route, and in some cases we know the day and even the hour of the day at which he arrived at his many destinations. Our traveller had a simple theme, a lugubrious message to convey to all men of religion wherever he went. In the previous year Count Wifred of the little Pyrenean county of Cerdaña had died at his monastery of Canigou, and our messenger was the bearer of the news of his death, soliciting far and wide prayers for his soul's health. He trudged up and down through the valleys of the eastern Pyrenees; then along the South coast of France, visiting the ancient towns on the Roman road as far as Arles; afterwards, by a direct but unfrequented route, he went northwards from Carcassonne to Poitiers, passed thence into the busy valley of the Loire and through the important towns of Tours and Orleans; from there he went north again to Paris, and then pushed north-east through Soissons and Laon to the valley of the Meuse, along which he travelled as far as Maastricht. This brought him to the border towns between the land of French and German speech, and the change was the signal for his return. He made a wide detour through Aachen to the Rhine valley, down which he passed as far as Coblenz, where he joined the valley of the Moselle. He made his way up this river, and reached once more the land of familiar French speech shortly before he came to Metz. In his long trek from Maastricht to Metz he added only three religious communities to his long list—an indication that he was on alien soil—but after Metz he was on more friendly ground, and we can follow him, though sometimes imperfectly, through the mountains of Auvergne to the south coast, and so home to Canigou.

He has left no record of his experiences during this long journey, no impressions of the people he met or the talk he heard, but what he left is—though less exciting—perhaps even more interesting. Through all his journeyings he carried on his back a roll of parchment, which grew longer and longer as he put the miles behind him.[1] On it, one religious house after another recorded his arrival, and made the event an occasion for the display of literary talent and the expression of pious sentiment. Individually, the compositions are not of much importance, but they have the merit of letting us see something of the tastes and learning of a large number of men who have no place in history.

The fact which we notice immediately from these humble efforts is the broad distinction between the land of written and of customary law, between Langue d'oc and Langue d'oïl, between the

[1]This document, with many others of a similar kind, is printed by Léopold Delisle, Rouleaux des Morts du IXᵉ au XVᵉ Siècle (1866).

country which faced towards the Mediterranean and that which depended on the great provincial centres of the Loire, the Seine and the Meuse. This broad geographical distinction was reflected in the literary and religious habits of these two great areas. Wherever he went in the South, the messenger acquired an addition to his roll couched in the heavy diction of an archaic style, generally in prose but sometimes in ponderous hexameters, replete with hard and book-learned words, impressively sonorous. With elaborate detail, the monasteries of the South mark the circumstances of the messenger's arrival, describe all that they have done in offering their prayers, and solicit the same charity for their own dead. The following is the beginning of the entry made in the Benedictine monastery of Grasse, in the diocese of Carcassonne:

When, on the last day of April, the fulgent orb of Titan had reached its western bourne, your messenger with wordy scroll came to us announcing the deaths of Wifred and others of your Fathers. Which when we heard, we prayed the One and Trinal God, that he would give them now a heavenly robe and, as the prophetic voices here foretold, two hereafter when the Last Day comes, that throughout endless ages they may sing hymns and praises to the Lamb.

No amount of circumlocution in English can do justice to the heavy roll of the Latin periods, expressive of the antique dignity of the South. But no sooner did the messenger come within reach of Poitiers than a different kind of composition prevails, and persists with remarkable consistency throughout the North. The characteristics of this style are its ease and naturalness of language, a light, and sometimes frivolous playing with ideas. The writers treat the messenger's theme with a sometimes callous freedom. There is an atmosphere of literary competition which replaces the solemnity of the South. Quite often more than one writer in a community tries his hand at expressing his sentiments and those of his fellows: at the cathedral church of Liége, which was famous for its poetry, the occasion let loose a torrent of versifying: fourteen separate compositions were added to the unfortunate messenger's burden; and at the neighbouring monastery of St. Lawrence in the same city, another nine. The collegiate church of St. Servatius at Maastricht was responsible for eleven pieces, and other churches advertised the richness of their literary talent with similar, though less extensive, displays. To pass to these compositions from those of the South is rather like passing from the prose of Sir Thomas Browne to the poetry of Dryden. The comparison is less far-fetched than it might appear: for the compositions of the South are almost the last representatives of the literary culture of the Carolingian age, which had its roots in classical models and added thereto a love of the strange wordplay for which Irish scholars were especially famous. But the compositions of the North reflect the freedom and lightness which are two of the most prominent characteristics of the civilization which was slowly emerging in the eleventh century.

These characteristics, which are already discernible in the roll of Wifred of Cerdaña, are remarkably developed some sixty years later in that of Matilda, the daughter of William the Conqueror, who died as Abbess of Holy Trinity, Caen, in 1113. This later roll circulated through England and northern France as far south as Angoulême—almost, that is, throughout the whole of the *Langue d'oïl*—and its entries present a vivid picture of the lively and irresponsible spirit of the northern schools, which found expression in satire and in the free use and abuse of scholastic terms. Considering the purpose of the roll and the status of the dead Abbess, such compositions as this (by a nun at Auxerre) are striking witnesses to the freedom of expression of the new generation:

> All Abbesses deserve to die
> Who order subject nuns to lie
> In dire distress and lonely bed
> Only for giving love its head.
> I speak who know, for I've been fed,
> For loving, long on stony bread.[1]

These compositions give us, of course, only one side of the distinction between North and South: they are of purely clerical, and largely monastic, origin; they tell us nothing of secular society. A literary competition between the lay rulers of the two areas would have left a quite different impression. We can feel fairly confident that the rulers of the South would have made a better showing than those of the North. While the literary culture of the religious com-

[1] Delisle, p. 276-7.

munities of the South, which found its expression in Latin, was archaic, there was developing a precocious vernacular literature in the courts of secular rulers.

In the pages which follow we shall be chiefly concerned with developments in the area North of the line from the Gironde to the Jura mountains. Without underestimating the importance of what was happening elsewhere, medieval civilization as we in England have known it and experienced its deep and subtle penetration into the texture of our life and institutions, is peculiarly a product of this Northern half of the Romance world—the world which had its main centres during our period in the valleys of the Loire, the Seine and—though possibly only insular prejudice compels us to add—the Thames.

II

THE RELATIONS OF LATIN CHRISTENDOM WITH THE OUTSIDE WORLD

The position of Latin Christendom with regard to its neighbours underwent a radical change in the course of our period. At the beginning, the windows on to the outer world were few, and the view from them was short and uninviting. The communities which owed ecclesiastical obedience to Rome were hemmed in on every side by hostile powers, which controlled the seas and threatened the land. All frontiers presented great but incalculable dangers. During the ninth and tenth centuries the greatest dangers came from the North and East, and we may start by considering these frontiers.

A. THE NORTHERN AND EASTERN FRONTIERS

In 972, the menace from the East was still a particularly vivid memory: less than twenty years had passed since, in two great campaigns separated by only a few months, Otto the Great had repelled the Magyars on the river Lech in the neighbourhood of Augsburg (10 August 955), and defeated the Wends in the marshes of Mecklenburg (16 October 955). Since this date there had been no great threat from the East, and a line of newly founded archbishoprics, bishoprics and settlements testified to the strength of the German missionary and colonizing effort in this direction. But in the

North-East, the position was still uneasy and dangerous. Just ten years after the death of Otto I a series of risings wiped out the German settlements of Havelburg and Brandenburg and laid Hamburg in ruins for the better part of a generation. These blows were not irreparable, but they enforced the lesson that the firm frontier of Latin Christendom still lay along the line of the Elbe and the Saale: beyond this line the organization of Christendom was shadowy and insecure.

Seawards, along the Baltic and North Sea, the dangers were even more obvious and unpredictable. The sea gave a mobility and a fitful unity to the people who could use and control it. The northern sea routes were in the hands of bold and vigorous Scandinavian traders and pirates, whose sphere of action formed a wide arc stretching from the Norwegian settlements in Ireland round the northern coast of Scotland, through the Baltic and down the great rivers, by which contact was made with the principality of Kiev and the remote Empire of Constantinople. At a time when, in Christian Europe, political power was being painfully built up on the dominion of the soil and the command of the meagre surplus of a primitive agriculture, the rulers of the North could draw on the resources of a far-flung trade and a ruthless piracy, and could exploit the fame of a personal glory won in many exhibitions of superhuman strength. Even when these rulers had received the first impress of Christianity, they remained alien and hostile to Christian Europe. The early career of Norway's national saint, King Olaf, is very suggestive in this respect: the early years of the eleventh century saw him, already a Christian, pursuing a profitable career of destruction and violence in any country where opportunity offered, from the Baltic to the Bay of Biscay. The Danish king at this time was slowly devastating and conquering England, and a good deal of Olaf's fighting took place in this country—though it is not always clear on which side he was fighting.[1] The conquest of England provided the most terrible proof of the vitality of the sea-faring adventurers of the Baltic. When the conquest was completed in 1017, it must have seemed a grave question whether it was only a prelude to a new outbreak of the fury of the Northmen, which had devastated Western Europe

[1] There is a very careful and interesting account of the saint's early career of violence by Alistair Campbell, *Encomium Emmae Reginae* (Royal Historical Society, Camden Series, vol. 72, 1949), pp. 76-82.

two centuries earlier. But, as it turned out, the vital force was spent.

Despite all temporary recoveries, the ancient heathendom of Scandinavian and Slavonic lands was slowly dissolving, and as it dissolved, there came into existence a chain of new Christian kingdoms and principalities: Norway, Sweden and Denmark to the North; Poland, Bohemia and Hungary to the East. With their formation Latin Christendom reached the limit of its northward and eastward expansion. Areas which had by repulsion exerted so strong an influence on Western Europe in their pagan days, became, for the greater part of our period, receiving areas for cultural, political and religious influences. Geographically, there was everything to suggest that Germany would be the source of these influences, and in great part it was. But propinquity often worked in the other direction. The rulers of these new Christian lands preserved a tradition of greatness older than their religion, and they were quick to seek their religion from sources which threatened them with no diminution of their political power. It is probable also that, like other newly converted people, they took a pride in being up to date, and were only partly satisfied by the conservatism of Germany. At all events, there grew up during our period, a web of relationships between these new countries and every corner of Christendom—with Rome in the first place, but also with France and England.

The relations between Rome and the countries on the periphery of Christendom were, throughout our period, peculiarly close. The Scandinavian countries and Poland, as well as England, all paid a form of tribute known as Peter's Pence, which was the foundation of more or less determined claims to Papal overlordship; the crown of Hungary owed its origin to the initiative of the Pope; and, when Bohemia finally became a kingdom, its new status was guaranteed by a Papal confirmation. Countries which, in 972, appeared so menacing had become by the end of our period an integral part, and to all appearances a permanent part, of Western Christendom.

Nowhere was the change more swiftly apparent than in Hungary where the first Christian king, Stephen, was also a ruler of genius. The country lay on the route of thousands of crusaders and pilgrims to Jerusalem in the eleventh and twelfth century. When Frederick Barbarossa passed that way on his crusade in 1189, he was received by a king, whose tastes were similar to his own, and whose queen was a sister of the king of France and the widow of an English king. These connexions with France and England went back a long way. It was a Frenchman, a member of a Hungarian monastery of French origin, who in the last years of the eleventh century wrote the first national history of Hungary.[1] The family connexions of the English royal house with Hungary go much farthur back, to a time shortly after the conversion. For when in 1016 Edmund Ironside died and Canute became sole King of England, Edmund's two sons fled to Hungary; one of them married a Hungarian wife and their children returned to England as the sole survivors of the old English royal family. Two of these children had names—Margaret and Christina—at this time unknown in England, and the rapid growth in the popularity of these saints and their legends owes something to the Hungarian connexions of these royal ladies. Margaret became Queen of Scotland and her daughter married Henry I of England; and so, after this Hungarian episode, the House of Wessex was grafted once more on to the English crown. Medieval history is full of these remote and unexpected contacts which, though they did nothing to alter the main current of events, yet exercised a persistent influence on thought and sentiment, and played a part in the consolidation of Christendom.

Yet the main gift of the countries on the Northern and Eastern frontiers of Europe was not a gift of ideas, but of men. The name Slavs, from which the word *slave* is derived in various forms in the languages of Europe, reminds us of the part which Europe's eastern neighbours played in the primitive European economy: they were a readily exportable product and swelled the exiguous surplus of more peaceful toil. The contribution of these wretched victims was however a wasting asset by the end of the tenth century and it does not compare in importance with the rôle of the Northmen. Having destroyed large parts of Europe in the ninth and tenth centuries, they proceeded in the eleventh and twelfth to play a massive part in the formation of European politics and civilization. From their bastion in Normandy, they went out to conquer England and Southern Italy, and to take a leading part in the Crusades. They seemed to have a knack of being in a vital spot at the right time. They came to

[1]For the relations between the monastery of St. Giles in southern France and the abbey at Somogyvár in Hungary founded by King Ladislaus in 1091, and for the influence of this monastery with its strong French connexions on the early historiography of Hungary and Poland, see a review by J. Hammer of recent work by the Polish scholar M. Plezia in *Speculum*, 1949, 291-7.

England at a time when the country was wavering between a closer approach to, or a wider alienation from, the culture and organization of Latin Europe, and they settled the question in favour of the first alternative for the rest of the Middle Ages. They went to Southern Italy in a dark and troubled time when Latin, Greek and Moslem influences jostled uneasily side by side, and they settled the question in favour of the first of these influences once and for all. They were the friends of the Popes at a time when the Popes needed every friend they could get, and having defeated the Moslem rulers of Sicily they were powerful agents in the transmission of Arabic influence to the West. This ability or luck which enabled the conquering but christianized Northmen to touch and influence some of the central themes of medieval history gives them a permanent place in that history out of all proportion to their numbers or the originality of their contribution to Western thought. Indeed, it was the Northmen who remained in their homeland, isolated and cramped, cherishing under a thin crust of Christianity the stories and ideals and experiences of their pagan past, who preserved in literary form the old, clear pagan light of epic achievement—it was they who, in their sagas, ultimately made a more original contribution to the record of human experience than the Normans who were absorbed in European affairs. But the knowledge of this literature outside the small communities in which it originated lay in the distant future: by contrast, the influence of the Normans who made their home in France, England, Italy and Palestine was immediate and often decisive.

B. THE MEDITERRANEAN

In 972, the Mediterranean, like the Baltic, was a hostile sea. Along the coastline of the western Mediterranean, the Moslem powers of Spain and North Africa pressed close upon the main land-block of Europe. The islands—Majorca, Corsica, Sardinia, Malta, Sicily— were all theirs. The Spanish peninsula was theirs almost to the Pyrenees, and the danger of a general forward movement which would overflow into the southern provinces of France seemed to thoughtful men by no means remote. Southern Italy was controlled by the Moslem rulers of Sicily and it was not yet clear how far North that control might be extended. From the Adriatic eastwards, Latin Christendom lost contact with Mediterranean coastline: the

Empire of Constantinople extended to the Dalmatian coast and stretched out its claims, if not its authority, to include Venice and Southern Italy.

In the western Mediterranean, Christian shipping was, if not quite at a standstill, at least paralysed for want of anything to carry. In the eastern Mediterranean, Venice was more favourably placed. Her long connexion with Constantinople gave her a privileged position among the traders of that great city and her ships provided a slender, but very tenacious, link between East and West. It was a link of vital importance for Europe, not so much for the precious cloths and condiments which it brought in, as for the artistic and intellectual influences which accompanied these goods. Venice was a town dedicated by its position, its history and its lack of other means of support to keeping open the communications between the West and the great centres of wealth and trade in the eastern Mediterranean. The very existence of Venice is a guarantee that there was continuous contact between Latin Christendom and its Mediterranean neighbours. The great hindrance to this contact was not religious or political animosity—the contacts grew steadily stronger as the animosities became more violent—but the poverty of the West: trade languished because there was little to trade with; but so long as there was anything at all, Venice was by far the best placed of all the towns of the West to handle the goods. The sea had great dangers, but it also held out the prospect of great gains, and the desire for profit was the most powerful agent in drawing western Europe from its shell.

By 1204, the territorial picture had quite changed. Two-thirds of Spain had been reconquered, and the Christian kingdoms of Castile and Aragon had advanced from the perilous footholds south of the Pyrenees of two centuries earlier. Southern Italy and Sicily together formed one of the most compact and desirable kingdoms of Latin Europe. Sardinia, Corsica, Crete, Cyprus and Malta had all been drawn within the orbit of western politics, and the Balearic Islands were soon to fall an easy conquest to the King of Aragon. There were Latin feudal states in Greece, in Macedonia, and even for a short and disastrous time in Constantinople itself. Only in the Holy Land had the tide turned against the expansion of Latin Christendom: since 1187 Jerusalem, after being ruled by Christian kings for eighty-eight years, had once more become a Moslem town. But he would have been a pessimist indeed who would have predicted that it would never again, except for an insignificant period of fifteen years in the thirteenth century, be the capital of a Christian state. There were still important Christian states in Palestine and the loss of Jerusalem was a challenge to fresh efforts, and not—for contemporaries at least—the symptom of an approaching end.

The territorial aspect of western expansion is not however its most important one. The increase in territory offered the possibility of greater freedom of movement. It was a symptom of the growing wealth and power of western Europe, and, in part at least, it was the outcome of a crusading zeal which embraced some of the most deeply felt convictions of the age. Above all, this territorial expansion brought the Latin mind into closer contact than it had ever been before with the results of Greek science and speculation as transmitted through Arabic and Byzantine channels. Whereas, on the northern and eastern frontiers, the traffic in ideas was all outwards, on the Mediterranean frontier the flow was in the opposite direction: at every point of western expansion along this frontier—in Spain, in Sicily, at Constantinople, in Palestine—intellectual and artistic influences were encountered which profoundly modified the course of European history.

The West learned much from Constantinople and from Moslems in Spain, in Sicily and elsewhere. Part, at least, of what these neighbours had to offer was eagerly accepted. But progress in understanding these, neighbours themselves—their beliefs, their way of life, and position in the world—was slow and reluctant. With regard to the Moslem world there was a distinct advance in understanding during the twelfth century, but the Eastern Empire remained in western eyes an ever-deepening mystery which simply invited destruction, not comprehension. We shall deal with these two neighbours in turn.

The Eastern Empire. Any account of the European attitude towards Byzantium in our period must start with the evidence of Liudprand, Bishop of Cremona from 961 to 972.[1] He was better equipped to understand the Byzantine point of view than any westerner of his time, and his evidence takes us to the root of the

[1]For Liudprand's works, see *Liudprandi episcopi Cremonensis Opera*, ed. Joseph Becker, (M. G. H., Scriptores rerum Germanicarum in usum scholarum, 1915). There is a translation by F. A. Wright in the Broadway Library (1930).

sharpening tension between East and West which characterized the next two and a half centuries. Liudprand was a north Italian of good birth, born about 920 into a family with a tradition of service to the Lombard kings, with whom good relations with Constantinople were a fixed point of policy. Their capital at Pavia was, as we shall see, the great centre of commercial exchange between north-western Europe and the East, and this trade provided a notable part of their revenues. Liudprand's family were well aware of the importance of the Byzantine connection. His father and stepfather, who brought him up after his father's death, had both been on embassies to Constantinople, and his stepfather seems to have trained him to be an intermediary between the Greek and the Lombard capitals. Liudprand gives a touching account of his guardian's anxiety for him to learn Greek: he was willing, he said, to spend half his wealth to give him the opportunity, and when his chance came in 949 to go on an embassy to Constantinople, his stepfather sent him at his own expense. It was not long after this that, with the assumption of the Imperial title by Otto I in 962, a new and disturbing factor entered into the diplomatic relations between East and West and when Liudprand next went to Constantinople in 968, he went as the representative of one who, in Byzantine eyes, was a usurper of their ancient rights and dignity.

Liudprand has left accounts of both these embassies of 949 and 968, and the difference in tone is very striking. When he wrote his account of the first visit and inserted it in his history of his own times, he was still strongly under the influence of that education which had taught him to look at Constantinople with friendly and dispassionate eyes. His wide view of affairs is betrayed in many ways —even in so small a detail as his description of the position of Frankfurt, where he started to write his book, as twenty miles from Mainz and nine hundred miles from Constantinople. His History is unique in weaving together in interlocking sections the histories of Italy, Germany and the Empire of Constantinople. Liudprand knew them all and he saw them as a whole. He gives a vivid account of the court at Constantinople as he saw it in 949, and he returned loaded with the coveted Greek silk cloths, for which there was so great a market in the West. It was a friendly visit which passed without a hitch.

It was very different in 968. Liudprand came to Constantinople as an ambassador from Otto I with the task of arranging a marriage between Otto's son and a Greek princess. The mission was a failure: indeed there were so many causes of dissension—theological, political and ceremonial—that the purpose of the embassy scarcely came into the picture at all. Every meeting with a Greek dignitary from the Emperor downwards was a signal for most bitter recriminations and abuse. When Liudprand wrote his report for Otto I, he no longer showed (as in his previous account) any readiness to explain the conventions and symbolism which formed such an important part of Byzantine imperial rule; he wrote only with contempt and indignation. His troubles reached a climax as he was on the point of departure. He had hoped at least to repeat his former success in taking with him some of the great cloths of purple silk, which were the pride of Byzantine craftsmanship and the wonder and envy of the world. But his baggage was examined by the customs officials and the cloths removed. The dialogue which ensued has a deeper interest than a mere study in recrimination: it reveals a deep cleavage which only became broadened by the negotiations and discussions of the next two centuries.

The customs officials appealed to a long-standing (though not always strictly enforced) law which forbade the export of these precious materials and which restricted their use to certain sections of the Imperial hierarchy.[1] In vain Liudprand pleaded his earlier immunity from this restraint: "that", he was told, "had been in the time of a negligent ruler". In vain he protested that the Emperor had given him permission: "The Emperor," he was told, "must have meant something different. These things are forbidden. It is only fitting that this distinction of dress should belong to those alone who surpass other nations in wealth and wisdom." Perhaps this explanation was as good a short answer as could be expected in a custom-house, but not unnaturally it excited Liudprand's angry retort: "In Italy our lowest prostitutes and fortune-tellers wear this colour"; and to Otto I he wrote:

> So, you see, they judge all Italians, Saxons, Franks, Bavarians, Swabians—in fact all other nations—unworthy to go about clothed in this way. Is it not indecent and insulting that these soft,

[1] For the Byzantine silk regulations and the symbolism which inspired them see R. S. Lopez, *The Silk Industry in the Byzantine Empire* (Speculum, XX, 1945, 1-42).

effeminate, long-sleeved, bejewelled and begowned liars, eunuchs and idlers should go about in purple, while our heroes, strong men trained to war, full of faith and charity, servants of God, filled with all virtues, may not! If this is not an insult, what is?

Of course, anyone might write like this after a brush with customs officers. Moreover, in estimating the difference between Liudprand's early attitude to Constantinople and his attitude in 969, we must remember that from an ambitious young man at an Italian court with which the Byzantine Emperor was anxious to preserve good relations, he had become a prelate deep in the counsels of one who had usurped (as it appeared at Constantinople) the title of Emperor, laid hands on ancient Byzantine possessions in Italy, and was presuming to negotiate with the ancient Empire on equal terms. But there was in the change something more important than this. In 969 Liudprand was writing what he thought would please Otto I; but what he wrote also fitted the mood and conditions of the future. In his careful training for Greek diplomacy he had no successors, but there were many inheritors of his petulance. Liudprand's angry epithets are forerunners of those which the Latin writers of our period loved to shower on the Greeks in sober earnest. Two centuries later a most clear-sighted historian of the Second Crusade can find space in a short narrative to record on many occasions the flattery, perjury, perfidy, blasphemy, heresy, arrogance, servility, deceit, pride, cunning and infidelity of the Greeks.[1] These were not words of anger inspired by personal loss, they were the mature considerations of a statesman. So far had the process of disintegration gone in two centuries.

If the matter were simply one of words, perhaps we could ignore these outbursts—for, after all, Otto's son *did* in time marry a Greek princess[2]—but behind the words was the reality of the falling asunder of the two halves of a hitherto united Christendom. Liudprand and

[1] Odo of Deuil, *De Profectione Ludovici VII in Orientem*, ed. and transl. by V. G. Berry (Columbia University Press, 1948. See especially pp. 27, 41, 55, 57, 59, 69, 87).

[2] There is a large literature on the projected marriage between Otto II and a Greek princess which was the object of Liudprand's mission in 968. In 972, a marriage took place between Otto II and the Greek princess Theophano, but it appears probable that she was not the princess "born in the purple" asked for in 968, but a niece or grand-niece of the Emperor John I Tzimisces, of unknown parentage. (See F. Dölger, *Wer war Theophano?* in *Historisches Jahrbuch*, 1949, 646-58 for a summary of the literature.)

his hosts in 968 freely denounced each other's heresies and errors, but they belonged to one Church, however diverse in liturgy, language, theology and discipline. It was only after 1054 that disunity was an acknowledged fact—but (as with the loss of Jerusalem) nobody thought of this as a decisive act which would still, after nine hundred years, cast its shadow on the history of the world. The breach was a more or less casual incident which the ecclesiastical statesmen of every generation confidently expected to see repaired, but it obstinately resisted every expedient which ingenuity and statesmanship could devise. Ostensibly the question was one of obedience to Rome, but the difficulties and misunderstandings went deeper than this. More important than any single issue in shaping the course of events was a profound lack of comprehension, which slowly hardened into obduracy. We have seen how easily this could happen with a man trained, as Liudprand had been, to regard Constantinople as an intimate part of the world in which he moved, speaking its language and familiar with its history. How would it be with those who had none of these advantages? Even Liudprand seems to have had no idea of the strategic importance of Constantinople, nor of the connexion between its fate and that of Western Europe. He appears quite indifferent to the fact that the Emperor whom he despised had just, in a series of notable campaigns, been stabilizing a frontier in Asia Minor which might affect the fortunes of Southern Italy and the Eastern Mediterranean. To any large strategic conceptions Liudprand was quite blind, and this blindness was shared by western statesmen till the end of our period. The world position of Byzantium was a closed book to men who were accustomed to large principles but to small fields of action, and unpractised in weighing and measuring practical issues on a large scale.

It is only this habit of mind, at once too short-sighted and too long-sighted for true statesmanship, which can explain the astonishing blindness which deluded the leaders of the Fourth Crusade into thinking that the Eastern Empire could be scrapped, divided into a medley of primitive feudal properties, and that the land could then peacefully learn its Latin liturgy as if it were in the depth of Leicestershire and not at the centre of an envious and ruthless world. The modern awe and reverence for Byzantium and its age-long mission of preserving the intellectual wealth of the past would have found no echo in the medieval breast. The wealth of the past which the western

Christians most valued in the Byzantine storehouse was the fund of relics of the True Cross, the Crown of Thorns, and the bodies of Apostles and Martyrs on which they cast covetous eyes from the time of the First Crusade. But Byzantium preserved inviolate the secret of its political longevity and bureaucratic stability, and remained the lonely and intolerant guardian of a political and intellectual order which had elsewhere been destroyed. Western Europe was not at home with its past, had not identified itself with its past, as Byzantium had done; but this Byzantine sense of being one with the past shut out all the more rigorously those who had strayed away from or had never known this past. Byzantium in western eyes aroused wonder, envy, hatred, and malice, and a sense of perplexity at the difficulties which were raised by all attempts at reunion; but it did not arouse respect or encourage understanding. The consequences of this hostility, as we shall see, were very serious.

Islam. The Moslem world presented a different problem. With Byzantium, western Europe was in constant contact throughout our period; and though discussion about points of disagreement might lead to very little result, yet some of the issues were well understood and were discussed at a very high level of intelligence. But what was known of the Moslem world or way of life? At the beginning of our period, almost nothing at all. In some ways indeed the Moslem world was more accessible than Byzantium: it was closer; and relations were not disturbed by rival political pretensions. There must have been merchants who knew Cordova, and sailors who knew the North African ports; there were churches with African carpets or Spanish silks, and individuals with Spanish combs or ivory writing tablets; and there were occasional diplomatic exchanges. But a single example will show how little all this amounted to in terms of human relationships.

In 953, John, a monk and later abbot of Gorze near Metz, was sent by Otto I to Cordova and he stayed there nearly three years. His biographer has left us a long account of his experiences.[1] The main purpose of his mission is significant: it was an attempt to enlist the help of the Caliph in suppressing the nest of Saracen marauders

---

[1]The life of John of Gorze, written (between 978 and 984) by John, abbot of St. Arnulf of Metz, is printed in M. G. H., *Scriptores*, IV, 337-77. The details of Recemund's mission to Otto I at Frankfurt are elucidated by E. Dümmler in the volume of the *Jahrbücher der deutschen Geschichte* devoted to Otto the Great (Leipzig, 1876.)

who had established themselves in the Alpine passes and imperilled the routes between Italy and the North. This purpose was a good deal more modest than that which inspired the mission of Liudprand to Constantinople fifteen years later, and altogether the two missions stand in marked contrast to each other: the atmosphere at Cordova was not one of violent debate, but of cool indifference on the one side and anxious uncertainty on the other. There seems to have been almost no intelligible contact between the ambassador and the important personages of the court. He had to rely on the friendly hints of visitors for information about ceremonial and procedure; he acquired a healthy fear of the consequences of any breach of etiquette, but nothing at all seems to have been accomplished. It all reads rather like a visit to the Kremlin.

But, negligible though the intellectual exchanges with Islam were, John's visit illuminates some other relationships of more interest. At Cordova, for instance, he found a Christian community with which he could hold some intercourse. Such communities were to be found all over the Moslem lands of the Mediterranean; by the end of our period they were the object of widespread interest in the West, and the source of some very unfounded hopes. But at this time they were regarded with very little curiosity. They were a challenge neither to action nor to thought. Nevertheless they had some contact with Latin culture, and John of Gorze had reason to be grateful for their help. It was probably from them that he learned that his letters of introduction to the Caliph would lead him into serious danger: they contained reflections on Islam which were punishable with death. There was no disputing the point, and the Christian bishop of Elvira, Recemund, undertook to return to Otto I for a more tactful document, while John remained in mild captivity at Cordova. Recemund met Otto I at Frankfurt in the Spring of 956 and achieved his object. By a curious chance he also met Liudprand who, after his first mission to Constantinople, had fallen into disgrace at Pavia and was now in exile in Germany. It was Recemund who inspired Liudprand to write his History, and Liudprand dedicated it to the Spanish bishop. So it came about that Liudprand, living in Frankfurt, but with his thoughts in Italy and at Constantinople, and with an impulse from Cordova, began to write. His History bears witness to a real, though faint, pulse of life across the estranged communities of Islam and Christendom.

A stronger pulse even at this time was provided by the activity of merchants, and both John of Gorze and Recemund benefited from this in their long journeys. They both took as guides merchants from Verdun. It is to Liudprand that we owe the information that the men of Verdun made huge profits in exporting slaves—men no doubt from the eastern boundaries of Europe—to Spain.[1] Whether or not John travelled with a slave convoy we cannot tell, but when he got to Cordova he found the results of the slave trade very much in evidence, for he remarked with astonishment that *sclavi cubicularii* were the only normal channel of communication with the Caliph.

After a wait of nearly three years, John (with his revised letters) obtained an interview with the Caliph and returned home. So far as we know, the mission was barren of all results, except the fortuitous inspiration to the writing of Liudprand's history. The time for fertile exchanges on Spanish ground had not yet arrived. Moslem and Christian met at many points along the frontiers of Christendom, but they met as patrols of hostile forces might do, who were anxious not to stir up the latent energies of the other. There were in the tenth century few, if any, traces of the crusading zeal which later added passion to a cold hostility. When, for instance, in 1002 one of the last Moslem waves swept over the county of Barcelona, Christian writers wrote of it rather as of a natural disaster, the result of a force which they feared but did not resent. They had no thought of revenge.

This situation changed in the course of the century and especially after the First Crusade; but, strangely enough, as the hostility became more intense and took more practical forms, the desire to understand something of the enemy also grew—and at the same time the opportunity for satisfying the desire. The popular versions of the life of Mahomet and the principles of his religion which became current among Christian writers from the time of the First Crusade were naturally not very edifying or instructive; but alongside these there are traces of some serious attempts to understand the rival faith. This was a formidable task, and it was not made easier by the existence of so much in Mahometan teaching which was familiar to Christians —familiar attributes of God, familiar counsels, familiar names of Prophets and Old Testament rulers—but all in so strange, so elusive and so incoherent a form as to baffle investigation. There was only

[1] *Liudprandi Opera*, ed. Becker, p.156.

one way in which this chaos (as it must have appeared) of truth and falsehood could be treated by a twelfth-century thinker if it were to be brought within the range of his equipment: it must be treated as a heresy, more mysterious in its operation than other heresies which had appeared in the course of Christian history, but like them a more or less deliberate perversion of the true faith, which required refutation by the ordinary rules of argument.

This was the spirit and purpose which inspired a remarkable effort to come to grips with the mind of Islam in the second half of our period.[1] In 1141 the abbot of Cluny, Peter the Venerable, was making a tour of the Benedictine monasteries of Spain when he met two scholars from opposite ends of Europe. The one was an Englishman called Robert, probably from the village of Ketton in Rutland; the other, Hermann, from Dalmatia. Neither of these men had been drawn to Spain by any interest in the contemporary Mahometan world: they were scholars on the look-out for works on astronomy and mathematics. But Peter the Venerable—whether on a sudden impulse or in pursuit of a long conceived plan we cannot tell—engaged them to prepare translations of fundamental Mahometan documents. They had the assistance of two local men, Peter of Toledo and Mahomet the Saracen, and laboured for the next few years on the Abbot's plan. The result was a collection of documents for the understanding of Islam, which retained its value as late as the sixteenth century. The collection comprised: a translation of the Koran; a brief universal history from a Moslem standpoint; a collection of Moslem legends about the Creation, the Patriarchs, the family of the Prophet and the circumstances of his birth; an exposition of some points of Mahomet's teaching, known as the *Dialogue of Abdia*; and an early work of Christian-Moslem polemics known as the *Apology of Al-Kindi*.

At one stroke, this collection multiplied by many times the Latin literature for understanding the great rival religion. It represented a great plan successfully carried out, but its effect was not commensurate with the largeness of the intention. Peter the Venerable himself

---

[1]For what follows, see Mlle M. Th. d'Alverny's important study of Peter the Venerable's collection of translations from the Arabic: *Deux Traductions latines du Coran au Moyen Age* (Archives d'Histoire doctrinale et littéraire du Moyen Age, XVI, 1948, pp. 69-131). This completes and corrects in many respects the more general account in U. Monneret de Villard, *Lo studio dell' Islam in Europa nel XII e nel XIII secolo* (Studi e Testi 110, Vatican City, 1944), which is nevertheless of interest for the wider picture of Christian-Moslem relations.

wrote a short *Summary of the whole heresy of the diabolical sect of the Saracens* on the basis of these translations; and some other writer supplied the collection with glosses conceived in a profoundly hostile spirit. And that—until the thirteenth century, when wider views prevailed—seems to have been all. The spirit of the enquiry was too narrow to inspire great results: we do not feel that we are face to face with real people, but only with arguments regarded at best as absurd, and at worst as filthy, deceitful and insane. When for instance, the text of the Koran read: "Do you not see that the birds in heaven are not sustained otherwise than by God?" the glossator commented: "See the simplicity of the madman who thinks that flying birds are supported not by air but by the miraculous power of God. But (as we know) fishes are supported by water and birds by air, according to an original decree and ordering of God, and not (as he thinks) by a special and invisible miracle." These are the words of a man in the Schools, seeking points of controversy, not points of contact. In the Schools, this might be well, for the common basis of agreement was wide and firm; but the great issues of a world-wide controversy could not profitably be brought indoors in this way.

It was St. Francis, two generations later, who decisively enlarged the context of the controversy, when he preached to the Sultan of Egypt outside Damietta during the Fifth Crusade. Meanwhile, it was neither in the Schools nor in the mission field, but in the world, that the main progress in comprehension was made. To men in habitual contact with the enemies of God, in Palestine and elsewhere, the creatures who had appeared at first like devils capering behind their bars, had a way of turning out to be very human after all. In a ruler like Saladin the Franks found more traits they could understand and appreciate, than in the complicated Emperors at Constantinople. They found him chivalrous, impetuous, and passionate, and these were qualities nearer to their hearts than the elaborate formalism of Constantinople. It was natural that those who had to live side by side with Moslems would fall into habits of easy familiarity, and there were some among them who came under the strange spell of the East, learned Arabic, adopted Arab dress and became almost strangers to their own countrymen. This growth in sentiments of humanity and in rational interest in the great enemies of Christendom, has a small but distinct place in enlarging the ideas of Christians about the world around them.

At the end of the twelfth century we find Giraldus Cambrensis, a scholar and writer of strong practical sense, reporting the existence of an explanation of some of the salient features of Mahometanism which stands in marked contrast not only with the account which had been current in Christendom since the time of the First Crusade, but also with the account offered by the Moslem sources translated for Peter the Venerable. Two of the points which struck an observer of Mahometan customs most strongly were the obligatory abstention from wine and from pork; and, from the beginning of the twelfth century, Christian writers gave a simple and trenchant explanation of these observances. Mahomet, they said, had met his death by getting drunk and being eaten by swine while he was in his drunken stupor; hence the distaste which his followers felt for these agents of his downfall. On the Moslem side, the explanation which was available in Latin after 1143 was even more colourful: according to the *Dialogue of Abdia* two angels had been sent down from Heaven to reconcile a man and his wife. They supped with them and drank wine; as a result, they tried to seduce their hostess; the hostess obtained from them the password to Heaven, was transported to the throne of God, and became the planet Venus. To prevent a similar occurrence, the use of wine was henceforth forbidden to the faithful. From these fantasies Giraldus brings us back to earth. Men, he lets us know, were beginning to say that the abstinence from pork was due to Judaic influence, and the prohibition of wine was to be attributed to the hot climate, which made wine harmful to health.[1]

This cool and reflective manner of reasoning was born no doubt of experience. It cannot however have affected more than a very few, and, even if known, would have been looked on with distrust by the great majority. In no sense can we talk about a growth of 'toleration'. What there was, was an enlargement of the area of vision, an accumulation of practical experience, and an exchange of ideas which was immensely fruitful in the West. To this result, the growth of trade, the Crusading activity, and the researches of scholars all contributed.

I. TRADE

The growth of Mediterranean trade in our period undoubtedly affected the way of life of many people. Directly, it meant that the

[1]Giraldus Cambrensis, *De Principis Instructione*, Distinctio I, Cap. XVII. (R. S., vol. 8, p. 68.)

pervading flavour of pepper, cinnamon and ginger could cover a multitude of shortcomings in the kitchen; it meant that great men on their deaths could be embalmed in spice instead of being rudely preserved in salt; it brought a host of private luxuries for the rich—clothes and ornaments for the person, hangings and rugs for the house. Indirectly, it brought into existence commercial powers which could rival in wealth and influence the old-established powers of land and church; it brought new forms of industrial and financial activity, and in districts quite remote from the stir of commerce it meant that the peasant with three or four sheep in the open fields could find a ready market and receive a cash payment for his wool. It was the taste for spices and the charm of luxuries which brought this whole complex of activities into existence; and it was to satisfy this taste that merchants travelled, sailors perished, bankers created credit and peasants raised the number of their sheep. As so often happens, the secondary effects are of more interest than the primary ones: the satisfaction of the instincts for which the whole cycle existed is a thing of the past, private and incommunicable; the activities and organization which existed to satisfy the demands of the relatively few coloured the whole history of the Middle Ages, and are the foundation of modern commerce and industry. It is no part of the purpose of this book to attempt a history of medieval commerce: we are here simply concerned with it as one of a number of activities which bound Latin Christendom to its neighbours.

We have seen that, at the beginning of our period, there was a trade route between Eastern Germany and Moslem Spain, of which Verdun seems to have been the central point. There must have been similar links between Italian ports and the mouth of the Nile—significant links but in bulk of traffic scarcely considerable. The most regular and best organized route was the one between Constantinople and the West. We must picture caravans every year moving down through Europe, fed with the goods of England and the Low Countries, the Rhineland and Germany, struggling across the Alps with a miscellaneous cargo of horses and slaves, woollen and linen cloths, spears and shields, and coming at last to the great meeting place of merchants at Pavia, the ancient capital of Lombardy. Here they met merchants who had come from Venice, or from the South Italian ports of Amalfi, Salerno or Gaeta, with the domestic and ecclesiastical luxuries of the East—silks, spices, ivory combs or crucifixes, gold-work and precious stones. We have a vivid description from the very beginning of the tenth century of the tents of the merchants pitched in the fields by the side of the river Ticino on the outskirts of Pavia, and of the hawking and bargainings over precious stuffs which went on with the arrival of a new batch of customers.[1] Even at this time there was a small specialized class of men who knew the ways of the markets and the comparative values of wares in Constantinople, Venice and Pavia, and had ventured their lives in strange lands and on strange seas. This was the Heroic Age of trade; success could lead to wealth and nobility; failure meant death or slavery in a foreign land.

There is evidence that the English took a considerable part in this early traffic. An Italian document of the early eleventh century tells us of the dues which merchants coming into Lombardy were required to pay to the royal treasury at Pavia.[2] There was an elaborate system of customs posts at the outlets of the Alpine Passes, and all traders coming into Italy were obliged to pay ten per cent of their goods by way of toll. But the English, to whom the document gives a prominent place, had grown violent at the opening of their bags and baggages by customs officials. The Kings of Lombardy and England had had discussions about the situation, and as a result they made an arrangement which provided for a flat rate of payment by the English merchants every three years: fifty pounds of pure silver, two fine greyhounds with gilded and embossed collars,[3] two shields, two swords, two lances; and to the official in charge two fur coats and two pounds of silver. If we suppose that this represents roughly the value of ten per cent of the goods carried by English merchants into Italy over a three-year period, we shall

[1]For this incident and other evidence for the trade between Constantinople and Venice from the ninth to the eleventh century, see F. L. Ganshof, *Note sur un passage de la vie de S. Géraud d'Aurillac* (Mélanges N. Iorga, Paris, 1933, 295-307).

[2]*Instituta regalia et ministeria camerae regum Langobardorum et honorantiae civitatis Papiae* (ed. A. Hofmeister in M. G. H., Scriptores, XXX (1934) p. 1444). The document has recently been discussed by J. Lestocquoy, *The Tenth Century* (Economic History Review, 1947, 1-14); but he does not understand that the *gens Anglicorum et Saxorum* who appear so prominently in the document are the Anglo-Saxons, and not "those of England and Saxony". See also E. H. R. 1935, vol. 50, p. 165-6 for a short note on the document by the late C. W. Previté-Orton, who inclines to the view that it refers to an earlier pact than the one between Canute and Conrad II referred to below.

[3]Examples of these hounds (which were apparently more like mastiffs than modern greyhounds) can be seen with their great collars in the Bayeux tapestry in the retinue of King Harold.

probably be as near to an estimate of the size of the trade from this country as the materials allow. It was not a large trade—not enough to affect the lives of many people—but it was evidently not negligible, and the agreement has great interest as the first commercial treaty in our history, of which exact details have been preserved.[1] There is an added interest in the fact that the information of the Italian document can be supplemented from the English side. We know that King Canute was present at the coronation of the Emperor Conrad II in 1027, and the two rulers talked together about the conditions of trade between England and Italy. Canute sent his people an account of these conversations and particularly of the concession which he had obtained for them "that they should not be hindered by so many customs barriers nor harassed by unjust tolls". It is, I think, probable that this is a simplified and somewhat roseate account for the general public of the agreement, of which the details are given in the Italian document.

There was then in the early eleventh century an international trade of modest dimensions of which the plain of Lombardy was the centre. We may also note that while the whole community of English merchants paid into the Lombard treasury the money and goods mentioned above, each Venetian merchant coming to Pavia owed an annual tribute of a pound of pepper, cinnamon, galingale and ginger, and to the wife of the official in charge an ivory comb, a mirror and some trimmings for a dress. The two sides of the bargain could scarcely be better illustrated than by the items extracted by the customs officials from the English and Venetians respectively.

In the course of the next two centuries, the volume of international trade was multiplied many times. Tenfold . . . twentyfold? It is impossible to say. Statistically no estimate can be made, but there are other ways in which the changing relations between western Europe and its neighbours can be observed.

In the first place, there was an increase in Europe's productivity. In all probability this increase was taking place in every branch of production between the tenth and thirteenth centuries: new land was being taken into cultivation; there were improvements in agriculture which increased the yield from land already cultivated; great land-holders developed the art of estate management, and

[1]For the evidence of earlier negotiations between King Offa and Charlemagne see Sir Frank Stenton, *Anglo-Saxon England*, 1943, p. 219-20.

began a process of planning and improvement which was to have a long history; finally, the conditions of relative peace brought stability and confidence. All these factors contributed, and indeed were essential, to the increase of international trade. But just as it was England's coal which made this country an industrial area in the nineteenth century, so it was the large-scale production of wool and manufacture of cloth which made Western Europe an important export area in the Middle Ages. There were other objects for export which accumulated at the Mediterranean ports—timber and arms, for instance—but the cloth industry was the basic industry of the Middle Ages.

The industry had its centre in the Low Countries, where it can be traced back as a specialized activity to the eleventh century, but doubtless it existed earlier. The region had natural advantages some-what similar—bearing in mind the difference in the fundamental raw materials—to those which later started England on its industrial career. The saltings of the mouths of the Rhine and Meuse were particularly favourable to sheep farming, and until the eleventh century the fame of the region for its finished cloths probably depended on its native raw material. But at the turn of the eleventh and twelfth centuries we find two new factors. Firstly, there was a general increase in population, of which the pressure seems to have been felt especially severely in Flanders. There was no considerable area of waste land on which the new population could find a living: hence we find Flemish emigrants to England and Wales and as far afield as eastern Germany. Secondly, just at this time, we first find Flemish agents penetrating the neighbouring countries in search of wool. Now it so happened that just across the Channel, in England, there was a country which was already a considerable wool producer, and which had moreover great possibilities of expansion in this direction by the taking in of waste land. We have then, at the begin-ning of the twelfth century, the two factors necessary for the develop-ment of a large-scale Flemish cloth industry: a surplus population which could not readily be absorbed on the land, and an easily accessible source of raw material for the industry which was already well established.

The Anglo-Flemish combination is a vital factor in the industrial history of the Middle Ages. We leave it at the end of our period with the better part of its long life still ahead of it—a life which was to become increasingly involved in war, politics and high finance. In 1204, this side of the story had scarcely begun, and we are concerned with it here simply as an example of the way in which, slowly in the eleventh and with increasing rapidity throughout the twelfth century, western Europe became an important export area capable of supplying the needs of its eastern Mediterranean neighbours on a scale never contemplated before. If we were to take our stand in 1204, and peer into the future, we might wonder whether this great machinery of production was not in danger of over-reaching itself, whether the expansion could continue indefinitely without flooding the market, whether the rulers of the main producing countries might not come to prefer military glory and large political designs to the more concrete, but less personal, rewards of their country's exports. The later Middle Ages provided the answers to some of these questions; but in 1204 these complications were quite remote. The only fact which was clear was the amazing ability to produce, which had been shown during the last century and a half.

This astonishing growth in productivity, which transformed the face of Europe and radically altered its place in the world in the course of our period, can be illustrated from the story of two other commodities: gold and silver. The precious metals had a very important place in the Middle Ages, not only in the form of money, but also as a means of display, which itself was a guarantee of solvency. There was an easy fluidity between the ornaments of a great church or the plate on a great man's table, and the coin into which they could so easily be transformed. These essential ingredients of grandeur declared a man's state, proclaimed his credit and were at the same time a reserve of ready capital which was often broken into to pay debts or to raise new loans.[1]

Throughout our period, the division between Latin Christendom and its Moslem and Byzantine neighbours was reinforced and emphasized by a broad currency division: there was what we may call a silver *bloc* and a gold *bloc*. Latin Christendom had a multiplicity of coinages, but they had this in common: they were, with the exception of occasional pieces made for purposes of ceremony or

[1]For the following paragraphs, see Maurice Lombard, *L'or musulman du VII au XI° siècle* (Annales: Economies, Sociétés, Civilisations, II, 1947, 143-160) and Marc Bloch, *Le problème de l'or au Moyen Age* (Annales d'histoire économique et sociale, V, 1933, 1-33). For Liudprand, see the edition of his works cited above, pp. 155, 158, 210-11.

display, exclusively of silver. We must imagine coinages composed for the most part of pieces worth perhaps half-a-crown or five shillings, though no modern equivalents can really give much help in expressing the value of medieval currency. They were coins unsuitable for very small transactions and inconvenient for very large ones. They served well the needs of an agrarian community buying and selling cattle and corn, laying in stores for the winter, or paying wages by the day. Packed in barrels and loaded on carts they were an essential part of the war-train of a king, and loads of this kind must have been a common sight on medieval roads. But large-scale commerce required something less cumbrous than this: in particular, a coin of higher value and less weight than the silver penny would have been a convenience. But this, as we shall see, was not easy to come by.

Immediately beyond the frontiers of Latin Christendom, in Spain, North Africa and the Eastern Empire, lay countries where gold coins were an ordinary medium of exchange. The financial centre of the gold area was Constantinople, where for centuries the Imperial administration had retained undebased the classical gold coin, the *solidus*. Financially Constantinople was the centre of an area much more extensive than the Empire of which it was the capital. It was the commercial capital—if the phrase may be allowed —of an area, linked by sea and caravan routes, stretching from the far East to the Western Mediterranean. Viewing the matter from Constantinople in the tenth century, Europe must have appeared as an undeveloped hinterland, the source merely of a few commodities such as slaves and arms. In European eyes, Constantinople presented an appearance of strange abundance and even stranger shortages. When Liudprand went there in 949, he took with him (as a man well versed in the state of the market) breast-plates, shields, swords, lances and javelins, two cups of silver gilt, and—most precious of all—four eunuchs. All these he offered to the Emperor, and in return he received a pound of gold coins and a great cloth of silk. Twenty years later, when he went again, he made an observation of considerable economic interest: he noted with disgust that the bishops of the Greek church were rich in gold, but poor in servants. Their coffers, he says, were full of gold; but in the midst of this plenty, they were their own stewards and their own masters of horse, they opened the the door for their guests, and they did their own shopping. The servant problem in a highly developed economy is evidently not new: but it was a thing unknown in Europe, where retainers were as plentiful as they were in the undeveloped Highlands of Scotland in the eighteenth century.

This abrupt distinction between an area of silver and gold coinage had not always existed. In Roman times, western Europe had had a gold coinage, and this had been continued in various forms by the barbarian invaders. But one by one throughout Europe, these gold coinages ceased to exist, until, by the middle of the eleventh century, they had all disappeared from ordinary use. Small silver coins were henceforth the only ones in common circulation, and this state of affairs continued until the middle of the thirteenth century when the gold coinages of Italian cities began to make their appearance.

The reason for the disappearance of the gold coinages is not difficult to see. The productivity of Western Europe as a whole left little surplus for exchange—certainly not enough to satisfy the avid desire for the apparently inexhaustible riches which reached the Mediterranean ports from Africa and the East. There was therefore a steady draining away of the precious metals from Western Europe to the great sources of production elsewhere. There is considerable evidence that this process had been going on for several centuries before our story begins. Probably there was less gold and silver in use in Europe in the tenth century than at any time since the days of the later Roman Empire: the combined effects of the export of specie in return for goods, and the exactions of Scandinavian pirates in the two preceding centuries must have seriously depleted the stock of precious metals.

So far as silver was concerned this deficiency could slowly be made good from indigenous supplies. There were silver mines in many parts of Europe. But the native supplies of gold were very small: it is a measure of the hunger for this metal in the tenth and eleventh centuries that there was an elaborate organization for extracting gold from the deposits of the River Po. But the only way in which the scarcity of gold could ever be met was by a reversal of the process which had brought it about in the first place, by an expansion of the productivity of western Europe to meet the needs of the countries which had access to supplies of gold. The sharp distinction between the areas of gold and silver coinage was only a symptom of a much more significant distinction between the area of relatively active commerce bound together by the long sea routes from the Indian Ocean to the Mediterranean on the one hand, and the area of low productivity, primitive commerce and the torture of bad roads and Alpine passes on the other.

Steadily throughout the eleventh and twelfth centuries, the contrast between the two areas was softened. Western Europe, from an economic point of view, became more and more integrated with the eastern Mediterranean. By 1204, this integration had not yet reached the point when gold currencies had once more become a common medium of exchange. But during the next hundred years new gold coinages made their appearance in one country after another in western Europe. They were the heralds of a new economic situation in which Europe was established as an important export area. The position of two centuries earlier had been reversed: instead of the European consumer scraping the bottom of the till to pay for the spices and luxuries of the East, the Italian merchant was seeking new markets for the ever-increasing flow of goods from beyond the Alps.

Venice in the first place, but increasingly in the twelfth century Genoa and Pisa, were the great agents in effecting this change in the commercial position of Europe. As the thin trickle of goods which had passed along the narrow lane between Venice and Byzantium swelled in volume, and as the activities of the Latin merchants were extended in area to the Black Sea, and to the markets of Syria and North Africa, so the towns on which these merchants were based developed new and aggressive commercial policies. With commercial power came plans for—or rather an instinctive drive towards—conquest and colonization: the fall of Constantinople and the demolition of the Eastern Empire in 1204 brought these instinctive policies into the light of day. This portentous event brings us to the second complex of activity which linked western Europe to the eastern Mediterranean in the course of our period.

2. THE CRUSADES

Where and when the Crusading zeal of the West was born, it is hard to say. Certainly it was not born in the border lands where Christian and Moslem met: in these lands we find rather the spirit of live-and-let-live, a certain tentative friendliness even, produced by the desire to avoid unnecessary trouble. The impulse to attack was generated further back, in the power-centres of Europe, partly at Rome, partly among the great families of Northern France, partly in prophetic souls. Perhaps it will never be possible to trace the early stages in the growth of the new spirit. The First Crusade burst on a world which had long been preparing for it in the recesses of its being, but there had been few outward signs of the work of preparation. Pope Urban II at the Council of Clermont in 1095 spoke the words which turned restlessness into action, but his words could have achieved nothing if this spiritual and material restlessness had not been there.

To this restless spirit the thinking part of Europe had long offered opposition. The passionate acceptance of the Crusade as an established aim of Latin Christendom, which characterizes the twelfth century, did not come to birth without a struggle, and it is not irrelevant to note that the Eastern Church remained permanently antipathetic to the ideal. The monastic ideals of the eleventh century were in the main hostile to the idea of the Crusade. To a St. Anselm, for instance, or a St. Peter Damian, the Crusade made no appeal. There could be no place for it in the world which St. Anselm pictured as a vast, turbulent, impure river, carrying off to destruction those who became immersed in it: against this destructive flood there stood only one safe refuge with peace within its walls—the Monastery.

> I advise you—he wrote to a young man hesitating between a monastic life and a military career in defence of the tottering Empire of Constantinople—I counsel you, I pray and beseech you as one who is dear to me, to abandon that Jerusalem which is now not a vision of peace but of tribulation, to leave aside the treasures of Constantinople and Babylon which are to be seized on with hands steeped in blood, and to set out on the road to the heavenly Jerusalem which is a vision of peace, where you will find treasures which only those who despise these (earthly) ones can receive.[1]

In the monastic refuge, restlessness had no place: protected by its saints and fortified by its discipline it offered a centre of rest where the struggle with evil could be fought out in secret.

[1] P. L. 158, Ep. II, 19. (Schmitt no. 117), written probably in 1086. For the understanding of this passage it is necessary to bear in mind the interpretation of Jerusalem as 'Vision of Peace'.

Yet of course there was restlessness in the world, and one symptom of it was the popularity of the pilgrimage to Jerusalem. A monastic writer of the early eleventh century who watched the growing stream of pilgrims from France tells us that the movement started in the middle of the tenth century: it appears that a certain nobleman of Aquitaine called Hugh went to Jerusalem about that time as an act of penance, and this was 'almost before anyone else in these times' had done so.[1] Hugh was a forerunner of many great and successful men of blood, who in this century and the next established the fortunes of their families, though not without incurring the blame for every form of the sin of violence. Fulk Nerra, the greatest and most formidable of the early Counts of Anjou (987-1040), and Robert I, Duke of Normandy (1027-35), were pilgrims of this type. Such men not only went to Jerusalem themselves, but they paid for others to go, and through their activities the interest even of those who did not go became thoroughly aroused.

The spirit of these pre-Crusading days, the religious and secular spirit, the interaction of patrons and pilgrims and the world in which they moved, can be shown by a pilgrimage undertaken at the expense of Richard II, Duke of Normandy, in 1026. The Duke's party was led by a well-known religious leader, Richard, Abbot of St. Vannes at Verdun. These pilgrims were joined by groups from Angoulême, Trier and elsewhere, until they made up a considerable party.[2] They travelled by the land route which had been opened up during the previous generation by the conversion of Hungary, and after a journey of about six months they reached Jerusalem on Palm Sunday 1027. Holy Week was spent in visiting the scenes of the Saviour's trial and crucifixion, and in a long round of religious services. This was the climax of the pilgrimage, and the words of the biographer of the Abbot of St. Vannes show that the visits to the Holy Places were

[1] This remark about Hugh occurs casually in the Life of Abbo, abbot of Fleury, by the monk Haimo. (P. L. vol. 139, 398.) Hugh was a nobleman in the district of Limoges, who made his way by successful violence. He had a large number of sons, for one of whom he bought the bishopric of Cahors. The son had scruples and consulted Abbot Abbo, and in this way the family obtained a small place in history.

[2] See Dom Hubert Dauphin, *Le Bienheureux Richard, abbé de Saint-Vanne de Verdun* (Bibliothèque de la Revue d'histoire ecclésiastique, fasc. 24, 1946), pp. 272-96. The details of the abbot's behaviour at Jerusalem occur in the *Life* based on the information of those who had known the abbot, printed in M. G. H., Scriptores, XI, 288-9.

not a perfunctory business undertaken in a spirit of formal penance:

> At length he (the abbot, came to the venerable place towards which he had so long journeyed thirsting for the sight of it. It is not for me to describe the flow of tears with which he watered the places which were the object of his veneration: when he looked at the Pillar of Pilate in the Praetorium and went over in his mind the binding of the Saviour and the scourging; when he reflected on the spitting, the smiting, the mocking, the crown of thorns; when, on the place of Calvary, he called to mind the Saviour crucified, pierced with the lance, given vinegar to drink, reviled by those that passed by, crying out with a loud voice and yielding up his spirit —when he reviewed these scenes, what pain of heart, what founts of tears do you imagine followed the pangs of pious reflection?

These tears on which the biographer dwells at length, this strong feeling for the sufferings of Christ and the places associated with these sufferings, have a greater importance than appears on the surface: without them there would have been no Crusade. The civilization of the twelfth century owes a great deal to the tears which were shed in the eleventh. They were the forerunner of a new world of sentiment, of devotion, and even of action.

On their way, the pilgrims met many interesting people, whose personal histories are a mirror in which we find reflected the great events of the time. Only two of these people can concern us here. The first was a hermit in Hungary called Gerard. He was a Venetian by birth, who had set out on a pilgrimage to Jerusalem a few years before this time. King Stephen persuaded him to stay in Hungary, and for seven years he lived the life of a hermit at Bél. It was at this period of his life that our pilgrims met him. Like many other men in solitary and out-of-the-way places, he was a pioneer in forms of piety which only became popular during the next two or three generations. He was a strange mixture of East and West, and a voluminous writer of rambling and effusive works. He gave one of these works to the Abbot of St. Vannes, and perhaps in this way a faint influence of his ardent spirit reached the West. Gerard's works, however, were soon forgotten, though his name lived in Hungarian history. He became bishop of Csanád and met a martyr's death in 1046. His appearance gives us a brief glimpse of one of the men who were turning

Hungary into a Christian country in the reign of King Stephen.[1]

The second figure was a man who made a mark in western history. The pilgrims met him in Antioch and he told them a tale of strange adventures. His name was Simeon, the son of Greek-speaking parents from Syracuse. He had received a good education at Constantinople and had, after many vicissitudes, become a member of the monastic community on Mount Sinai. By a curious chance, this monastic house had a close connexion with the distant Duchy of Normandy: the Duke had perhaps come in contact with monks from this house during his own pilgrimage to Jerusalem, and he continued to make it an object of his liberality. The monks of Mount Sinai periodically sent one of their members to Normandy to collect the Duke's alms, and it was on this task that Simeon was engaged when he met the party at Antioch. He had taken a Venetian ship from Egypt, which had been attacked by pirates, and he was cast ashore in a strange land where the inhabitants spoke neither Egyptian, Syrian, Arabic, Greek or Latin. Simeon managed to make his way to Antioch, where he met the pilgrims' party and travelled with it as far as Belgrade. But here he was the victim of a diplomatic situation. The Serbs were hostile to the Eastern Empire and Simeon must have been conspicuous as a Greek: consequently he was turned back, and had to find his way by sea to Italy. He got to Normandy at last to find that the Duke had died, and after some more adventures and journeys he spent the last few years of his life as a recluse in the Roman gateway at Trier. When he died in 1035 he was formally canonized by the Pope.[2]

All these men—Duke Richard II of Normandy, Abbot Richard of St. Vannes, Gerard the Venetian hermit in Hungary and Simeon of Mount Sinai, are examples of the cosmopolitan society of the first half of the eleventh century. The interests of all of them ranged over a wide area and brought them in contact with men from the ends of Christendom. In different ways they illustrate the relations between Latin Christendom and its neighbours. There is a notable

---

[1]Gerard, Bishop of Csanád, and his writings were brought to life in a short note by G. Morin, *Un théologien ignoré du XIe Siècle: l'évêque-martyr Gérard de Czanád, O.S.B.* in the Revue Bénédictine, XXVII, 1910, 516-21. C. A. Macartney has discussed his early biographies in his *Studies on the Earliest Hungarian Sources* in Etudes sur l'Europe centre-orientale, no. 18, 1938.

[2]The Life of Simeon is in Mabillon, *Acta Sanctorum Ordinis Sancti Benedicti*, aec. VI, i, 367-81, and only partially in P. L. vol. 154, 1245-8.

lack of barriers in the intercourse between East and West: we find the Abbot of St. Vannes in cordial relations with the Eastern Emperor and the Patriarch of Jerusalem; the Duke of Normandy is a person well known on Mount Sinai; Venetian ships are trafficking with Egypt. In the reverse direction, the career of the Greek monk Simeon contains no hint that we are on the eve of a great split between East and West: he was listened to with respect by a French provincial Council, on his death he was venerated as a saint at Rome, and his name lived on at Rouen as the reputed source of important relics of St. Catherine brought from Mount Sinai. In all this there is nothing which suggests the atmosphere of the Crusades. We come nearest to the temper which made them possible when we follow the Abbot of St. Vannes round the Holy Places; and we come nearest to the situation which made them seem necessary when we read of Bedouins throwing stones at the Abbot as he celebrated Mass under their town walls. But Europe had a long way to go before the Crusade could appear either a reasonable or a likely possibility.

This was in 1027. Seventy years later the first Crusaders were already on the move. What had brought about this change? The worsening position of the Eastern Empire, and the genuine desire of some to save it; the even more potent though secret desire of others to profit by its disintegration; the dim realization that Islam constituted a widespread and growing threat to Christendom; the sharper realization that the enemies of Christ were triumphing at the scenes of his earthly life. Some hoped to be saved by going; others didn't care if they were damned so long as they found new fields for profit and adventure. There was something in the Crusade to appeal to everyone. It provided an idealistic background for the enterprise of the new aristocracy, which was beginning to find its feet in western Europe, and especially in France. It made knighthood, of which as yet very little good could be said, not only respectable but glorious. Twenty years before the First Crusade, Pope Gregory VII had suggested a way in which knighthood could be rescued from the radical defects attaching to its human and sinful origin, by dedication to the service of St. Peter and particularly to the defence of the Patrimony of St. Peter. But this was never a call with much popular appeal: it attracted a few men in Gregory's own day, but it was swept into oblivion by the larger issues and wider prospects opened out by the First Crusade. Naturally, in their early phases, the Crusades were deeply impregnated with the language and ideals of the men who were the mainstay of the movement. Men who were accustomed to the obligations incurred by holding land in return for military service found it easy to imagine themselves the feudatories of an injured God, seeking in a most literal way to exchange by military service a life tenancy on earth for a perpetual inheritance in heaven:

> God has brought before you his suit against the Turks and Saracens, who have done him great despite. They have seized his fiefs, where God was first served and recognized as Lord.

> God has ordained a tournament between Heaven and Hell, and sends to all his friends who wish to defend him, that they fail him not.

> God has fixed a day for you to be at Edessa: there the sinners will be saved who hit hard and who serve him in his need.[1]

This was the kind of language which made sense to men of the two generations which followed the First Crusade. Crude, narrow, external though the view of religion might be which it implied, yet it commanded the respect and support of contemplatives and mystics. St. Bernard lent the force of his eloquence and largeness of vision to tracing the outlines of a holy order of knighthood, and men discovered that God had need of knights in a cause which they could understand.

Yet several causes were at work, even before the end of our period, to alter the early attitude towards the Crusade—changes in the society in which the crusading energy was generated, and changes in the situation confronting the Crusaders in the field. As to the first, the main change was that the straightforward feudal-contract view of society was giving way to something more complicated and indeterminate. The crusading literature reflects this change: the hearty appeal to the knightly masses lost ground to statesmanlike judgments on men and kingdoms, measured by their response to the crusading ideal. There was less of action and more of satire and romance, and reflection on the ways of men:

[1] The quotation comes from a song of the Second Crusade composed in 1147 and printed by J. Bédier and P. Aubry, *Les Chansons de Croisade*, (Paris, 1909) pp. 8-11.

When men are hot with drinking wine
And idly by the fire recline,
They take the cross with eager boast
To make a great crusading host.
But with first glow of morning light
The whole Crusade dissolves in flight.[1]

This was the mood of the mid-thirteenth century. And indeed men had more than the thought of domestic ease to hold them back. Jerusalem had fallen in 1187 and, with a few rapid strokes, Saladin had reduced the Frankish conquests in Syria to the area of a few sea-ports and strongholds. These blows permanently altered the methods and outlook of the Crusaders. Slowly it became apparent that Islam also was capable of waging a Holy War; slowly also, and increasingly, there developed a new and grim feeling that Christendom stood with its back to the wall. It took a long time for this attitude to work itself out fully in thought and action, but after 1187 the old optimism disappeared. Until Saladin, there had been no check sufficiently serious to make men reconsider the whole position. The manifold and divergent impulses which lay behind the Crusade had been held together in a single purpose so long as the purpose was simple, and, above all, victorious. To win Jerusalem had proved amazingly easy: to hold it at first seemed equally simple —a mere matter of applying the formula of feudal government. Then suddenly, inexplicably, the whole structure collapsed. The kingdom was blown away in a single battle.

The Third Crusade (1189-92) did little to restore the position: strategically it was planned on the old lines of an unsophisticated assault on Jerusalem—and the old ideas proved a failure. It was disheartening and bewildering to find that the way was less simple than it had been in earlier days. New ideas were clearly called for. During the disappointing years which followed the failure of the Third Crusade, the view gradually gained ground that the key to Jerusalem lay in the capture of the great strategic points of the Middle East. The centre of the Moslem power in Egypt was clearly the primary object of any plan made on this theory. But an assault of this kind, which involved a naval expedition, a descent on enemy

[1]These lines are translated from a French poem composed in 1266 by the poet Rutebeuf (J. Bastin and E. Faral, *Onze poèmes de Rutebeuf concernant la Croisade*, Paris, 1946, p. 74). Rutebeuf repeated this sentiment in his long poem, *La nouvelle complainte d'outre-mer*, in 1277 (ibid. p. 126).

territory far from any friendly base, and an immediate contact with the full weight of the enemy power, meant endless planning. The more men planned, the greater the difficulties appeared, and the more gigantic the necessary preparation. Preparation stifling action, and action inadequate to the situation, is the history of the thirteenth-century Crusade. It does not lie within our scope to follow the story of the failure of so much thought and activity, but we may illustrate the situation as it appeared in the early years of the thirteenth century by some remarks on the Fourth Crusade.

The Fourth Crusade (1202-4)[1] is the climax of the period, so far as the relations of Latin Christendom and its neighbours are concerned. It was the fruit of a great deal of thought, and of feeling towards a new solution to the crusading problem; and, in the event, it illustrated the disruptive effect of over-ambitious planning. It was the first of the Crusades to follow the new strategic plan of an indirect approach to Jerusalem. Yet in one way it reverted to the pattern of the earlier Crusade: its leaders were a set of great men, mostly from Northern France, who boasted that they were the greatest uncrowned heads in Europe. Unlike the leaders of the Second and Third Crusades, there were no kings among them. They were, in their way, men of vision: the hot-heads were all for the straightforward plan of attack which had failed ten years earlier—to land at Acre and strike out from there to Jerusalem. Perhaps, looking back, they were right, and the headlong approach offered the best hope of success: but once reflection had set in, this was not a course which could commend itself to far-sighted men. So, at least, the leaders thought.

It seemed that the moment had come to use the predominance of the Latins at sea (which was recognized by Arab commentators as their own greatest weakness) for some bold stroke which offered hope of a lasting success. Hence, in pursuance of this idea, the plenipotentiaries of the crusading leaders made, in April 1201, an agreement with the government of Venice for the transport of the crusading army to Cairo in the following year. It was a bold arrangement, involving the guarantee of a large sum of money to Venice in return for an assured provision of ships and supplies, and the success

[1]The chief source for the history of the Fourth Crusade is Villehardouin, *La Conquête de Constantinople*, ed. and transl. by E. Faral in Les Classiques de l'Histoire de France, 2 vols., 1938, where there is also a good discussion of the various views of the Crusade which have been put forward. Innocent III's letter of 25 May 1205 is found in his Register under this date (P. L. vol. 215, 637-8).

of the whole plan turned on the arrival of sufficient numbers of Crusaders at the port of embarkation to fill the ships and to pay the bill.

Failure at this point meant failure everywhere: and failure of course there was. Miscalculation is a common hazard of warfare at any time: in the circumstances of the early thirteenth century the only surprising thing is that the number of Crusaders fell short of the required number only by about one-half, and that, of the money promised to the Venetians, only about one-third was finally lacking. Considering how little control the leaders had over the parties of Crusaders making for the Holy Land; considering also, in a plan of this kind, which required secrecy and the over-riding of objections, how many people must inevitably have considered themselves left out of the deliberations or their advice ignored; above all, considering the great difficulty of calculating numbers and arranging for payment in advance—one cannot say that the miscalculation was discreditable.

Yet it was fatal. The unpaid debt was a mill-stone round the necks of the crusading leaders; it took away their freedom of action and delivered them into the hands of the Venetians. From this moment, the Crusade drifted from one expedient to another; a whole host of side-issues, which only the momentum of attack could have held in check, dominated the conduct of the army. And, with every expedient, the gap between promise and achievement became wider. First of all, to secure a moratorium on the debt, the Venetians must be helped to reconquer the Dalmatian town of Zara—an operation which brought the Crusaders to the end of the year (1202) which should have seen them already in Egypt.

Then a flattering prospect opened itself to the harassed leaders: a refugee member of the Byzantine royal family appeared with startling promises of financial and military help, union of Eastern and Western Churches, the prolonging of the Venetian contract for a further year to see the Crusaders safely in Egypt—if only they would first restore his family to the Byzantine throne.[1] Here indeed

[1]The refugee, Alexis, was the brother-in-law of Philip of Swabia and nephew of the reigning Emperor at Constantinople. He had arrived in the West, probably at the end of 1201, and had lost no time in trying to enlist support for himself on all hands. How far the Crusading leaders (particularly Boniface of Montferrat, who had been elected leader of the expedition in September 1201) were committed to the cause of Alexis before the expedition left Venice is one of the riddles of the Crusade; but these commitments would have been of no avail had not events impelled the main body of Crusaders in the same direction. For the complex background of these commitments see L. Bréhier's article on Boniface of Montferrat in D.H.G.E. and the same author's Le Monde Byzantin, i, 1947, 362-5.

was a dazzling vision for men sorely tried by adverse circumstances and labouring under Papal censure for their attack on Zara. If only a little of this could come to pass, in how different a light would all their actions appear! Despite some grumbling and defection, the leaders took the plunge. In April 1203 the crusading host sailed from Zara; in June they arrived in sight of Constantinople; on 17 July they succeeded in setting their candidate, Alexis IV, on the Imperial throne All seemed well: the gamble had succeeded.

Now, however, fresh difficulties appeared: the original contract with the Venetians was on the point of expiring. The Crusaders depended on their imperial protégé for its renewal. But equally the Emperor depended on the presence of the Crusaders for the maintenance of his position. The means for carrying out his promises to them were for the present lacking; but, if they would wait until Easter 1204, he would pay the Venetians, and all would yet be well. What could the Crusaders do but stay? They stayed, but the situation got rapidly worse. Soon they convinced themselves that the Emperor had not the will to keep his promises to them. Indeed, very little thought might have convinced them that, even if he had the will, he lacked the power to submit the ancient Empire to the purposes of the western intruders. The Crusaders were too far committed to draw back: only the use of force could now help them, and they did not shrink from it. The first three months of 1204 were a period of confused violence and intrigue, and on 12 April the crusading army burst into Constantinople: four weeks later Baldwin Count of Flanders became Emperor.

For a brief instant the Western leaders stood at the summit of affairs and saw a large prospect unfolding before them. Even men who were disgusted by the horrors of destruction and brutality perpetrated by the crusading army might excusably for a moment suppose that, despite everything which could have been wished away, a century of effort had been crowned by success, and that a brighter future was opening out. They had the vision of a church united by the submission of Constantinople to Rome, of the doorway to Palestine at last firmly in the hands of an active crusading power, of the Byzantine barrier to the extension of western commercial interests in the Middle East and along the shores of the Black Sea finally removed. It was a dream to flatter the spiritual and temporal aspirations of many, from the Pope downwards, who had viewed the progress of the Crusade with deep distrust. On 25 May 1205 the Pope wrote to all the Masters and Scholars of Paris:

By many means and in many ways, God in his mercy calls us to awake to life from the sleep of death, and to raise ourselves from the slough of misery to the hope of everlasting glory. We rejoice therefore, and rightly does the whole congregation of the saints rejoice, that He who is mighty hath visited us from on high, so that a great part of the eastern Church—indeed almost the whole of the Greek Empire—which for very many years has refused to follow the footsteps of the holy Roman Church, has in our own day turned from disobedience to obedience, and from contempt to devotion. And to fill our cup of joy to overflowing, that most Christian man, our most dear son in Christ, Baldwin, the illustrious Emperor of Constantinople, strives with all his might, and labours with ardent and diligent solicitude to sustain the Christian religion, so that the building, which is now in large part constructed, shall not fall to the ground. Lately (wishing, from the devotion planted in his heart, to bring forth the fruit of good works) he has humbly prayed us to encourage and advise you through our apostolic letters to go to the Greek Empire and there to exert yourselves to reform the study of letters, which as you know had their origin in Greece. We, therefore, lending a more ready ear to the Emperor's petitions inasmuch as we have in greater matters proved the sincerity of his faith, earnestly ask you all, and advise you through these apostolic letters to ponder diligently the many and great difficulties which your ancestors experienced in obtaining a grounding in the liberal arts in their youth, and we urge that many of you should go to that land filled with silver and gold and precious stones, rich in corn, and flowing with wine and oil and an abundance of all good things, in order to bring benefits to yourselves and others, to the glory of Him from whom comes every gift of knowledge, and to the receipt not only of temporal honours and riches, but also of the reward of everlasting glory.

These words are the culmination of the easy optimism of the early crusading period. During the succeeding years, events gradually forced men to see that they were founded on a great illusion. As yet, the leaders of western Christendom had little idea of the problems which faced them when they broke out of their narrow bounds. Their political conceptions had been formed behind the protective barrier afforded by the Empire they had just destroyed. These homely conceptions laid more stress on personal rights than on large strategic designs; the idea of the State as an expression of organized force was still weak. This weakness was a source of strength in the development of the complex political tradition of Europe, but it left the Crusaders curiously baffled by the phenomenon of the Eastern Empire. They fell on it as savages might fall on a watch—giving the case to one, the jewels to another, and the disjointed mechanism to a third. The disjointed mechanism was the portion of the new emperor: five-eighths of Constantinople, Thrace, the north-west corner of Asia Minor and some islands of the Dodecanese fell to him. The chosen leader of the Crusade, Boniface of Montferrat, took Salonika and its adjacent territory. Venice took the jewels—the remaining three-eighths of Constantinople and numerous islands and ports scattered between the Adriatic and the Sea of Marmora.[1] The Crusaders were accustomed to the splitting up of fiefs and they adopted the plan of division as the only possible one under the circumstances. Fifty-seven years of miserable life were to teach them what it meant to hold the gateway to the western world, on which the ambitions of many nations converged.

In the whole sweep of European history, the fall of Constantinople in 1204 is only a minor landmark. It meant that for just over half a century (until 1261) there was a French Emperor and a Latin patriarch

[1]The principle of the division was laid down in an agreement made between the Crusading leaders in March 1204, before the assault on Constantinople. This gave the Emperor, who was still to be elected, one quarter of all conquered lands, both inside and outside the city. The remaining three-quarters were to be divided in two equal parts between Venice and the other Crusaders. Villehardouin (§234) gives a brief account of this agreement, of which the complete text is printed from a Venetian source, in G. L. F. Tafel and G. M. Thomas. *Urkunden zur älteren Handels- und Staatsgeschichte der Republik Venedig* in Fontes Rerum Austricarum, 2e Abt., XII, 1856, pp. 445-501. The details of the division were worked out by a Commission during the later part of 1204: the very remarkable and intricate results of these deliberations are contained in a document entitled *Partitio Romaniae*, printed by Tafel and Thomas, pp. 464-88. In the division of Constantinople itself, the Emperor seems to have received the three-eighths due to the other Crusaders as well as his own quarter, so the proportions here were: Emperor, five-eighths; Venice, three-eighths. (See Tafel and Thomas, vol. 2, p. 283.) The results of these arrangements are elucidated in E. Gerland, *Geschichte des lat. Kaiserreiches von Konstantinopel*, 1204-16, (1904), pp. 29-31. But the plans of partition were disturbed almost from the first by the creation of a principality for Boniface of Montferrat, and by the failure of the Crusaders to secure the Empire intact. (See Map LXXIV, by J. B. Bury in R. L. Poole *Historical Atlas of Modern Europe*.)

at Constantinople, and that for varying periods there were principalities of a western, feudal type at Salonika, at Athens and in Achaia. The Greek world was broken open, its wealth dispersed, its ports and strategic points surrendered to the Venetians. The representatives of Byzantine government and civilization were scattered among the three fragments of the Empire with their centres at Nicaea, Trebizond and present-day Albania, which escaped from the control of the invaders. The continuity of Byzantine history was broken, though it is quite doubtful whether the final disaster of 1453 was at all advanced by the events of 1204. Yet in the history of the Crusades and as a symptom of the forces at work in western Europe the fall of Constantinople has great significance. Whatever judgment we pass on the instruments of its destruction must in great part be extended to the leaders of western Christendom as a whole. The crusading leaders were the instinctive interpreters of the impulses running through the society of which they formed part. It seems clear that they were not following a well-laid plan to make use of the Crusade as a weapon against the Eastern Empire in the interests of Venice or any other single power. The final catastrophe emerged from a long series of decisions taken in concert by men who were a very fair cross-section of the chivalry of Europe. There was no master plan; each new turn of fortune imposed the need for a new major decision. The overthrowing of the Empire did not become a matter of practical politics until November 1203—perhaps not even until after the death of Alexis IV in February 1204: on 12 April it was accomplished. There was no time, and, even had there been time, circumstances were too pressing for thought. The Crusaders had to follow their instincts.

That their instincts finally led to the capture of Constantinople is deplorable, but not surprising. In a sense it was an object which had floated before the eyes of the very earliest Crusaders, and it had been a standing temptation ever since this time. As early as 1099 a letter purporting to have been written by the Greek Emperor to the Count of Flanders had circulated in the West: it drew a tempting picture of the wealth of Constantinople, and half invited the Latins to partake of it.[1] Already the charm was working. In 1189 Frederick

---

[1] This letter is printed by C. Riant, *Alexii Comneni ad Robertum I Flandriae Comitem epistola spuria* (1879). Its date and purpose have been much discussed. The letter purports to have been written by the Emperor Alexis to the Count of Flanders, appealing for military help about the year 1091; but it is probably a forgery composed between 1098 and 1099 as an incitement to Crusading zeal.

Barbarossa toyed with the idea of taking the city on his way to the Holy Land, and it is very likely that this formed part of the large ambitions of his successor Henry VI. But when it happened it was the work of smaller men brought up on no great imperial dreams: in a moment the long dream became an accomplished fact, and no one either then or later has been able to point to the moment of decision or to its author. Like the Crusades themselves this tragic climax in their history was the work of no single man and no single force: yet there is a dramatic symbolism in the fact that, while it was Pope Urban II who called up the latent energies which made the First Crusade, the presiding genius of the Fourth Crusade was the ancient, deep and resourceful Doge Henry Dandolo of Venice.

3. THE TRAFFIC IN IDEAS

When men in western Europe between 1098 and 1204 wrote of the wealth of Constantinople they were generally referring not so much to its stores of gold and precious stuffs as to a less material form of wealth: its spiritual wealth. And when they talked of its spiritual wealth, they were generally thinking not of its stores of ancient literature, or of the acquaintance with the works of antiquity which was to be found among cultivated people in the Eastern capital, but of the prodigious stores of relics which were reported to be possessed by the churches of the city. The unworthiness of the Byzantines to be the custodians of this sacred treasure was one of the arguments by which the Crusaders' assault on the city was justified. Naturally, therefore, the fall of the city led to a wide dispersal of this wealth throughout the churches of the West.[1] Many of the objects which were held in particular veneration in the thirteenth century—the Holy Rood at Bromholm, the Holy Blood at Westminster, the Crown of Thorns at Paris—came to these places directly or indirectly as a result of the events of 1204. It was through these objects of devotion that the fall of Constantinople entered into the lives of many people who had no further concern with the Empire or its fate.

There is no legend of the widespread transfer of Greek books and

[1]For the avidity with which Constantinople was ransacked for relics, and for their dispersal after the Fourth Crusade, see C. Riant, *Exuviae sacrae Constantinopolitanae*, 2 vols., 1877-8. The experiences of a Canterbury monk who brought relics of St. Andrew from Constantinople to Rochester in about the year 1090 are related in an account published in C. H. Haskins, *A Canterbury Monk at Constantinople*, E. H. R., 1910, 293-5.

literature to the West as a result of the fall of Constantinople in 1204. It might be inferred from this that there was a lack of interest in the thought and literature of ancient Greece, of which Constantinople was the chief guardian, and to the influence of which Byzantine civilization was the living witness. But this is not so. There was certainly little or no interest in Greek letters, such as there was two and a half centuries later: but among a small circle of scholars there was, and had been for more than a century, intense interest in the results of Greek scientific and philosophical enquiry. For every one person interested in Greek thought there were perhaps a hundred interested in Byzantine relics, but this small class of scholars was busy re-laying the foundations of western science. Nor were they blind to the part which Constantinople could play in providing material for this work, as a single illustration will show.

One of the most important events in the history of the twelfth-century scientific thought was the translation into Latin of Ptolemy's *Almagest*. This was a work which superseded all the books of astronomy at that time known to the West. It is therefore interesting to find that it was first known to the Latin world by means of a copy brought from Constantinople to Palermo about 1160, as a present from the Eastern Emperor to the King of Sicily, in the course of some diplomatic exchanges. Even more interesting is the discovery made by the late Professor Haskins that it was first translated into Latin by a scholar, who heard of the arrival of the manuscript while he was studying medicine at Salerno, and straightway hurried across to Sicily to catch a sight of the great work.[1] The intellectual wealth of Constantinople was therefore not unknown, and the news of the arrival of an important scientific work travelled far and could arouse great enthusiasm.

Why then was Constantinople not more valued as an intellectual treasure house? The answer is twofold. In the first place, though the Latins were interested in Greek science, and some at least of them were prepared to go to great lengths to obtain the scientific works of antiquity, they were not at all interested in the literary culture of Byzantium; and even if they had been, they had not enough Greek to make it accessible to them. At Constantinople science had stood still, but nearer home there were centres of learning where the ancient Greek scientific works were available, and where a body of

[1] C. H. Haskins. *Studies in the History of Medieval Science*, pp. 157–65.

scientific teaching had grown out of them which was greatly desired for its own sake. These were the centres which had developed under Moslem rule in Spain and Sicily. The drawback that the Greek works were here found at one remove from their original language —in Arabic—was more than balanced by finding them surrounded by a body of living thought. There was also what appears to us a strange blindness among the Latins to the disadvantages of making translations from translations: their standards of translation were not high, and they probably depended more than we know on discussion and verbal explanation, rather than on the mere letter of the text. Hence the Arabic contribution to western thought was, during our period, far more valued and far more impressive than the Byzantine contribution. The fate of the translation of the *Almagest* which has just been mentioned is significant in this respect: although the first translation was made directly from the Greek, this translation soon disappeared from sight, and its place in general esteem throughout the Middle Ages was taken by a translation from the Arabic made some fifteen years later.

This fruitful contact between the Moslem and Christian worlds developed after the beginning of our period, and its greatest days were over by the time our period ends. At the very end of the tenth century the first faint traces of Moslem influence on Christendom are to be found in some Arabic numerals in two Latin manuscripts, which had their origin on the Spanish border. These numerals are a curiosity at this time for they did not become common in western Europe until the fourteenth century; but they show that the silent penetration had begun. We can be sure that it had not begun much earlier because between about 960 and 970 the greatest scholar in Europe lived in Northern Spain without feeling in any noticeable way the impact of Arabic studies. Gerbert (the later Pope Silvester II) was possessed by an avidity for books and learning which made him scour the libraries of Europe for unknown texts, with an enthusiasm reminiscent of the later searches of Renaissance scholars. He had gone to the border country near Barcelona for the express purpose of studying; and two of his favourite subjects—mathematics and astronomy—had been intensively cultivated by Moslem scholars. But he left without knowing anything of their discoveries in these fields. The body of knowledge on which he built his reputation in later years was entirely of Latin origin.

Between Silvester II and Innocent III every generation saw some fresh addition to the scientific knowledge which Latin scholars owed to Arabic sources. Gerbert's own pupils were in possession of one of the major contributions to science which came by this channel: they possessed the instrument known as the astrolabe which for the first time made possible accurate measurements of the elevation of the stars. During the next generation, in the middle years of the eleventh century, the stream of medical learning, of which the principal centre at this time was the South Italian health resort at Salerno, began to flow from Arabic into Latin.

These were only the beginnings of a one-way traffic in ideas which, hesitatingly in the eleventh century, but with rapidly increasing impetus throughout the twelfth century, transformed the scientific knowledge of the Latin West. Wherever the receding tide of Moslem or Byzantine power, in Spain, Sicily and Southern Italy, left men who knew Arabic or Greek and could serve as intermediaries between Christendom and the outside world, there were Latin scholars anxious to make use of their new opportunities. Scholars came to these centres from England, France and Italy in search of knowledge; and slowly by their efforts and those of their collaborators a new scientific library was built up more extensive than that which the Latin world had ever known.

It may help to give some idea of the extent of the revolution which was thus effected to make a brief comparison between the scientific works which were available in Latin to scholars in various subjects at the beginning and end of our period.[1]

Taking the 'literary' subjects (grammar, rhetoric and logic) first, there is no great change to record except in logic: here the scholar owed all the more advanced books of Aristotle (the *Prior and Posterior Analytics*, the *Topics* and *Sophistici Elenchi*) to translations made during our period from Greek or Arabic or from both. Yet the revolution here was not as great as this broad change might

[1]For what follows see G. Lacombe, *Aristoteles Latinus*, Pars Prima (Rome, 1939) —the first volume of a great survey of Aristotelian texts in the Middle Ages. Also C. H. Haskins, *op. cit.*, for the work of the great twelfth century translator Gerard of Cremona. For the growth of scientific knowledge at the end of the twelfth century, see A. Birkenmajer, *Le Rôle joué par les médecins et les naturalistes dans la réception d'Aristote au XIIe et XIIIe Siècles* (published in Warsaw in 1930 in *La Pologne au VIe Congrès International des Sciences Historiques, 1928*); T. Silverstein, *Daniel of Morley, English cosmogonist and Student of Arabic Science* (Medieval Studies, X, 1948, 179-86); and Lynn Thorndike, *The Sphere of Sacrobosco and its Commentators* (Chicago, 1949).

make it appear; for though these books of Aristotle had previously been unknown, the outline of his doctrine was (as we shall see later) accessible to the tenth-century scholar from other sources. It is when we come to the scientific subjects that the change in the position is so great as to sweep away the old landmarks: in mathematics the study of geometry had been practically founded by the translation of Euclid in the early twelfth century; in astronomy the fragmentary reports contained in Latin writers on the seven arts such as Martianus Capella had been replaced by the fundamental work of Ptolemy, the translation of which has already been mentioned. In medicine, the translations of the works of Galen and Hippocrates and a whole host of Arabic writers—largely the result of the indefatigable labours of one man, Gerard of Cremona, working in Toledo between 1175 and 1187—had entirely superseded the few elementary works available at the beginning of this period: a well-stocked medical library of the thirteenth century might well have contained no single work known to the Latin world two centuries earlier. Beyond these subjects there was a range of sciences which had no place in tenth-century schemes of knowledge: physics, optics, mechanics, biology—all of them had their origin, so far as Latin Europe was concerned, in translations from Greek and Arabic made during the twelfth century. In 972 none of Aristotle's works on natural science were known in Latin. By 1204, there were translations (in several cases, more than one translation) of Aristotle's works on Physics, on the Heavens, on Meteorology, on the Soul, on Sensation, on Memory and Remembering, on Sleeping and Waking, on Longevity and its opposite, on Youth and Old Age, on Respiration, on Life and Death. So far as we know, all these translations were made in the half century between about 1150 and 1200; and to this body of scientific works which made their way into Christendom in this brief time, we should add the works of Moslem scholars, who henceforth became familiar in the West under strange names—Albumazar, Alfragani, Alfarabi, Avicenna, and soon, and most potent of all, Averroës.

It is clear that these changes constitute a considerable revolution, made possible by the changing relations between Latin Europe and its neighbours during our period. Despite the Crusades—partly even as a result of the Crusades—Christian and Moslem scholars met on common ground in scientific enquiry. The large-scale hostility produced or permitted a measure of collaboration which had been quite unknown in the tenth century. The case was similar with regard to the Jews, who played a notable part in the work of translation and interpretation: here also the twelfth century witnessed an appalling development in outbreaks of hysterical violence against the Jewish community—and, at the same time, many acts of individual co-operation for scientific ends. The heightening of tension between Christendom and the bodies which existed outside it was one symptom of that growth in power and confidence, of which the pursuit of scientific knowledge beyond the ancient boundaries of the Latin tradition was another.

One is tempted to add that the collaboration was of more permanent importance than the hostility. Perhaps it was, but the importance of the activities which have just been described lay in the future. Most of the developments in thought and experience which we shall have to describe later in this book drew their strength from the native tradition of Latin Europe, and owed little to the science which became available in the translations of our period. The work of translation and even of comprehension is after all only a first step; it remained to be seen to what use these translations would be put, and how they would affect the general conditions of thought among scholars and among that wider public which studied but left no name in the history of scholarship. This story belongs to the thirteenth and later centuries. Before the end of our period we can record no single scientific name, no pregnant idea or observation in the field of science, which emerged from the great labours of research and translation. This is only what might be expected: the new world had to be discovered before it could be settled. These translations represented a great adventure in exploration opening out a world quite as new as that which was discovered by the voyagers of the fifteenth and sixteenth centuries. A great wealth of new knowledge was unearthed, but (for all the explorers knew) treasures far richer than any which were ever to be discovered might have lurked in the next book to be turned from Greek or Arabic into Latin. By 1204 the great period of acquisition was coming to an end: the period of digestion was beginning.

C. THE DISTANT HORIZON

Beyond the periphery of Europe, of which, at the end of the

tenth century, the extreme limits were Constantinople and Jerusalem, lay lands known to the Latins only from the testimony of ancient books.[1] Classical writers, of whom Pliny was the chief, handed down to the Middle Ages picturesque and distorted versions of the knowledge which had been gathered about these lands by the ancients. It was from these books that men learnt of the existence

> of the Cannibals that each other eat,
> The Anthropophagi, and men whose heads
> Do grow beneath their shoulders.

Othello claimed to know these peoples from personal experience: with more modesty, but with no less conviction, medieval geographers claimed only literary authority for the existence of this strange world. The maps which illustrated their theoretical reconstructions of these distant lands presented a schematized picture of a world divided into three inhabited continents, Europe, Africa and Asia, separated by a T-shaped system of waters representing the Mediterranean, the Dnieper and the Nile:

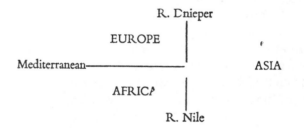

In essentials, the general picture of the world did not change in the course of our period. Although there was a great extension in the area of Latin Christendom, it took place in lands which were already comparatively well known in the West in the tenth century—whether

[1]For the whole subject of medieval geographical ideas see C. R. Beazley, *The Dawn of Modern Geography*, 3 vols., 1897-1906 (vol. 2 covers the period 900-1260) and J. K. Wright, *Geographical Lore in the time of the Crusades*, (New York, 1925). L. Olschki, *Marco Polo's Precursors* (Johns Hopkins Press, Baltimore, 1943) has a stimulating account of the widening of the geographical horizon which culminated in the great journeys of exploration of John de Plano Carpini and William of Rubrouck in the middle of the thirteenth century. There are translations of the original accounts of these journeys in Manuel Komroff, *The Contemporaries of Marco Polo* (London, 1938).

as a result of pilgrimages to the Holy Land, or of wars against the Slavs on the eastern frontier, or from travellers' accounts of the Scandinavian North. Even in the tenth century stray travellers occasionally found their way to the West from more distant parts. We hear, for instance, of an Armenian monk, who wandered from the farthest outpost of Christendom, East of the Black Sea. He turned up in the Lateran church at Rome while Pope Benedict VII (974-83) was holding a council, and his strange appearance and manners excited the anger of the Roman crowd. He was saved from violence by the interposition of Papal authority, and lived to continue his wanderings through Italy, France and Spain, and to bring a rumour of strange lands to the religious houses in which he stayed. He died in a monastery at Mantua in 1016.[1] Such travellers probably added little to the general stock of knowledge: they were like the exotic animals which sometimes found their way to kings' courts as part of some princely gift—dumb witnesses to the existence of lands beyond the range of present experience.

Even the Crusades only touched the fringe of this hostile world. But they had one great effect: they opened men's minds to the size of the unconverted world. Until the First Crusade men instinctively thought of Constantinople as a bulwark beyond which it was unnecessary to look. Gregory VII pictured himself leading an army of the faithful in defence of Constantinople, and many scattered bodies of men found their way into the service of the Greek Emperors from the West. But the Crusade destroyed any prestige which the Eastern Empire might still have in the West, and directed men's eyes to the enemies beyond. It was the work of Urban II to accomplish this change of view. We have several versions of the speech which Urban made at the Council of Clermont in 1095, and though they differ in many details they agree in this: he drew a vivid picture of the wide sweep of the lands which threatened Christendom. His words left a deep impression. Thirty years after the speech was delivered, the English historian William of Malmesbury produced a remarkable elaboration of Urban's words. The Pope's speech, reconstructed in the mind of a scholar who had digested the experience of the First Crusade and who knew his ancient authors,

[1]The monk's name was Symeon. He was soon venerated as a saint, and his life is printed in Mabillon, *Acta Sanctorum O.S.B.*, saec. VI, i, 151-64 and by the Bollandists in *Acta Sanctorum*, Jul., VI, 324-34.

painted a picture of the plight of Europe, threatened by the vast manpower of Asia and the sharp wits of Africa:

The world is not evenly divided. Of its three parts, our enemies hold Asia as their hereditary home—a part of the world which our forefathers rightly considered equal to the other two put together. Yet here formerly our Faith put out its branches; here all the Apostles save two met their deaths. But now the Christians of those parts, if there are any left, squeeze a bare subsistence from the soil and pay tribute to their enemies, looking to us with silent longing for the liberty they have lost. Africa, too, the second part of the world, has been held by our enemies by force of arms for two hundred years and more, a danger to Christendom all the greater because it formerly sustained the brightest spirits—men whose works will keep the rust of age from Holy Writ as long as the Latin tongue survives. Thirdly, there is Europe, the remaining region of the world. Of this region we Christians inhabit only a part, for who will give the name of Christians to those barbarians who live in the remote islands and seek their living on the icy ocean as if they were whales? This little portion of the world which is ours is pressed upon by warlike Turks and Saracens: for three hundred years they have held Spain and the Balearic Islands, and they live in hope of devouring the rest.[1]

The passage of time intensified this awareness of the inexhaustible resources of the enemy they had so light-heartedly engaged. To the South and the East of the Mediterranean as far as the mind could reach or report could verify, there were Moslems. Was there anything beyond—anything which could bring a ray of hope in a world where the general prospect of Crusading success was becoming clouded and uncertain? As the twelfth century wore on, there is evidence that men's eyes turned more frequently to the distant horizon anxious for any message of hope which it contained.

It is in the light of these anxieties that we must examine a curious series of incidents which aroused increasing interest towards the end of the century:

In 1122 a mysterious figure appeared in Rome. It seems that he professed to be the Christian king of an unknown land, and that he impressed a half incredulous Papal court with an account of his

[1]William of Malmesbury, *Gesta Regum*, ed. W. Stubbs, R. S. vol. 2, p. 395.

empire. After this brief appearance he vanished from history, and the whole incident might be dismissed as one of those inexplicable approaches of worlds moving in different orbits and disturbing only for a moment the even tenor of their course, were it not for what followed. A generation or so later the Latin world was again disturbed and intrigued by a flamboyant letter purporting to come from the same mysterious ruler—now given the name of John, and popularly known as Prester John—addressing himself to the potentates of Europe. He gave them a dazzling account of his state and power, called on them to become his subjects and promised them in return some posts of consideration about his court. The letter was no doubt a hoax, though its purpose and the circumstances of its composition have eluded investigators; but it obtained sufficient credence to call for an answer from the Pope. On 27 September 1177 he wrote to Prester John in temperate terms, expounded the Petrine claims, promised further explanations from the bearer of the letter, and entrusted this task to a physician of the papal court called Philip. Philip sailed from Venice, disappeared over the horizon, and we hear no more about him.[1]

All this may seem the merest chasing of a will-o'-the-wisp, but these shadowy events have a wider significance. They are indications of a movement in men's minds. Just a few months after writing to Prester John, the same Pope, Alexander III, addressed a treatise on Christian doctrine to the Moslem Sultan of Iconium in Asia Minor—apparently in answer to letters from him—exhorting him to become a Christian and promising the dispatch of teachers in the faith.[2] Like the earlier letter, this also remained without effect: it is possible that the Sultan's approaches to the Latin church had a political purpose, which a shattering victory over the Eastern Emperor had already fulfilled before the dispatch of the Pope's letter. But these two letters

[1] The subject of Prester John has been extensively treated in F. Zarncke, *Der Priester Johannes* (Abhandlungen der Königl. Sächsischen Gesellschaft der Wissenschaft, Göttingen, VII, 1879). The letter of Alexander III to Prester John is preserved by most of the English Chroniclers of the time ("Benedict of Peterborough", Roger of Howden, Ralph Diceto, Roger of Wendover) under the years 1178 or 1179.

[2] Alexander III's letter to the Sultan of Iconium is preserved in the correspondence of Peter of Blois, P. L. vol. 207, 1069-78. The approximate date of this letter is given by the rubric which appears in several manuscripts of good authority: *Hanc epistolam misit Alexander papa tertius dum essem in curia eius.* Peter of Blois spent several months at the Papal court from the autumn of 1177 to July 1178, and it was probably during this time that the letter was written. He was also in Rome for the Lateran Council of 1179 but there is no evidence that he stayed long on this occasion (cf. J. A. Robinson, *Somerset Historical Essays*, 1921, p. 109).

are indications of the emergence of two new approaches to the Moslem problem in the late twelfth century which obtained a dominating position during the succeeding century: the attempt at conversion, and the attempt to pierce beyond the surrounding wall of Islam. In their different ways they are evidences of larger views of the relations between Latin Christendom and its neighbours.

In all that concerns these wider prospects, the twelfth century was a time of preparation, not of achievement. Imaginations were stirred and the conditions were created which made action possible. When we read quite by chance that, during Richard I's absence from England on Crusade, his powerful Chancellor William Longchamp was accused of setting up to be a Prester John—as we might say 'a little Hitler'—we may be sure that the popular imagination had been caught by the figure of this haughty wielder of supreme spiritual and temporal authority in a far-off land.[1] And when we find, a few years earlier, an English scholar, Robert of Cricklade, Prior of St. Frideswide's, in Oxford, making for his king an abridgement of Pliny's Natural History (the work to which the West owed most of its facts or fictions about the distant unvisited lands), we may think that this is one more example of the attraction which those lands were beginning to exert. There was everywhere a groping beyond the immediate frontiers of Christendom to the vast world beyond that with which Christians came into contact in the markets of the Levant and in the war with Islam. The persuasion that beyond the ring of unbelievers there was a land of long-forgotten Christians had very little foundation in fact, but it was a belief which contained the seeds of future action. The great travellers of the thirteenth century who set out to find these brethren did indeed discover, scattered between the Black Sea and the boundary of China, groups of Christians very different in faith and outlook from anything that was known in the West. Their importance as a buttress to the Christian cause was negligible—the unpleasant truth had finally to be faced—but they played a large, though unconscious part in the opening out of the world by the great travellers of the thirteenth century. These efforts lie beyond the scope of our story: we are concerned only to record the mixture of confused fact, conjecture, myth and spasmodic contact with unknown peoples, which gradually in the course of the twelfth century enlarged the mind and imagination of Europe.

[1] Giraldus Cambrensis, *Opera*, ed. J. S. Brewer, R. S., IV, 425.

CHAPTER II

THE BONDS OF SOCIETY

WE turn now from the description of the relations between Latin Christendom and its neighbours to consider the state of the lands which owed obedience to Rome. It is necessary to bear the broad picture of external relations in mind, because in some ways these relations controlled the course of internal development. In particular, the enclosure of Western Europe at a critical moment in the development of social and political institutions, the practical exclusion from the Baltic, and very limited access to the Mediterranean, meant that the land was the unique source of political power, and almost the only source of wealth. Even at the end of our period, when there were in Europe some centres of intense commercial and industrial activity, Europe was still overwhelmingly a peasant society. The annals of village life are short, yet no more substantial work was accomplished in our period than the building up of a village life which, though full of hardships and shortages, was not without dignity, colour, and the independence which comes from a well-established routine. So much depended on the establishment of this routine, and so little can be said about it. We can dimly see throughout our period the filling up of the countryside, the waste receding, slow improvements in equipment, regular three-year rotation of crops emerging from more primitive arrangements. More clearly we can see that village churches, which were rare at the beginning of our period, are common by its end. Yet it was not until the thirteenth century that village life, both in its material and spiritual aspects, is illuminated by any large mass of documents. As so often happens, the period of growth is one of silence.

By the thirteenth century, however, the main features of village life were established as they were to exist for another five hundred years. Materially, there was probably remarkably little difference between the life of the peasant in the thirteenth century and in the village before it was transformed by modern mechanisms: the produce of the land had increased six fold or ten fold during these centuries, but very little of this increase went into the pocket or stomach of the individual peasant. Compared with the rest of the community, he remained immune from new wants, or the means of satisfying them. Everywhere the peasant kept himself alive on a diet whose scarcity and monotony was broken only by intermittent feastings, at harvest time, at pig-killing time, and when people got married or died. There were great differences in the fortunes of individual peasants: families rose and fell, holdings grew and withered away again, following laws similar to those which governed the rise and fall of kingdoms. Over the fortunes of all, high and low, there presided the unpredictable factors of marriage and child-birth. The rules of succession, infinitely various and complicated, often modified, but with the general authority of centuries of growth behind them, were the framework within which the pattern of village—as of national—life was woven.

The continuity of village life goes back visibly to the thirteenth century. For an earlier period, the records for the most part simply fail us. There are no farming accounts, no court rolls, no treatises on agricultural method, little clear information about the land or its crops. The six hundred years which lie on the other side of the thirteenth century are in these matters a time of great darkness. There are a few surveys of great estates from the landlord's point of view for the eighth, ninth and tenth centuries. After that we must rely on scattered documents: the passing remarks of chroniclers on famines, murrains, droughts, storms and years of plenty; charters which throw light on the most deceptive of all standards of a people's well-being—their legal status; miracle stories and crime stories which show that there was plenty of ready violence—murders committed and houses broken into on small pretexts; men maimed, blinded or emasculated judicially for small offences. The village, from these accounts, seems to have had for its narrow means a strange capacity for supporting men cruelly afflicted in the course either of nature or of law. But to extract a coherent story from these records is beyond our power. Yet the village communicated to society at large in all its activities the rhythm and standards of workmanship of a peasant community. The patient, elaborate skill of the arts, the intricate complexity of law and custom, the slow, remorseless procedure of the courts, the heavy, annually revolving routine of monastic life, the respect for ancient authority in the sciences and for solidity as opposed to novelty in scholarship—all these familiar features of medieval life betray the impulse of an agrarian society. Trade might come to quicken the responses of the community and to create those accumulations of wealth which made possible the art and learning of the later Middle Ages; but at least until the thirteenth century, village life is the basis of every activity, and scholars and artists carry into the world of the spirit the qualities learnt in the stubborn struggle with the land.

But if the society with which we are concerned was predominantly a peasant society, it was also everywhere an aristocratic one; and the aristocracy imposed a unity of a different kind on the face of things. By the end of our period we may picture this unity as one of knightly and political ideals in which the aristocracy of the greater part of Europe concurred. But the way for this diffusion of rules of conduct and guides to statesmanship was prepared by something less intangible than ideals—it was prepared by the bond of marriage. Nothing was more effective in giving men the sense of belonging to a society beyond the horizon of their ordinary interests than the recollection of their distant kinsmen. Women were less rooted in the soil than men; they brought new influences from distant parts and established bonds between men of little or no identity of purpose or of interest. These new influences were often, both in the Middle Ages and later, greeted with cries of distrust and suspicion. The marriage of Henry III of Germany to Agnes of Poitou in 1043, was viewed by solid German churchmen with about as much enthusiasm as English puritans showed for Charles I's marriage to Henrietta Maria: "now we see the shameful habits of French folly introduced into our kingdom" wrote an indignant abbot.[1] These suspicions were not without foundation: a great lady had her own clerks, her own household staff, a large say in the dispensing of religious endowments, and circumstances might easily make her a ruler among unknown people. There was a moment in the eleventh century when the regent in Germany was the French Agnes, and in France the Russian widow of King Henry I.

The career of Agnes[2] illustrates the way in which a woman in a great secular position could overcome the local limitations, which

[1] See the letter of Siegfried, Abbot of Gorze, to Poppo, Abbot of Stablo, in Giesebrecht, *Geschichte der deutschen Kaiserzeit*, (5th Edition) ii, 714-8.

[2] For the life of the Empress Agnes, see M. L. Bulst Thiele, *Kaiserin Agnes* (Beiträge zur Kulturgeschichte des Mittelalters und der Renaissance, vol. 52, 1933).

pressed more hardly on a man, and could absorb more easily than a man, with his more exacting political responsibilities, the disturbing ideas of the time. She was the daughter of William V of Aquitaine, who died in 1030 when Agnes was about five years old. Her mother was a masterful woman, also called Agnes, who later married the Count of Anjou, and made a name for herself for ruthless activity and strong piety. For thirteen years after her father's death, the life of the young Agnes was one of utter obscurity. Then, in 1043, the greatest ruler in Europe sought her hand. She became the wife of the German King, who was soon to become the Emperor, Henry III, and her world shifted to Goslar, Aachen, Kaiserswerth and Speyer. Thirteen years later, at the age of about thirty, she was left a widow, and regent of Germany for her infant son. After six years' rule, a sudden revolution ousted her in 1062, and for the remainder of her life she was one of the small band of devoted adherents of the reforming Popes. She became known throughout Italy for her religious generosity, and she was the chief ambassador between the Papal court and her son Henry IV. It would be hard to imagine a more cruel position: her affection for her family appears to have been strong, but she had to labour in a thankless task of reconciliation in which no permanent success could be achieved, and finally she had to acquiesce in the deposition of her son pronounced by Gregory VII in 1076. It was fortunate for her that she died in the next year, in the false after-glow of Canossa when the reconciliation seemed at last to have been effected, however drastically. Yet it was in these hard years that she found herself. Her friends and spiritual advisers were the French and Italian churchmen who were discovering new forms for the expression of Christian piety—Peter Damian and John of Fécamp; and, in the practical life, Hugh of Cluny, and later, with over-mastering influence, Gregory VII. She was in the inner counsels of a group of men of stern and uncompromising purpose, who watched themselves and others for any sign of weakening in the spiritual cause to which they were committed, and yet relied on the encouragement of the woman who had given up everything in serving their ideal:

Return (wrote Peter Damian to Agnes during one of her missions abroad, using words of Jeremiah with innocent enthusiasm) *turn again, O virgin of Israel to these thy cities. How long wilt thou go about hither and thither*? Although thy journey is not to be ascribed to wandering, but rather to obedience and solid reason, yet I will say to thee in the voice of the Roman Church: Return, return, O Shulamite, return, that we may look upon thy face . . . and that our lord pope may see his desire, and that his great staff and stay Hildebrand, and this broken reed, myself, may all—like Jacob at the coming of Joseph—be strengthened by thy sight.[1]

It could not often happen that a woman by marriage was brought into the centre of such a massive conflict as that between the claims of Empire and Papacy, or that her background and personal preferences were so widely at variance with the traditions and interests of the society into which she was transported by marriage. The gap was too great for her mediation to be of any avail. But less dramatic and less tragic cases than that of Agnes are not uncommon. At a time when the spread of ideas was achieved more through the movement of people than through the impersonal circulation of books, the migrations of ladies of noble birth and the small company of advisers who surrounded them were a potent factor in drawing together remote parts of Christendom. The picture at the front of this book is an illustration of the point. For more than seven centuries, from 1094 to 1805, it formed part of one of the most treasured manuscripts of the monastery of Weingarten not far from Lake Constance, and there is evidence that it served as a model for the important school of artists connected with that monastery in the twelfth century. But it was far from its original home, for it was a product of England. It had been made, probably at Winchester, for a Flemish lady, Judith, the sister of the Count of Flanders, who came to England about 1051 as the wife of one of the sons of Earl Godwin. Her husband, Tostig, Earl of Northumbria, was killed at the battle of Stamford Bridge in 1066, and she returned to her native land. In 1072 she married Duke Welf of Bavaria and took with her to southern Germany manuscripts and relics which she had collected in England. When she died she left these treasures to the monastery of Weingarten, which thus unexpectedly became in a small way an agent in the dissemination of Anglo-Saxon artistic influence in a distant land.

[1] A. Wilmart, *Une Lettre de S. Pierre Damien à l'impératrice Agnès*, Revue Bénédictine, 1932, XLIV, 125-46. Dom Wilmart has also clarified the relations between Agnes and John, Abbot of Fécamp, in his article *Deux préfaces spirituelles de Jean de Fécamp* (Revue d'Ascétique et de Mystique, 1937, XVIII, 1-44).

The wide net cast by the prohibited degrees of marriage often forced a very great man to look far afield for a wife, unless he would make a disparaging match or fall under ecclesiastical censure. These prohibitions continued to be very comprehensive until the end of our period. There was a generally accepted belief drawn from a variety of sources—Biblical, Roman and Germanic—that the prohibited degrees of marriage were seven in number, and throughout the tenth, eleventh and twelfth centuries these degrees were interpreted in their greatest amplitude: that is to say, a man and woman were considered to be within the prohibited degrees if they had had a common ancestor during the last seven generations. There were many reasons why this very comprehensive rule could not have been strictly observed, and the simplest of these reasons was that even so late as the twelfth century only a few of the greatest families could trace their ancestors back through seven generations. Yet the rule was not a dead letter, as we may see from the experience of King Henry I of England—

Henry I had many illegitimate daughters, and he forwarded his intricate policies by marrying them to members of the Norman and French baronage. Two of the marriages which he projected for them were with William of Warenne, earl of Surrey, and a certain Hugh fitz Gervase. But before proceeding to the first of these marriages he found it necessary to submit a genealogical tree to Archbishop Anselm; and some hostile or scrupulous relatives of Hugh fitz Gervase performed a similar office in sending a family tree to Bishop Ivo of Chartres. The result of these two communications was as follows:—

A Forester?

1. Richard I, D. of Normandy (d. 960) = Gunnor	1. Senfria	1. Unknown
2. Duke Richard II	2. Josceline	2. Beatrice
3. Duke Robert II	3. Roger of Montgomery, 1st Earl of Shrewsbury	3. William of Warenne, 1st Earl of Surrey
4. King William I	4. Mabel	4. William of Warenne, 2nd Earl of Surrey
5. King Henry I (d. 1135)	5. Hugh fitz Gervase	
6. Illegitimate daughters		

On this showing, King Henry's daughters were clearly well within the prohibited degrees in regard to both their proposed husbands, and the marriages were forbidden by ecclesiastical authority. The common ancestor who was responsible for the legal barrier had lived two hundred years earlier, and his name seems to have been as unknown to the parties concerned as it is to us. The capacious memory of family genealogists had been able to retain no more than the fact of his existence. The case took men back to the days when the greatest of feudal families were just emerging from obscurity, but even so it did not reach to the limit of the prohibited degrees.

It would seem that these very wide restrictions were founded on a misunderstanding of ancient civil and canonical texts which had the intention of prohibiting marriage only within the third and fourth degrees. Already in the eleventh century, the renewed study of Roman law caused some voices in Italy to be raised in favour of the narrower restrictions of earlier days. But these advocates of reform were defeated for the time being by the allegorical and Scriptural reasoning of Peter Damian confirmed by Papal authority, and it was not until 1215 that the Fourth Lateran Council limited the prohibited degrees to the first four generations from the common ancestor. From this time onwards, therefore, both the marriages projected by Henry I would have been lawful.[1]

But if the law did nothing, dynastic interest did more to make the marriage connexions of any great family very extensive. These connexions were the foundation of public policies and they affected men's ideas in many subtle and unpredictable ways. It is to these public policies that we now turn.

I

THE GROWTH OF GOVERNMENT

Politically, the great question in the tenth century, outside Germany, was how far the disintegration of authority would go. The immediate cause of the disintegration was lack of loyalty, and with lack of loyalty to persons went a decay and confusion of the

[1] For this account of the prohibited degrees of marriage during our period, I have followed A. Esmein, *Le Mariage en Droit Canonique* (2nd edit. ed. R. Génestal, 1929) vol. i, pp. 371-93. On the sisters and nieces of Gunnor, see G. H. White in *The Genealogist*, N. S. XXXVII, 1921, pp. 57-65, 128-132. The main contemporary sources for the marriage proposals of King Henry I are letter no. 261 of Ivo of Chartres (P.L. vol. 162, 266) and letter IV, 84 of St. Anselm (P. L. vol. 159, 243; Schmitt, no. 424).

ideas for which the persons stood. It was a time when claims of allegiance and duty, however well founded in law or in history, counted for nothing when they went beyond the bounds of effective personal power. It was easy for the Count of Anjou to throw off his obligations to the King of France. Would it prove equally possible for the lord of Loches or of any of the castles of the Loire to throw off the authority of the Count of Anjou? How far would the process go? The answer depended partly on the range of those small bodies of armoured, mounted soldiers who were growing up round the strong points of government. Partly it depended on the extent of the sacrifices people would be prepared to make for peace and security. It was no accident that after the confusion of the tenth century the strongest governmental units appeared where there was least in the way of marsh, mountain or forest to separate one community from another—in the open plains where the competition for power was most intense, and where the need for organization was consequently most keenly felt. But even in the most favourable geographical conditions, man's technical equipment was so primitive that this helplessness before Nature—which added to his misery in one way—saved him from the misery of organized tyranny. There was a mercifully large gap between the will to rule and the power to do so, and it may be that bad roads and an intractable soil contributed more to the fashioning of familiar liberties than any other factor at this time.

Perhaps more simply than anywhere else in Europe, the shaping of a new political order may be seen in the valley of the river Loire. There was here so clean a sweep of ancient institutions, title deeds and boundaries, that the emergence of new forms of loyalty and authority was facilitated. Elsewhere the same processes are to be observed, men have the same objects in view, but they work towards them less directly and less swiftly. We shall observe the ambitions, and the restraints imposed on the wills, of some of the most powerful personalities of their time, in studying the emergence of one of the strongest new political units of the eleventh century in the Loire valley.

The County of Anjou.[1] The history of this county from the late

[1]For what follows, see L. Halphen, *Le Comté d'Anjou au XI Siècle,* (Paris, 1906), J. Chartrou, *L'Anjou de 1109-1151* (Paris, 1928), and J. Boussard, *Le Comté d'Anjou sous Henri Plantegenêt et ses fils (1151-1204)* (Bibliothèque de l'école des Hautes Études, CLXXI, Paris, 1938). The chronicle sources are published in *Chroniques des Comtes d'Anjou et des seigneurs d'Amboise,* ed. L. Halphen and R. Poupardin (Collection des Textes pour servir à l'étude d'histoire, 1913).

tenth to the mid-twelfth century provides a rich portrait gallery of the makers of a medieval 'state'. Like other families, the counts took a great interest in their past; they were proud of it, and in the course of years they left a large collection of documents, which illuminate their history. Towards the end of the eleventh century, there was a historically minded Count, Fulk Rechin, who set himself to record the traditions of the family and his own recollections of his predecessors. Looking back from the eminence which the family had attained in his time, he could dimly perceive the origins of their good fortune in the career of an ancestor two hundred years earlier. Nothing was clearly reported about this ancestor except that his name was Ingelgarius, nor was much known about his descendants for nearly another hundred years; but the later panegyrists of the family were able to fill this gap by proclaiming that Ingelgarius was descended from an ancient Romano-British family of high rank. No amount of research or invention could discover how the family had lived in the intervening period since the fall of Rome, but it was concluded that "the matter is unimportant for we often read that senators have lived on the land and emperors have been snatched from the plough". This classical background was a twelfth-century addition to the history of the family—it reveals the romantic prejudices of that period—but in essentials the historians of the family were right. They saw that the effective origins of the family were to be sought in the later years of the ninth century—a time when, as one of them remarked, "the men in established positions relied on the merits of their ancestors and not on their own", and allowed themselves to be elbowed out of the way by new men pushing their way to the front by superior energy and military effectiveness.

The family of Ingelgarius were among these new men. War made them conspicuous, grants of land established their position, marriage consolidated it, and the acquisition of ancient titles of honour cloaked their usurpations. Ingelgarius gained the first foothold in the valley of the Loire, but it was his son Fulk the Red—with a name and physical characteristic which kept reappearing in his descendants—who made the family a power to be reckoned with in the neighbourhood: marriage added to his possessions, force held them together, and the comital rights (for what they were worth), which had previously been shared, were now acquired outright. Two more generations, covering the period from 941 to 987, gave the family a place in legend and in general repute, establishing them in a subtle way in men's minds as well as in their physical experience. The time of Fulk the Good (941 to c. 960) was looked back to as a period of growth, though it was not a time of territorial expansion: it was now that the unnatural fertility of the soil—the fruit of long years of depopulation—was discovered, and prodigious crops rewarded the labours of new settlers. The prize of the Loire valley, the capital city of Tours, still lay outside the range of the count's authority, but the family had great claims to the gratitude of the church in that city. It was said that Ingelgarius had restored to it by force of arms the relics of its patron saint, thus starting the family tradition of goodwill towards the church of Tours. Fulk's reputation in this respect was of a more scholarly kind. It was reported that he delighted to take part in the choir services with the canons and that he was the author of a famous rebuke to a king who ridiculed his clerical tastes. The story is exceedingly improbable, but it illustrates the way in which the family was adding to itself fame of a more than military kind. Fulk's son, Geoffrey Greymantle, who was Count from about 960 to 987, added to this legendary reputation: he was one of the select band of tenth-century heroes whose names were handed down to form part of the stock-in-trade of twelfth-century poetic memory. He was pictured as the standard bearer of Charlemagne in the *Song of Roland*, and in his own right he was the hero of various stories, in which his prowess and counsel saved the kingdom from its enemies.[1]

By 987 the family was ready to emerge from its legendary and epic age on to the stage of history. At this moment there appeared one of those powerful figures, who combined all the qualities and ferocity of his race and consolidated the achievements of the last four generations: Fulk Nerra, the Black, Count of Anjou from 987 to 1040. We cannot do better than look at him through the eyes of his grandson, Count Fulk Rechin. This is what he records of Fulk Nerra:

1. He built thirteen castles, which he can name, and many more besides.
2. He won two pitched battles, against his neighbours to East and West. (Continued on p. 86)

[1]For the place of Geoffrey Greymantle in epic tradition, see F. Lot, *Geoffroi Grisegonelle dans l'Épopée* in Romania, 1890, XIX, 377-93, and *Traditions sur Geoffroi Grisegonelle et sur Helgaud de Montreuil* in Romania, 1920, XLVI, 376-81.

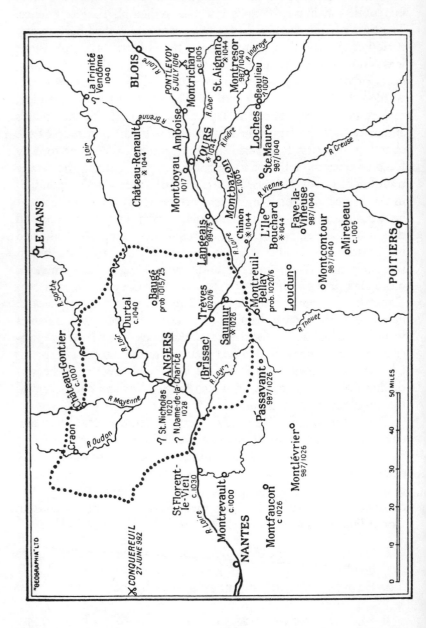

LE MANS

BLOIS

La Trinité Vendôme 1040

Château-Renault X 1044

Montrichard

PONTLEVOY 5 July 1016

St. Aignan X 1044

Montrésor 987/1040

Beaulieu C./1007

R Indroye

R Cher

R Bra>enne

Amboise

R Loir

Montboyau 1017

TOURS X 1044

R Indre

Loches

Ste. Maure 987/1040

Montbazon C. 1005

R Creuse

Langeais 994/5

Chinon X 1044

R Loire

L'Ile Bouchard X 1044

Faye-la- Vineuse 987/1040

R Vienne

Montcontour 987/1040

Mirebeau C. 1005

POITIERS

R Sarthe

Baugé prob 1015/25

Durtal C.1040

Trèves 1020/6

Montreuil- Bellay prob.1020/6

Loudun

R Thouet

Château-Gontier C.1007

R Loir

ANGERS

(Brissac)

Saumur X 1026

R Layon

Passavant 987/1026

R Mayenne

St. Nicholas 1020

N Dame-de-la-Charité 1028

Craon

R Oudon

Montlévrier 987/1026

St. Florent- le-Viel C.1030

Montrevault C.1000

R Loire

Montfaucon C. 1026

NANTES

X CONQUEREUIL 27 JUNE 992

GEOGRAPHIA LTD

0   10   20   30   40   50 MILES

ANJOU IN THE TIME OF COUNT FULK NERRA, 987–1040

The map is designed to illustrate the formation of the County of Anjou in the time of Fulk Nerra, in relation to the neighbouring capitals at Nantes, Le Mans, Blois and Poitiers.

1. The boundary of the old Carolingian County is marked with a dotted line. (For a detailed description of the line of demarcation, see C. Port, *Dictionnaire Historique, Géographique et Biographique de Maine-et-Loire*, i, 1878, pp. iii–iv.)

2. The aspects of Fulk Nerra's work shown on the map are his monastic foundations, his battles and his castles:

    i. The monastic foundations are marked thus: **?** —Beaulieu and St. Nicholas at Angers were the work of Fulk Nerra himself. N. Dame-de-la-Charité was a nunnery founded jointly by Fulk and his wife. Holy Trinity, Vendôme, was founded by Fulk's son Geoffrey Martel, but the preliminary steps were taken in his father's life-time.

    ii. Fulk Nerra's two pitched battles against the Counts of Brittany and Blois respectively are shown thus: *CONQUEREUIL* and *PONTLEVOY*.

    iii. All the other places shown on the map are sites of castles either in the Count's hands or dependent on him. The dates indicate the castles built by the Count. When no date is given, the castle was certainly in existence before Fulk's time, except for Brissac which is shown in brackets because it is first heard of in 1067. When the date is preceded by an asterisk the castle was captured by the Count at this date. In addition to those castles captured by Fulk, the last strongholds of the Count of Blois in Touraine, captured by Geoffrey Martel in 1044, are also shown: this was the culmination of Fulk Nerra's work.

3. Castles which are underlined were the centres of comital local government (*prévôtés*) in the twelfth century. It will be seen that, of these nine centres, four (Baugé, Saumur, Langeais and Montbazon) were castles either built or captured by Fulk Nerra, and one (Tours) was captured by his son in 1044. The foundations of the later government of Anjou were thus largely laid by the military operations of Fulk Nerra. (For details of most of these castles, see L. Halphen, *L'Anjou au XIe Siècle*.)

3. He built two abbeys, one at Angers and the other near Loches, the great outpost of his power in the South East.
4. He went twice to Jerusalem (this is an understatement: it is almost certain that he went three times); and he died on his way home during his last journey.

Each one of these items, properly considered, stamps him as a man of note: taken together they convey a vivid impression of a pioneer in the art of feudal government. In the first place, the castles: they were the guarantee of the stability of the régime. Fulk was a pioneer in the building of stone keeps, and one formidable example of his handiwork still survives at Langeais. The inexpugnable fortresses solved at once the problem of defence and of government—they made loyalty easy. The battles were more speculative—brilliant gambles based on the solid capital of defensive positions. It was a time when he who committed himself to open battle, committed his fortune to the winds. But the reward of successful enterprise was great, as befitted the uncertainty of the outcome; and the battle of Conquereuil in 992 against the Count of Brittany was one of the foundations of Angevin greatness.

We pass to the expressions of Fulk Nerra's religious zeal. He and his contemporary Duke of Normandy were the greatest of the pilgrims who set on foot the movement to Jerusalem. In them the alternation of headlong violence with abrupt acts of remorse and atonement, which characterises the early feudal age, has its full play. Perhaps more than in anything else, the nature of the man is revealed in the documents which recount his religious benefactions. They breathe a vigorous and autocratic spirit, unencumbered by any feeling after intangible things, yet accessible to a sense of guilt and stirred by a sense of littleness before the miraculous disturbances of nature. These documents deal with stark facts:

I give them (says Fulk's charter to Beaulieu) the blood, the thieves and all evil deeds, of whatsoever kind they are (that is to say, jurisdiction over, and the profits arising from the punishment of, murderers, thieves and other criminals), between the rivulet *de Concere* and the oak of St. Hilary, and between the vegetable garden and the elm on which men are hanged. And wheresoever, on my land, the abbot does battle for anything, if his champion is beaten, he shall go free and pay no fine to my reeve or any official.[1]

So far as Fulk speaks to us at all, he speaks to us in words like these. Yet, when all is said, we are very far from understanding a man like Fulk Nerra. It is only occasionally that we are allowed to see behind the façade of ruthlessness and activity to the not over-confident humanity which guided arm and hand. It takes some extraordinary event to reveal these men in their more domestic moods. They must often have sat with their wives at the upper windows of their newly built castles, but it is not until a meteor falls into the garden below that we have a picture of Fulk's formid-able son Geoffrey Martel and his wife Agnes (the mother of the Empress) racing down to the spot where it fell and vowing to found an abbey dedicated to the Holy Trinity, in memory of the three glowing fragments which had flashed before their awestruck eyes. It was in the face of the miraculous that they became most human. When the Duke of Aquitaine heard that a rain of blood had fallen in his duchy, he did not reflect that he was hostile to the royal pretensions—he humbly wrote and asked the king if he had any learned men who could explain the event. And their answers were such as to make any man pause in a career of wrong-doing.[2] But, on the whole, the secular leaders of the early eleventh century must be judged by what they did, and not by what they thought or intended. Judged by this standard Fulk Nerra is the founder of the greatness of the County of Anjou.

His life-time brings us to an age of serious, expansive wars waged by well-organized and strongly fortified territorial lords. The confused warfare, haphazard battles and obscure acts of force of the first hundred years of the family's history had turned scattered and precarious rights into a complex, but geographically compact and militarily impregnable association, dependent on the Count. The process was directed by an instinctive feeling for strategic advantage, which perhaps lends to the history of these years an appearance of consistency greater than in fact it possessed. The methods were not refined, but they were practised with a consistency of purpose which inspires a certain respect. The swallowing of an important strong point might be preceded by many years of steady

[1] L. Halphen, *Le Comté d'Anjou au XI Siècle*, pp. 351-2.
[2] These letters were preserved among the correspondence of Fulbert of Chartres and they are printed in P. L. vol. 141, 239-40 and 935-8.

encroachment. It was necessary, first, to get established at some point within the territory to be threatened—an operation carried out by a careful marriage, a purchase which the documents represent as a gift, or an act of force or fraud. Then a castle was built as a base of operations. After that, watchfulness: a minority, the chance offered by the enemy's engagement elsewhere, or a lucky battle, might complete the circle. The town of Tours, for instance, was not swallowed until 1044, but in a sense the whole history of the family was a preparation for this event: the good relations with the church of the city seem to go back to the founder of the dynasty; the encircling of the town by a ring of castles at Langeais, Montbazon, Montrichard and Montboyau had been begun by Fulk Nerra fifty years before the final victory. How much was design and how much a kind of inspired opportunism it would be useless to enquire. Once started, the process went on as relentlessly as the operations of the Stock Exchange.

But by the middle of the eleventh century, easy progress by these familiar methods was no longer possible. The weak had been made dependent, the strongholds of intruding neighbours had been taken and, by the same token, distant claims of the Counts outside their own territory had been abandoned. To the west stood Brittany, to the east Blois, to the north—across the still debatable land of Maine—Normandy, to the south Poitou. They faced each other as equals. Although the armed peace was often broken, the chief interest of the next hundred and fifty years lies in the emergence of stable political institutions and the elaboration of a new system of law. The swashbuckling days were over, and the régimes which had emerged began to clothe themselves in habits of respectability. Up to this point, St. Augustine's dictum that secular governments are nothing but large-scale robbery seemed to be abundantly justified by the facts: but slowly something more complex, more sensitive to the positive merits of organized society, seemed to be required. Government became something more than a system of exactions from a conquered countryside, and there developed a routine for the peaceful exploitation of resources and for the administering of justice. For this, an expert and literate staff was needed, in addition to the menials and military leaders who had satisfied the requirements of a more primitive age. Government by means of the written word returned after a long silence. Until the time of Fulk Rechin, the Count seems not to have felt the need for having someone at hand who could write his letters. All the known comital documents were written by an outsider. It was quite natural that this should be so. The most frequent occasion for writing a document was to make a record of some act of generosity, by which the Count had endowed a religious house: it was the beneficiary who was interested in making the record, and to him fell the labour of making it. If on the other hand, as might sometimes happen, the Count wished to correspond with the Pope or the King of France, he called in some notable scholar for the occasion to write his letters for him. But slowly his needs outgrew this primitive expedient. The necessity for transmitting orders and preserving information became more pressing, and by the end of the eleventh century the Count was not only sealing or witnessing documents which had been written for him by those with whom he was in casual contact; he had men about him who could conduct his correspondence and were eager to manage his affairs. It is an important moment in history, not peculiar to Anjou but common to the governments of north-western Europe. The continuity of government was re-established. The work required trained men, and the presence of trained men— by a process with which we are familiar—made more work for more trained men.

The rise of the great schools of Northern France and Norman England coincided with and forwarded this movement in government. Slowly the ruling households of Europe, at all levels from the Papal Court to the household of a minor baron, were penetrated by men calling themselves 'Masters', men who had studied in the Schools—or as we should say university men. The flow of university men into the Civil Service and into technical positions from the 1870's to our own day is not more significant of the new part played by government in daily affairs, than the similar flow of 'Masters' into official positions which began in the early twelfth century and, by the end of our period, had transformed the operations and outlook of secular government. The revolutions in thought which transformed the mainly monastic learning of the eleventh century on the one hand, and the mainly clerical education of the early nineteenth century on the other, had, both of them, wide repercussions in the sphere of government. The 'Masters' of the twelfth century brought to government a training, a method and a breadth of vision which had been unknown in the previous century;

they were only the instruments of government, but they were finer instruments than had been known before.

With the refinement of the instruments of government, the range of effective government became greater. The intense localism of the eleventh century, in government as in other spheres of activity, gave place to a greater spaciousness. Anjou was as much affected by this extension of range as any other part of Europe. But the extension did not come by the old piecemeal method of encroachment—a castle here and a town there. It came in the first place as a result of a series of remarkable marriages which made Anjou part of a wide Empire: in 1128, Geoffrey Count of Anjou married Matilda the heiress of Normandy and England. It took nearly twenty years of war and uncertainty to make good her claim to these lands, but in the end it was made good in the person of Henry II, *Rex Anglorum, Dux Normannorum, Comes Andegavorum;* and—by his marriage with Eleanor of Aquitaine—*Dux Aquitanorum;* then finally (although the title was not officially used until the reign of his son, John) *Dominus Hiberniae*, Lord of Ireland by Papal authority. Henry II's complex association of lands and titles symbolizes the extension of vision of a late twelfth-century ruler. Events quickly demonstrated the insecurity of this great territorial combination, which was broken asunder by a few vigorous strokes of the French King Philip Augustus in the years 1203 to 1205. Anjou henceforth moved in the family orbit of the Kings of France. During the remainder of the Middle Ages, it formed part of more than one political combination; but whether it was part of the French royal demesne, or was joined in uneasy association with the Kingdom of Naples, its days of independent local development were over.[1]

No single pattern of political development holds good for the whole of Europe. There was not everywhere the clean sweep of ancient institutions, title-deeds and boundaries which facilitated the emergence of a new order in Anjou. It would be quite wrong to take Anjou as a typical case. Yet what happened there is unusually instructive for we can point to Anjou and say: this is what happened where the control exercised by the past was least effective, and where the disturbing elements of trade, large towns and active commercial

[1]The territorial connexions of Anjou after 1205 can be followed in A. Longnon, *La Formation de l'Unité Française* (Paris, 1922).

oligarchies were not conspicuous. Where these elements are present, the pattern of events is greatly complicated. For example, if we compare the history of the Counts of Tuscany with that of the Counts of Anjou, we find a broad similarity of development shot through with some remarkable differences of detail.[1] Like the Angevins, the Counts of Tuscany could not in the twelfth century trace their ancestry further back than the late ninth century. They also began as an obscure family of vassals who rapidly made their way forward in the tenth century. Their fortunes also were founded on royal favour, and it was their aim to form their scattered possessions into a compact territorial lordship. But the methods they had to employ were more tortuous than those of the Counts of Anjou, and their success was more limited. The royal, or Imperial, power counted for more in Northern Italy than in Northern France, and the Tuscan counts made their way more peacefully and less boldly on that account. They owed much of their land to grants made by churches, on conditions which were already obscure and no doubt ignored in the eleventh century. And, of course, marriage contributed its share to the accumulation.

When the great Countess Matilda died in 1115 she left, by her will, her lands to the Roman Church. It was a donation which had been in the wind for thirty or forty years: Gregory VII had negotiated it, and the friends of the Roman Church attached great importance to the expected event. The document of Gregory VII's time was lost—perhaps in the troubles of his later years—but in 1102 a new one was drawn up to make the gift as unambiguous and absolute as possible. To prevent a repetition of its loss it was carved on a marble slab and preserved in the crypt of St. Peter's, where fragments of it have come to light during the last century. Yet all these careful preparations and high expectations foundered because the diverse origin of the lands which made up the Countess's heritage had not been forgotten. The Emperor claimed his own. But here endless difficulties arose. The past was remembered sufficiently well to confuse the issue, not sufficiently well to clarify it. The question of distribution was never solved, and the problem added another

[1]For the origins of the house of the Counts of Tuscany, see H. Bresslau, *Jahrbücher des Deutschen Reichs unter Konrad II*, i, 431-6; and for the history of the family possessions, A. Overmann, *Gräfin Mathilda von Tuscien: Ihre Besitzungen: Geschichte ih es Gutes von 1115-1230 und ihre Registen* (1895). Mathilda's Testament of 1102 is printed in M. G. H., *Leges*, Sectio IV, i, 654-5.

cause of confusion to the tangled relations of Popes and Emperors for the next two generations. Like Anjou, but as a result of a quite different chain of events, the county of Tuscany from scattered origins in the tenth century achieved a limited cohesion and territorial compactness in the eleventh, and in the twelfth century was drawn into the field of wider politics and became part of the complicated sum of imperial rights and possessions. In law, no doubt, the territories should have been torn apart and returned to their original sources: in practice, the force of cohesion was enough to prevent this, and the lands continued to be treated as a whole, though not in the way that the Countess Matilda had sought to bring about.

It was the misfortune of Northern Italy generally that the past was remembered sufficiently well to suggest problems and to raise claims, which could neither be settled nor adequately defined; Imperial rights and Roman Law were never quite forgotten, but their application was doubtful in the extreme, as Frederick Barbarossa discovered to his cost. The county of Anjou was happier in that, in the tenth century, it had no history, and having no history, it produced new forms of organization unencumbered and uncontrolled by the theories which had guided men in the past.

There was indeed, at the time when Anjou was emerging as a recognizable unit of government, a great deal of theory about the duties and position of the secular ruler, but it contained nothing to help—and men of the stamp of Fulk Nerra saw to it that it did little to hinder—the activity of the Counts. The weightiest part of political theory was enshrined in the coronation rites used in the hallowing of kings.[1] And if the words used in these rites are to be trusted, the majesty of kingship had reached a height to which even the Tudors could not aspire. But this majesty of kingship only emphasized the nothingness of countship, unless (which was far from the truth) the count would be satisfied with the reflected glory of a royal official. The position of the count was based on violence, with the covering of such respectability as it could gather around it in the course of time. By contrast, the position of a king rested on eternal foundations: he was in the strictest sense God's anointed, endowed by God

[1]For the history of these ceremonies, see P. E. Schramm, *Die Krönung bei den Westfranken und Angelsachsen von 878 bis um* 1000 (Zeitschrift der Savigny—Stiftung für Rechtsgeschichte, LIV, Kan. Abt. XXIII, 1934, 117-242), and the same author's *History of the English Coronation* (transl. L. G. W. Legg), 1937.

with powers which combined important aspects of the powers of bishops and priests, as well as the sanctions of secular rule. He was anointed with the holy oil used in the consecration of priests; he was invested with the ring and staff conferred on bishops, with the power to destroy heresies and to unite his subjects in the Catholic faith; and he received the sword and sceptre with words which gave the highest authority to his use of violence. It was by virtue of this consecration that kings could call themselves—as they could without impropriety in the tenth century—*Vicars of Christ*[1]; and it was by this same virtue that an extreme advocate of old-fashioned views in the late eleventh century could write:

> Kings and Priests have a common unction of holy oil, a common spirit of sanctification, a common quality of benediction, the name and power (*rem*) of God and Christ in common... Both Kings and Priests are deified and sanctified by the grace of unction and by the consecration of their benediction . . . If therefore the King and the Priest are both, by grace, Gods and Christs of the Lord, whatever they do by virtue of this grace is not done by a man but by a God and a Christ of the Lord. And when the King gives a bishopric or a Priest a kingdom, it is not a man who gives them but a God and a Christ of the Lord.[2]

This is a strange language to our ears, but it would have been less strange in the tenth than it was in the eleventh, and less strange

[1]For the use of this phrase by King Edgar, see below p. 161.

[2]The quotation comes from the writer generally known as the "Anonymous of York". (M. G. H., *Libelli de Lite Imperatorum et Pontificum*, III, 663-5.) Recent work has shown that he almost certainly had nothing to do with York nor with Gerard, archbishop of that city, as was supposed by H. Boehmer, who in his *Kirche und Staat in England und Normandie im XI und XII Jahrhundert* (1899) first emphasized the importance of his work. He probably wrote at Rouen, and was in the main a thinker of old-fashioned principles, trying without complete success to achieve coherent theological and political views in a time of great stress and difficulty. (See G. H. Williams, *The Norman Anonymous of A.D.* 1100, in Harvard Theological Studies, vol. 18, 1951). A striking expression of the point of view of the "Anonymous of York", which is all the more valuable because it is found in a work entirely lacking in controversial bias, occurs in the *Life and Miracles* of the Northumbrian King and Saint Oswin, written at Tynemouth in the early twelfth century. The author describes Oswin's humility in the presence of Bishop Aidan, as specially remarkable, because *regiam majestatem pontificali dignitati praelatam esse novimus, tam ex spiritualis unctionis singulari sacramento, quam ex temporalis principatus excellenti dominio.* (*Miscellanea Biographica*, ed. J. Raine, Surtees Soc., 1838.) For further discussion of the effect of the royal unction, see F. Kern, *Gottesgnadentum und Widerstandsrecht im früheren Mittelalter*, 1914, pp. 53-123 (English translation with the title *Kingship and Law* by S. B. Chrimes, 1939, pp. 27-61), and E. H. Kantorowicz, *The King's Two Bodies: a Study in Medieval Political Theology* (Princeton, 1957).

in the eleventh than it became in the twelfth century. The man who wrote these words was struggling against a rising tide, against a new spirit of definition which would rigidly sever the powers and nature of a king from those of a priest, but the attitude he expressed never quite lost its hold. In the time of Henry II and Archbishop Becket, John of Salisbury could still complain of ignorant people who believed that the dignity of priesthood belonged to the royal office,[1] and it is possible that Henry II did something to encourage this belief. There were important political conclusions to be drawn from the meaning of the king's anointing, and what is remarkable is not that very generous conclusions were drawn therefrom in the early part of our period, but that they made so little impression on either the thought or the practice of the twelfth and thirteenth centuries.

This collapse of a long-established habit of thought was the more remarkable because it took place at the very moment when the Kings of France and England were successfully claiming a new addition to their supernatural powers in the form of a miraculous gift of healing, which (it was said) descended from king to king as part of the royal office. The origins of the belief in this miraculous power are very obscure: all that is certain is that the claim was being made in both France and England in the early twelfth century, and that it had developed in some way from miracles reputed to have been performed by Robert the Pious in France and Edward the Confessor in England in the first half of the eleventh century.[2] Once established the belief proved to be astonishingly tenacious, and it might have seemed to a far-sighted observer in the late eleventh century that the novel claim of miraculous power combined with the ancient semi-priestly character of the king heralded a very extreme form of royal ascendancy in the political sphere. This union of supernatural powers in a temporal ruler, so contrary to the political temper of western Europe as we know it, is one of the might-have-beens of history. There were many forces working against it, but it did not seem so remote a possibility in the time of Gregory VII.

The most important force working against this theocratic conception of secular authority was the real power of men like the Counts of Anjou, whose rule owed nothing to theory or to religion.

[1] Ep. 241 (P. L. vol. 199, 274).
[2] For the history of the royal power of healing, see M. Bloch, *Les Rois Thauma-turges* (Strasbourg, 1924). I have suggested some revision of his account of the early history in E. H. R., 1943, 389-91.

Their power belonged to a world of crude fact, shockingly uncon-
secrated and dumb. But if the counts found no words to justify
themselves, and took refuge from their secular misdeeds in works of
pilgrimage and pious benefaction, there were others who began to
find words for them. In about the year 1131, Hildebert, Archbishop of Tours, wrote to the Count of Anjou of that day—a
young man, recently married to the sole legitimate daughter of
Henry I, and the begetter of a long line of English kings—who had
recently laid himself under a vow of pilgrimage:

> You have laid yourself under a vow, but God has laid on you an
> office. Your vow demands a journey, but God requires obedience.
> Your journey will bring you to the memorials of the saints, but
> your obedience will make the saints themselves mindful of you.
> Consider well whether the fruit of this journey can compensate
> a breach of that obedience. If so, lay down your shield without
> delay, exchange your sword for a staff, go off at once and join the
> pleasant companions who, as Solomon says, are as good as a
> carriage on a journey. But if the fruit of government (*administra-*
> *tionis*) is much greater and more desirable than this—which no-
> one will dare to deny—stay in your palace, help the afflicted, live
> for all, that all may live for you: live for the State (*reipublicae*);
> work for it day and night. Let equity not acceptance of persons be
> the rule of your court. Rule yourself by law, and your subjects
> by love.[1]

Words like this would certainly have surprised a Count of the
old school of Fulk Nerra; he would scarcely have believed that ars
administration could be so respectable. But Hildebert, and scholhis
who came after him—men who knew what Cicero and Seneca had
said about the office of a ruler—were opening up a new vein of
political theory, based on human rights and needs, and the innate
dignity of the secular order of society. The view expressed in a few
words by Hildebert was developed in great detail in the next generation by John of Salisbury in his *Policraticus*, and afterwards by a long
series of distinguished writers. These writers gave new standards
of conduct to secular rulers and taught them, or at least the clerks in
their service, the dignity of just authority. They defined the limits
of the ruler's power, and distinguished the qualities of the just ruler

[1] Ep. 1, 15 (P. L. vol. 171, 182).

from those of the tyrant: in their hands the idea of a tyrant again became a political concept to be feared and fought over. They raised secular government from the dust of violence and self interest while they divested it of the cloak of a semi-priestly authority. In doing this they spoke not only as advocates of a new view of secular rule, but also as members of a Church which had lately come through a great crisis: churchmen who two centuries earlier would have emphasized the powers which the king received in his religious consecration, now shrank from the dangers which they saw lurking there; and kings, despite their consecration, were placed on the same footing as other secular rulers who derived no dignity from any holy unction.

This change of attitude was the greatest contribution of our period to the science of ordinary life. It affected government at every level. At the beginning of the period, the appeal to the supernatural was the most common of all the expedients of government. From the ninth century onwards we have a large number of liturgical forms designed to elicit a divine judgement in all kinds of doubtful cases, whether of crime or disputed ownership. Churches were repositories for the instruments by which the divine judgement was conveyed—the cauldron for the hot water, the brazier for heating the iron, and so on—and one of the commonest functions of the priest must have been the blessing of these instruments to their purpose. The disappearance of these instruments together with the religious ceremonies which surrounded their use was a slow process. Throughout the eleventh century we can mark no decline, and many curious cases can be cited of the use to which they were put: they decided the paternity of two children of Robert, Duke of Normandy; they convicted a bishop of Florence of simony; and the greatest church council of the century seems to have contemplated the use of the ordeal as a means of testing the orthodoxy of Berengar of Tours.[1] These were unusual cases but they illustrate the tendency to fly to the ordeal in any matter of doubt whatsoever.

During the twelfth century this habit of mind underwent a

[1]For the first of these instances, see Ordericus Vitalis, *Historia Ecclesiastica*, ed. Le Prévost and L. Delisle, IV, 82; for the second, see P.L. 146, 693-8, for the third, see Berengar's own account of the Council of 1079 in Martène and Durand, *Thesaurus Novus Anecdotorum*, IV, 103-9, which can, I believe, be defended against the criticisms of C. Erdmann in *Quellen und Forschungen aus Ital. Archiven und Bibliotheken*, XXVIII, 1937-8, pp. 48-74. There is a valuable and succinct account of the ordeal in F. Liebermann, *Die Gesetze der Angelsachsen*, II, 2, art. *Ordal*.

rapid change. The change took place at the same time as the change in the attitude to secular government, and some of the same causes were operating in both cases. The study of Roman Law opened men's eyes to the existence of an elaborate system of purely human proof; and the growth of a uniform Canon Law, which applied the methods of Roman Law, carried the lessons of the lawyers far and wide. Moreover, with the greater abundance of written evidence supplied by the growing activity of clerks in government, disputed facts about ownership, which had been one of the most fertile sources of appeal to the ordeal, became amenable to the test of human testimony. Above all, men came more and more to doubt the efficiency of judgement by ordeal. William Rufus appeared a monster when he sneered at the system; but his great-nephew Henry II could punish those who succeeded in the ordeal, without a murmur. When the Lateran Council of 1215 forbade priests to take part in the administration of the ordeal, it was here, as in so much else that it did, expressing a change of attitude which had been developing for a long time.[1] The effect, so far as the regular administration of justice was concerned, was immediate. Men were forced to prefer the probability arrived at by human agencies to the certainties of divine judgement. In many cases they did so unwillingly. Roger Bacon tells us that, half a century after the Lateran Council, there were still many men in various places saying prayers over hot iron and cold water and such-like things, by which the innocent were approved and the guilty condemned[2]; and ordeal by battle lingered on as an instrument of justice for many centuries. But, despite these exceptions, by 1215 the essential steps had been taken in making human justice and government an affair subject to human rules and dependent on the efficacy of human agents.

[1]Already in January 1212, Innocent III had forbidden the use of the ordeal for the trial of cases of heresy with the significant words: *Licet apud iudices saeculares vulgaria exerceantur iudicia, ut aquae frigidae vel ferri candentis sive duelli, huiusmodi tamen iudicia ecclesia non admisit, cum scriptum sit in lege divina: Non tentabis Dominum Deum tuum.* (P. L. vol. 216, 502.) This letter, addressed to the bishop of Strassburg seems to have been occasioned by a mass trial of heretics by ordeal of hot iron in this city, which resulted in the condemnation of about eighty men and women. (See J. Havet, *L'hérésie et le bras séculier au Moyen Age* in Bibliothèque de l'Ecole des Chartes, 41, 1880, p. 515, quoting Ann. Marbacenses, M.G.H. Scriptores XVII, 174. Havet, however, dated Innocent's letter 1211, and was thus misled as to the sequence of events.)

[2]*Opera Inedita*, ed. J. S. Brewer, R. S. p. 526.

This process of limiting the scope of the appeal to the supernatural in human affairs had, as its counterpart, a process of limiting the interferences of secular persons in spiritual affairs. To the second of these processes we have to return in a later chapter. As to the first, it is perhaps scarcely necessary to add that it had nothing to do with any lack of belief in the existence of a supernatural order: on the contrary, it was a symptom of a more refined spirituality which found something crude in the constant and automatic appeal to the supernatural in earthly matters. The same generation which laid bare the human basis of secular government, was also disclosing a new intensity of spiritual life in the study of the individual soul.

II

THE CONDITIONS OF MEN

There were two great and universal divisions in the society which emerged from the changes and innovations of the eleventh century: between freemen and serfs, and between freemen and noblemen. How sharp were these divisions? What benefits did the higher status confer, and what disabilities did the lower inflict? To answer these questions fully would require a more technical and complex treatment than can be attempted here. We can only try to seize the meaning of serfdom, liberty and nobility in some critical instances.

Once more it will be convenient to turn to the valley of the Loire, where social no less than political ties were specially open to the transforming influence of present necessity.

A. SERFDOM

The monks of the important monastery of Marmoutier, on the outskirts of Tours, kept a book in which they recorded the details of transactions by which men came under their lordship during a large part of the eleventh century. The following document of about the middle of the century is typical of many[1]:

Be it known to all who come after us, that a certain man in our service called William, the brother of Reginald, born of free

[1]A. Salmon and Ch.-L. Grandmaison, *Le Livre des Serfs de Marmoutier* (Société archéologique de Touraine, vol. XVI, 1864, p. 30.)

parents, being moved by the love of God and to the end that God—with whom is no acceptance of persons but regard only for the merits of each—might look favourably on him, gave himself up as a serf to St. Martin of Marmoutier; and he gave not only himself but all his descendants, so that they should for ever serve the abbot and monks of this place in a servile condition. And in order that this gift might be made more certain and apparent, he put the bell-rope round his neck and placed four pennies from his own head on the altar of St. Martin in recognition of serfdom, and so offered himself to almighty God. The following are the witnesses who saw and heard what was done. . . .

What was being done here? Let us notice the points on which the document dwells: the original freedom of William, which he inherited from his parents, the religious motive behind the surrender, the perpetuity of the new status, and finally the outward and symbolic acts which accompanied the transaction—the bell-rope and the pennies on the head.

It is hard to say which of the elements in the transaction seems strangest to our eyes—the pretence of a religious motive, the expectation of perpetuity, or the symbolic acts. As for the motive, we may in many cases consider that this was a mere form of words, and that the real impulse was quite different from the pretended one. But we shall see that serfdom *had* a religious side to it, and the appeal to religion in our document—though formal and therefore meaningless as a guide to individual motives—is not meaningless as a guide to the social theory of the time. Nor shall we understand the expectation of perpetuity without some reference to religion. There is indeed something awe-inspiring about this once-and-for-all attitude in social relationships. A man's freedom was hereditary and could not (in theory) be invaded arbitrarily: yet a single act on his part could destroy it for his whole family to the end of time. The consequences of this act would descend as a taint in the blood, like original sin itself. As, by man's first sin, all mankind was delivered to the slavery of sin, so by the action of men in the eleventh century the liberty of their descendants was lost beyond their power of recall. No doubt, during the course of our period, many came to be bound in the chains of serfdom, whose condition could be traced back to no definite act of surrender. But by the beginning of the thirteenth century, almost the only thing which could make a man a serf was the fact that his forefathers had been serfs before him. They were the victims of the Fall of some long forgotten ancestor.

The symbolic acts seem at first sight to add a macabre element to the proceedings which brought about this Fall, but they are an essential part—perhaps *the* essential part—of the business. What was being done was something very serious: it was intended to change the whole future of a man and his descendants. This was not to be done in a corner; it must have publicity—publicity of the only kind which the age recognized. There must be witnesses to some singular act which impressed the occasion and its significance on the memory. The act moreover must be appropriate to the thing it signified. Just as, when a man was freed from serfdom by an act of manumission, primitive law decreed that the owner of the serf should show him the open door and the open road, and place in his hands the weapons of a freeman, so, in the act of submission to serfdom, we have the bell-rope and the head money. The bell-rope round the neck served both as a means of publicity—for it seems from one document that the bell was tolled by the new serf[1]—and as a means of emphasizing his abject dependence on his new lord. The head money was the first-fruit of the man's servile condition, placed on the head—or, as we sometimes find, hung round the neck—as a sign of submission, not tendered by hand like a freeman's rent.

In many places the payment of this head money became, in the twelfth and thirteenth centuries, the determining factor in deciding whether a man was a serf or not. In itself it was little—an annual payment of a few pence only—but it made a clear line of distinction between free and unfree. It was good to have a simple rule: the gradations of society were infinite and there was no close relation between status and wealth; it might not always be possible to say whether a man was a sokeman or a sergeant, but at least he should know if he was free or unfree.

Yet the necessity for some superficial, straightforward rule like

[1]E. de Certain, *Les Miracles de Saint Benoît* (Société de l'Histoire de France, 1858) p. 206. These miracles, from the monastery of St. Benedict at Fleury on the Loire, contain several examples of ceremonies identical with those of the *Liber de Servis* of Marmoutier. In the case mentioned here a serf of St. Benedict, who had posed as a free man, was stricken with physical disability and brought to acknowledge his servitude. After offering the *aes servilis censionis* on the altar, he was tied to the bell-rope, and rang the bell three times in order to publicize his condition (*signi funiculo religatus collo, pandit sonitu trino nativo se reputatum naevo.*

this prompts the question: if such a small indication can decide such a weighty matter, can it really have been so important as it seems to us whether a man was free or unfree? The outward appearance and the name—which in the Latin documents before us is the same as the word for slave—are as bad as man can make them. But what did it all amount to? In many of these documents we read of men of some consequence who made themselves and their children serfs for one reason or another; but except for the small annual payment which symbolized their servitude their property was not affected. No new or burdensome services followed in the wake of their new status—at least not immediately; and, conversely, a man who held land by the most onerous services might yet be by status a free man. That the serfs of Marmoutier were often men of property is clear on every page of these records. We hear of one freeman, the feoffee of a vineyard, who became a serf in return for an additional vineyard of equal extent: and this new vineyard was to be so much his own property that he might sell it, provided he gave the monastery the first option.[1] Wherein did this man's servitude lie, and why were landlords like the monks of Marmoutier willing to make bargains which were, in effect, costly purchases of a man's liberty?

To understand this, we must ignore the old Latin name which they used, and see the transaction as a way of establishing a new claim to a man's loyalty and aid. Land was plentiful: labourers were comparatively few. The greatest problem for an estate manager was to ensure full cultivation. Landlords were not above competing for labour. The condition of serfdom, though it did not take away a man's property prevented him from moving elsewhere. Probably most of those who came into this condition were already working on the land as tenants of the lord to whom they delivered their freedom; henceforth the lord was assured of their continued service—and would pay a price for this assurance. When the employee of a great industrial concern today accepts a substantial sum on condition that he will not move elsewhere, he is doing in a grand way what thousands of men, large and small, were doing in the eleventh century. The modern firm is not interested in securing the services of its tied-man's children: and for good reason—they might be useless. The less selective eleventh-century landlord thought otherwise: the guarantee of service bound also the serf's children.

[1] *Livre des Serfs*, p. 112.

The securing of their labour was a vital part of the bargain.

From this there arose, by way of simple precaution, a custom which came to be regarded as one of the most degrading of all the incidents of serfdom—the payment made by a serf to his lord on the marriage of his daughter; the so-called merchet. In origin, this was the price of the lord's consent to the marriage; the guarantee of his control. This control was not a senseless humiliation. If the serf's daughter married away from the lordship, she and her children were lost to the lord. It was otherwise with the man: the woman came to live with him, the labour of the children was secure. The Marmoutier documents show clearly the difficulties which arose when the daughter of a serf married outside the lordship. A case arose sometime between 1064 and 1100, which shows that the rules about marriage were only slowly worked out under the compulsion of circumstances, and were at first not very rigid. The daughter of a serf of Marmoutier married a serf of the Count of Anjou, had several children and then died. She was an only child and, therefore, heiress to the lands of her parents in the lordship of Marmoutier. When *her* parents eventually died, her children proceeded to divide the inheritance. But the monks of Marmoutier objected: by their mother's marriage, her children were serfs of the Count of Anjou; all kinds of complications would arise if they were allowed to inherit Marmoutier lands. The case went from court to court, and attracted the interest of the Count himself, who declared that he would not allow serfs to be deprived of their inheritance. Finally the monks paid the claimants the truly enormous sum of £15, and allowed them to participate in the prayers of the monastery, on condition that they dropped their claim.[1] The monks of Marmoutier wanted their lands cultivated, but not by another man's serfs—the next step would have been to lose the land altogether.

It was not a special degree of misery which drove these men of Marmoutier into serfdom, but the need which was felt on all hands for a more lasting and intimate relationship between landlord and tenant for the cultivation of the soil, than that provided by the forms of free society. The new relationship secured advantages to both sides: to the lord, hereditary labour; to the serf a mixture of advantages, from a simple money payment or an additional holding of land to the benefits of religious fraternity. But things did not end

[1] *Livre des Serfs*, pp. 108-110.

here. The filling up of the land, the increasing hold of landlords upon the waste spaces, the elaboration of government, the growing definition and systematization of law, the influence of Roman Law, were the chief factors which during the twelfth and thirteenth centuries affected the position of the serfs. So far as status went, they all worked against the serf. Whether the history of the peasantry in those centuries would have been much different if the idea of serfdom had never been conceived may be doubted. But it is certain that the fact of serfdom was a convenient lever in enforcing the dependence of the peasantry. It was the one all-sufficient argument against any peasants who wanted to subtract their service, or any part of it, from their lords, and against any who resisted the remorseless pressure of landlordly control. We have seen that men in the eleventh century who were given the worst name that could be given to man—*servus*—were yet able to make good bargains with their masters and they could seek to enforce them in courts of law: such bargains would have been unthinkable a hundred or a hundred and fifty years later, and would indeed have been tantamount to recognitions of the man's freedom. By the end of the twelfth century, the processes of government had become more searching, the 'controls' were more elaborate, the status of serfdom was more rigidly defined. No doubt there were compensations—more rapid, more certain justice; rights which, though more restricted, were more assured; a share in a more general prosperity. We can never know whether the gains outweighed the inconveniences, and probably the men themselves would have been unable to tell us.

We are on surer ground when we enquire what they thought about serfdom. There were many ways of looking on it, but broadly we may distinguish a high religious view, and the view of the ordinary man. As to the first, it is relevant to observe the title used by the head of Christendom in all his acts: *servus servorum Dei*, which could be translated 'serf of the serfs of God'. There was nothing abhorrent in the idea of servitude—everything depended on its object. All men by sin have lost the dignity of freedom and have made themselves, in varying degrees, slaves of their passions: the way to freedom lies through a new subjection, the humiliation of self-negation. The teaching about serfdom in the Schools of the early twelfth century is well represented by some sentences which come from the influential circle of Anselm of Laon:

Servitude is ordained by God, either because of the sins of those who become serfs, or as a trial, in order that those who are thus humbled may be made better. For servitude is of great help to religion in protecting humility, the guardian of all virtues; and it would seem to be pride for anyone to wish to change that condition which has been given him for good reason by the divine ordinance.[1]

This was the teaching of a school which stood for a somewhat heartless and uninspired efficiency in scholastic matters, but here is a more urgent expression of the same point of view: St. Anselm is writing to a monk who proposed to make a journey to his native land in order to save his sister from a state of serfdom to which she had been unjustly depressed:—

What concern is it of monks—men who have resolved to flee the world—what does it matter to them, who serves whom in the world, or under what name? Is not every man born to labour as a bird to flight? Does not almost every man serve either under the name of lord or serf? And is not he who is called a serf in the Lord, the Lord's freeman; and he who is called free, is he not Christ's serf? So if all men labour and serve, and the serf is a freeman of the Lord, and the freeman is a serf of Christ, what does it matter apart from pride—either to the world or to God— who is called a serf and who is called free?[2]

It is easy to see that from this point of view secular serfdom had no terrors. The burdens and restrictions it imposed were of feather weight compared with those imposed by the radical servitude of unredeemed nature. At best, this human servitude was a preparatory discipline, teaching the motions of humility to a will not yet subdued; at worst, it added only one more lord, and the least tyrannous of them, to the array of lordly passions under which human nature already groaned. At best, it taught the first step in religion—humility; at worst, it lessened the dominion of self-will by subjection to the will of another. Hence it came about that the

[1] O. Lottin, *Nouveaux fragments théologiques de l'école d'Anselm de Laon*, in Recherches de Théologie ancienne et médiévale, 1946, XIII, p. 206.
[2] Ep. I. 15 (P. L. 158, 1081; Schmitt, no. 17). The letter is addressed to Henry, later prior of Christ Church, Canterbury, and Abbot of Battle. It appears from Ep. IV, 123 (P. L. 159, 267; Schmitt, no. 24) that he did not follow Anselm's advice.

ceremonies of initiation into serfdom were often used to symbolize initiation into the liberty of religion. We read of the young St. Odilo, later abbot of Cluny, entering a lonely church and offering himself as a serf to the Virgin, with the token offering of serfdom hung round his neck and with God as his witness. We read also of St. Gerard of Brogne going every second year to Rome 'with ten shillings hanging from his neck to offer himself as a serf to his Lord'. It was an idea which came naturally to the triumphant Crusaders when they entered Jerusalem in 1099, to go to the Holy Sepulchre and offer their *capitale tributum*—their head money—to the Lord.[1] The symbolism of serfdom seemed to these men a fitting expression of the demands made by religion. When theologians extolled the benefits of mundane serfdom as a doorway to religion, and condemned the attempt to throw off this condition as an exhibition of the sin of pride, this was not simply comfortable doctrine for the well-to-do, teaching the poor their place. It sprang from a deep sense of the place of man in the universe, and it was authorized not only by striking acts of religious devotion but by the countless unknown surrenders implicit in the monastic life.

Yet all this did not make for—rather it was incompatible with—any theory such as that of Aristotle that serfdom or slavery was a condition for which some men were marked out by nature. On the contrary, serfdom was regarded as an unnatural state, only justified by the even deeper disharmony in the state of man induced by sin and the conflict with God. This is a theme which recurs again and again in our documents: *lex poli*, so the jingle ran, is not the same as *lex fori*—

> by Heaven's high law all men are free,
> but human law knows slavery.

[1] The story about St. Odilo comes from the *Vita Sancti Odilonis Abbatis*, lib. II, cap. 1 (P. L. vol. 142, 915-6). To this may be added a similar story told by his contemporary Peter Damian (988-1072) about his own brother, Marinus, a layman, who offered himself as a serf at the altar of the Virgin with a rope round his neck. (*De Bono Suffragiorum*, cap. IV, in P. L. vol. 145, 566.) The account of St. Gerard of Brogne is in Odo of Cluny, *Vita sancti Geraldi*, lib II, cap. 17 (P. L. vol. 133, 680.) The behaviour of the Crusaders in 1099 is described in the *Gesta Francorum*, ed. and transl. by L. Bréhier in the series "Les Classiques de l'Histoire de France au Moyen Age", 1924, p. 206. According to the Anonymous author of this contemporary history of the First Crusade, the Crusaders, on entering Jerusalem, went immediately to the Lord's sepulchre, *et reddiderunt ei capitale tributum*. (This is the reading of the best MSS., though the editor has preferred the reading *debitum* for *tributum*.)

By what right does human law perpetuate this unnatural condition? If we went a hundred years beyond the limit of this book we should find men devoted to a primitive evangelical purity of life pressing this question with uncomfortable persistence. But in our period there was a sufficient, if not wholly satisfying, answer: God wills that the very sins of men shall turn to the relief of human misery; the man who in his pride and arrogance beats down the weak is a sinner indeed, but he establishes a kind of peace. Little good can be expected in the world, but even that little is only to be had by submission to the man who thus strangely becomes God's minister and beareth not the sword in vain. The choice of half a loaf is all that is left to man, and to resist is to throw away even this; the serf still has his life, his family, his livelihood and, by that special mercy which turns all things to good, in his very serfdom, an instrument for the exercise of his religion, the expiation of his sins, and the perfecting of his humility. And then—to emphasize that serfdom like other human institutions existed on sufferance only—there was always manumission. It was the duty of the serf to submit: it was the glory of the lord to free. "Whoever, in the name of the holy and undivided Trinity, moved by charity, permits anyone of his servile dependents to rise from the yoke of servitude to the honour of liberty, may surely trust that in the Last Day, he himself will be endued with everlasting and celestial liberty." These are the words of an eleventh-century act of manumission: they give the only answer to the problem of serfdom which the religious doctrine of the period allowed.

But there was another, less elevated, view of the matter which was shared by the majority of men, free and unfree alike. Even the monk to whom St. Anselm wrote, rejected his advice and made the long journey from England to Italy to try to save his sister from serfdom. To nearly all men serfdom was, without qualification, a degrading thing, and they found trenchant phrases to describe the indignity of the condition. The serf's family was always referred to by lawyers as his brood, his *sequela*, and the poets delighted to exercise their ingenuity in describing the physical deformity of the ideal serf. Hard words break no bones, but they are hard to bear for all that, and they became harder as time went on. Men well knew, however theologians might seem to turn common notions inside out, the difference between the yoke of servitude and the honour of liberty—or, to use the expressive phrase of Giraldus Cambrensis, the *hilaritas libertatis*: "There is nothing," he wrote, "which so stirs the hearts of men and incites them to honourable action like the light-heartedness of liberty; and nothing which so deters and depresses them like the oppression of servitude".[1] If we consider only the practical effects of serfdom and notice how little the lines of economic prosperity follow those of personal status; if we reflect on the many impediments to free action, to which even the mightiest were subjected in such delicate matters as marriage and the bequeathing of property, it may seem surprising that the pride of liberty was so strong, and the contempt for serfdom so general: yet such was the case. However much the hierarchical principle of society forced men into relationships at all levels of society in which rights and restraints were inextricably mixed up, the primitive line which divided liberty from servitude was never forgotten.

B. LIBERTY

What men feared and resented in serfdom was not its subordination, but its arbitrariness. The hatred of that which was governed, not by rule, but by will, went very deep in the Middle Ages, and at no time was this hatred so powerful and practical a force as in the latter half of our period. The supremacy of Will was itself an evil, whether the will was one's own or another's: the latter was more uncomfortable; the former more deadly. This instinctive distrust of the Will comes out in many ways. When Ivo, Bishop of Chartres, wrote to dissuade a canon, living according to the Rule of St. Augustine, from becoming a hermit, he raised the objection that the life of the hermit was a *vita voluntaria*.[2] By this he did not mean that it was a life voluntarily adopted, but that every detail of the life was at the will of the individual: the life governed by a well-established rule was higher, and essentially freer. When the thirteenth-century lawyer, Bracton, wanted a single phrase to sum up the attributes of serfdom, he said that the serf did not know today what he would have to do tomorrow—he was at the will of another. As a practical test this definition would have been quite worthless: most serfs knew very well what they would have to do tomorrow, probably better than their masters; but the idea of living according to

[1] Giraldus Cambrensis, *De Principis Instructione*, R. S., VIII, 258.
[2] Ep. 256 (P. L. vol. 162, 261.)

the will of another struck the imagination—it expressed better than anything else the degradation of serfdom.

The higher one rose towards liberty, the more the area of action was covered by law, the less it was subject to will. The knight did not obey fewer laws than the ordinary freeman, but very many more; the freeman was not less restricted than the serf, but he was restricted in a different, more rational way. Law was not the enemy of freedom; on the contrary, the outline of liberty was traced by the bewildering variety of law which was slowly evolved during our period. The irksome rules and tedious gradations of society did not appear, as they did to a later age, as so many strangle-holds on liberty. High and low alike sought liberty by insisting on enlarging the number of rules under which they lived. The most highly privileged communities were those with most laws. At the bottom of society was the serf, who could least appeal to law against the arbitrariness of his superiors. At the top was the nobleman, governed by an immensely complicated system of rules in his public life, and taught in his private relationships to observe an equally complicated code of behaviour.

It is significant that the men of our period were not greatly interested in the 'ordinary' freeman. There must have been many men who, to our eyes which are not adjusted to the fine distinctions of status, appear to have belonged to this miscellaneous group. But to the medieval mind the conception of mere freedom was colourless, almost meaningless, and it was consequently difficult to imagine a freeman without imagining him a member of some privileged group. It should now be possible to see why this was so. Freedom could only be defined by reference to the law, by which those who were free were governed. Freedom was not a status like serfdom; it was a quality which was attached to the status of all who were not serfs. This quality was the quality of rational order. The mere freeman, with no further qualification, was a man who stood on a zero line: it was not easy to decide on which side he stood, and he could easily be pushed across the line into unfreedom. It was only when the quality of freedom was articulated by being attached to the status of knight, burgess or baron that it could be observed, analysed and measured.

It is one of the most striking features of our period that on this subject of freedom common thought and practice joined hands with theological speculation: the conjunction gives solidity to the political experiments of the twelfth and thirteenth centuries. The barons of Magna Carta had little thought for generalities, but a theologian would have found no difficulty in giving their instinctive reactions the authority of a systematic argument. Liberty is a creation of law, and law is reason in action; it is reason which makes men, as we should say, ends in themselves. Tyranny, whether of King John or of the Devil, is a manifestation of the absence of law. The man who lives outside the law, whether under the rule of his own will or that of another, is bound by the iron chains of servitude. The gossiping Franciscan chronicler of the thirteenth century, Salimbene, distinguished five kinds of rule by which a man was disgraced: the rule of women, of serfs, of fools, of boys and of enemies.[1] The common feature of all of these forms of tyranny was lack of law; they were destructive of rational order. The inclusion of women in this list deserves notice, because it emphasizes the point that rule over free men should be rational. In practice of course women often exercised rule, and sometimes with conspicuous success. But equally in the theological and chivalric conceptions of the time, woman stood for that which was either below or above reason: woman, in the person of Eve, was the agent by which sin came into the world, and, in the person of the Virgin, the agent by which Salvation came; in courtly literature, women stood at once for that which was below reason—caprice—and for a higher principle than reason—love. But liberty, at least in this world's affairs, was a product of the masculine quality of reason, as expressed in law.

It was a characteristic of the higher forms of law, that those who submitted to them must do so by their own choice. There must be a personal act, an oath, a profession, a contract embodied in a public ceremony, renewed by each person in each generation, not descending in the blood like serfdom from some ancestral act. The highest law of all was that in obedience to which a man stripped himself of this world's goods and subjected himself to religious poverty and obedience. But this state had nothing in common—as the writers of the period were almost too anxious to point out— with that ordinary poverty, the common lot of the majority of men,

[1] Salimbene, *Chronica*, ed. O. Holder-Egger in M. G. H., Scriptores, XXXII, p. 65-6.

who of necessity were poor. The monk had chosen his poverty and servitude:

> O holy band of men living at unity with one another, what can I say that is worthy of you? You hunger and thirst and suffer penury for the name of Jesus. But it is an honourable and sober poverty, not compulsory but freely chosen . . . There is nothing freer, nothing more safe, than holy poverty.[1]

These words, written by a Cistercian monk in the early years of the thirteenth century, occur in a passage which already breathes something of the spirit of Franciscan poverty. But even in this final renunciation there was also the spirit of aristocracy.

Medieval society was prolific in creating forms of association to which entry was obtained by some form of oath. This connexion between freedom and individual acts of acceptance of its responsibilities again emphasizes the rational character of freedom. The serf's unhappy freedom from law was involuntary, but the submission of the knight, the baron, the clerk, the monk, the burgess, to their various codes of law was voluntary. The nobleman was bound by several codes of law—as a Christian, a baron, a knight, a subject of the king; and he could suffer all manner of penalties for a breach of any of these codes of law. Into all these obligations he had entered by an individual contract in the ceremonies of baptism, homage, knighthood and fealty. If he was punished, even by being burnt as a heretic, he could reflect that he was being punished for breach of contract.

C. NOBILITY

It follows from the foregoing discussion that whereas serfdom was transmitted in the blood, nobility—the highest form of liberty —was not. Between the eleventh and the thirteenth centuries there is no nobility of blood. This state of affairs was not one which had always existed, nor one which, in large parts of Europe, would continue to exist. At the beginning of the history of the modern European peoples there was a clearly marked aristocracy raised above the level of ordinary freemen by their blood-worth, which was

---

[1] A. Wilmart, *Les Mélanges de Mathieu, Préchantre de Rievaulx*, Revue Bénédictine, 1940, LII, p. 73.

passed on from generation to generation, and which went back perhaps to some mythological beginnings in a descent from the Gods. But by the beginning of the eleventh century this ancient distinction of blood had ceased to have any significance. At the other end of our period, though not universally, we see the dim beginnings of a new nobility of blood claiming legal privileges by virtue of descent. But during our period, nobility had only two roots: property, by which a man entered into a set of relationships determining his place in society; and knighthood, by which he assumed responsibilities and privileges denied to those outside the ranks of the fraternity. The property relationship was born in the act of homage; the knightly relationship in the act of initiation to knighthood. The first gave a man a place in a hierarchy; the second in a brotherhood. The man who had many lords by his homage was on an equality with the king by his knighthood. It is not surprising therefore that the first was the practical working bond between men, while the second had almost from the beginning something of romance and idealism and ineffectiveness.

The act of homage was purely secular and had immediate legal consequences. Being a simple and business-like proceeding it underwent no development, and remained immune from the influences of a changing society. With knighthood, the case is more complicated. It seems to have begun as a social act, perhaps convivial or even boisterous according to one's reading of the minds behind the rough ceremonies. Its first certain appearances are in the middle of the eleventh century and its origins are intimately associated with the rise of the art of fighting on horseback. It is no accident that the time when we first find dukes and counts depicted armed and on horseback on their seals is also the time when we begin to find notices of the knighting of their sons and vassals. Fundamentally knighthood was the rite of entry into the ranks of the mounted warrior. But, while homage gathered no new aura round it as time went on, knighthood responded to every wind that blew: without ever becoming religious it enjoyed the sanction and colour of a religious setting; it obtained a place in the philosophy of political and social life; it inspired a great literature and was swept into a romantic movement wholly alien to its origins. By the second half of the twelfth century, it is possible to talk as if the essence of the ceremony of knighting lay in its religious setting—the taking of the arms from the altar, the implied profession of obedience to the Church, the obligation to protect the poor and punish the wicked. But it is noteworthy that the few existing accounts of knighting suggest something much more secular, and it is hard to say whether, in the hard school of knightly exercises, practice kept pace with theory. Nevertheless, in the thirteenth century, the ceremony of knighting was commonly performed in a church, often on the occasion of a great festival and after a night of vigil: it was firmly fixed in an ecclesiastical—it would perhaps be too much to say, a religious—setting.

The middle years of the twelfth century marked an important stage in this development. It happens that there is a very full description of the ceremony of knighthood in the year 1128, which gives us a clear picture of the procedure at this date at the highest social level.[1] The occasion was the knighting of the young Geoffrey of Anjou by Henry I of England shortly before his marriage with the king's daughter Matilda. In this ceremony, there was no hint of any association with the Church, it was a purely secular affair, and this is the more striking since the occasion was a very great one and the author of our account gives full weight to the religious ceremonies of the marriage which followed. The day of the knighting began with a bath; then the young man was clothed in a linen undergarment, a tunic of cloth of gold, and a purple cloak, silk stockings and shoes ornamented with golden lions. So arrayed, he appeared in public together with the companions who were being knighted with him. Then followed a distribution of horses and arms. Round the neck of Geoffrey was hung a shield with the device of golden lions which also ornamented his shoes, and there was brought for him from the royal treasury an ancient sword, reputed to have been made by the smith Weland. The young men then proceeded to a display of warlike exercises which continued for a week till the wedding took place.

This may be taken as an example of all that was most splendid and 'proper' in the ceremony of knighthood in Northern France and England during the third decade of the twelfth century. But thirty years later, in the book of political wisdom called the *Policraticus* which he completed in 1159, John of Salisbury was able to speak of a new and solemn custom which had grown up, by which the new

[1]Halphen and Poupardin, *Chroniques des Comtes d'Anjou*, pp. 178-180.

knight went to church on the day of his knighting, placed his sword on the altar and took it up again as a token (says John) that he offered himself and his sword to the service of God. John of Salisbury's words deserve special attention because he has just been telling us what modern knights do *not* do: they do not for instance take the solemn military oath prescribed by ancient authors; they do not, it seems, take any oath at all. But John sees in their action in coming to the altar, something which is as good as an oath, something which for unlettered men has the same force as the written profession of obedience made by bishops and abbots to their superiors.[1]

It would appear therefore that by the middle of the twelfth century it was becoming common for an act of religious dedication to be added to the secular ceremonies. But, though common, it was not necessary. The essential feature was the bestowal of a sword by an established knight on the aspirant to knighthood. When, for instance, in 1173, the grandson of Geoffrey of Anjou was in revolt against his father, Henry II of England, he was knighted as a preparation for battle. The ceremony was performed by William the Marshal, and the author of the Marshal's life disposes of it in very few words: a sword was brought to the young man; he gave it to the Marshal, the best knight in his company; the Marshal girded him, kissed him, "and so he was a knight".[2] The circumstances were unusual for the injured king was hourly expected, but the incident shows what could be done in an emergency.

The addition of an ecclesiastical ceremony to the act of knighthood is somewhat similar to the addition of an ecclesiastical ceremony to the act of marriage, which was increasingly insisted upon by the authorities of the Church during the twelfth century. There were of course great differences: marriage was a sacrament which knighthood, except in the haziest and least technical of senses, was not; and marriage, unlike knighthood, was undeniably governed by the law of the Church. Nevertheless there is a parallel between the attempt to sanctify the institution of knighthood and the ecclesiastical additions to what was essentially a private contract between two persons in

[1] For John of Salisbury's account of knighthood, see his *Policraticus*, ed. C. C. J. Webb, vol. 2, 1-58 (esp. pp. 23-5). There are some interesting pages on the ceremony of dubbing to knighthood in M. Bloch, *La Société Féodale*, ii, 46-58, but he seems to miss the force of John of Salisbury's words, which point to a real change in habits during John's own lifetime.

[2] *L'Histoire de Guillaume le Maréchal*, ed. P. Meyer, 1891-1901, vol. 1, p. 76-7 (lines 2071-96).

marriage. When we recall the horror and aversion with which secular arms were regarded by serious writers in the eleventh century—an aversion which, as we shall see, played an important part in the crisis of the Investiture dispute—this work of sanctifying secular life appears as something of very great moment. It helped to soften the harsh division between the secular and spiritual aspects of society which is implicit in much of the best thought of the period.

The large conclusions which John of Salisbury drew from the addition of a religious sanction to the status of knighthood would perhaps not have been accepted by many laymen.

> For what purpose (he asks) is knighthood ordained? To protect the church, to attack infidelity, to reverence the priesthood, to protect the poor, to keep the peace, to shed one's blood and, if necessary, to lay down one's life for one's brethren.[1]

The phrases which, by contrast, might have come more easily from secular lips are such as these: to defend one's rights, to see justice done, to keep one's inferiors and superiors in their place, to be a wise counsellor and a bold fighter, a loyal vassal and a respected lord, and to make the exercise of arms (if one's interests lay in this direction) profitable. There is always a great difference between high theory and low theory. Nevertheless John of Salisbury, high theorist though he was, had conspicuously more room for knighthood in his scheme of things than Gregory VII or St. Bernard in the two previous generations. Gregory VII had sought a sanction for knighthood in the specific service of St. Peter: his *militia sancti Petri* was a desperate remedy, and one with a narrow appeal, justified as it seemed by circumstances of desperate disorder. St. Bernard's ideal of a knighthood dedicated to the cause of re-establishing Christ's kingdom in the Holy Land had a wider appeal, but knighthood was here sanctified by being drawn away from the possibility of doing mischief at home. With John of Salisbury, however, knighthood had its duties and found its fulfilment at home, on a man's native soil. It may seem a far cry from John of Salisbury, demonstrating the necessity for knighthood from Cato and Cicero, illustrating its virtues from the military authors of antiquity,

[1]*Policraticus*, ii, p. 23.

deducing its religious obligations from Roman Law, and finding a modern sanction in the ceremony at the altar, to the country knights—the 'county' folk—of the time of Henry II who sat as jurors, held enquiries into lands and rights, kept records of crime, and were in every way becoming increasingly involved in the work of local government. There is a world of difference here. But though John of Salisbury's learning makes him seem remote from real life, he knew well how things worked; he had not been the right-hand man of a very active archbishop of Canterbury for nothing. Both the *Policraticus* in its book-learned fashion, and the assizes of the English king—intensely practical, yet, in part at least, the work of learned men—bear witness to the important place in peace as well as war which knights were beginning to take in every aspect of government.

While knighthood was thus entering a period of staid and responsible respectability, it was also inspiring a literature which influenced conduct and manners in many important respects. The knights of this new literature had perhaps as much relation to the knights of the time as the private detectives of fiction to the policemen of everyday life. But the portrayal of knightly character in verse and song, in sermons and educational manuals, impressed a unity of social ideals on the Latin world. The themes of Charlemagne and King Arthur, of the Crusade and the formation of the Christian ruler, were all sustained by and developed round the character of the knight. From very humble origins the word 'knight' became charged with an emotional significance, which outlived the social environment of its birth. The literature in which the ideal of knighthood was set forth had probably little influence on the art of government or the practical life of society at large; its impact was on the individual in his social conduct, in the refinement of his emotions and manners. We shall return to this aspect of the knightly ideal in a later chapter.

We have spoken of serfs and knights because these were two distinctive products of the period from the tenth to the twelfth centuries and because it was round these two classes that the social thought of the period crystallized. But it would be wrong to think that most men belonged to these classes, or that they always took the obligations and restrictions imposed on them very seriously. If we were to divide men (leaving aside for the present the members of the ecclesiastical hierarchy and the religious orders) on practical rather than on idealistic lines, we should have to distinguish a whole host of men who either stood outside this classification, or whose condition was only faintly coloured by their being included in the categories of serfs or knights. There would first be the landless men, the most varied and in some ways the freest class of all, stretching from the son of a noble house in search of distinction on the field of battle or in a great man's household, to students, pedlars and labourers. After them would come men, whether serf or free, with only so much land as they and their families could work themselves, and who paid for their land either by rent or labour; then men with more land than they could work, and who either employed the casual labour of others or could demand services as a right from those who in their turn held land from them. There would be men at all stages of prosperity or decay who formed part of the long line of commerce which led from the sheep-runs of England or Spain, or the mines of Germany, or the forests of the Baltic, across half the world; and men who manufactured either for the neighbourhood or for distant markets. There were men who lived exclusively on the services of others either as money-lenders or as employers of labour at the loom or in the fields, or—grandest of all—those who enjoyed the services of men as knightly as themselves in war, in administration and in ceremonial duties.

New forms of specialization were constantly breaking up the conventional divisions of society. But it was only slowly that new social phenomena could be fitted into the framework of thought—the position of the merchant or the hired labourer was still an uneasy one at the end of our period. Men were not generous or imaginative in the acceptance of change. Two hundred years earlier knights and serfs had themselves been the product of an effort at specialization, and their position in society had been far from clear. Since then a great deal of law and literature had gathered round them. The age which saw the creation of military and social organizations like the county of Anjou also saw the formation of the two classes on which this organization depended: the knights and the serfs. But just as the county of Anjou was swept into the stream of larger policies in the course of the twelfth century, so knighthood and serfdom changed their character. They began as local adaptations to circumstances, with no clear ethical or legal status: both of them practical expedients. In course of time their practical bearing became obscure—serfdom could disappear in some areas and be reinforced in others without affecting in any clear way the position of the peasantry; at the same time knights lost many of their primitive functions. In the middle of the twelfth century it was still possible to speak as if only the knight could properly and with full responsibility and sanction take part in warfare: two generations later when knights formed only a fraction of a fighting force and when many skilled men were needed in warfare besides the fighter on horseback, such language would have seemed woefully out of date. Yet both knighthood and serfdom persisted and continued to reassert their importance in different ways throughout the Middle Ages and beyond. The local necessities which brought them to birth disappeared but left them as permanent features of the medieval landscape. Here as elsewhere we have to admire the solidity of the achievement of the tenth and eleventh centuries, which ensured the survival of the characteristic institutions of these centuries amidst the widely different prospects which were gradually opening out.

CHAPTER III

THE ORDERING OF THE CHRISTIAN LIFE

I

THE CHURCH AND THE WORLD

IF we wish to catch a glimpse of the old church life of Europe before it was transformed by the zeal of the late eleventh century, we cannot do better than turn to the counts of Catalonia.[1] The country between Barcelona and the Pyrenees long remained a little outpost of Carolingian civilization in a changing world; it was prolific in the production of documents at a time when they are not too plentiful in most parts of Europe; and the conservatism of the area (undisturbed by Reformation or Revolution) has helped to preserve the evidences of its past. In the late tenth and early eleventh century, when Northern France was being reorganized by a military aristocracy, the Spanish March remained set in the old ways. Its aristocracy was descended from a certain Wifred the Hairy, a nobleman of the late ninth century who, like others of his class (including the ancestor of the Counts of Anjou), had profited by the troubles of the Emperor Charles the Bald. But the history of the family had been widely different from that of the ruling families of northern France. Despite the proximity of the Moslems, the Counts of Barcelona were less obsessed by the idea of defence than (for instance) their Angevin

[1]The superb collection of documents for the history of Catalonia in the tenth and eleventh centuries, on which the following account is founded, are largely printed in Petrus de Marca, *Marca Hispanica, sive Limes Hispanicus, hoc est Geographica et historica descriptio Cataloniae, etc.* (Paris, 1688). These are supplemented by documents in Villanueva, *Viage literario a las iglesias de España,* (1803-51) VI, 302-6, 308, 320; VII, 281-3; XII, 214. For the general history of Catalonia in this period, see Ferran Soldevila, *Història de Catalunya,* 3 vols., 1934-5. There is a useful summary by Dom A. Lambert in the *Dictionnaire d'histoire et de Géographie Ecclésiastique* ed. A. Baudrillart, A. de Meyer and E. van Cauwenbergh, vol. 6, 723-38. The relations with the Papacy are dealt with by P. Kehr, *Das Papsttum und der Katalanische Prinzipat bis zur Vereinigung mit Aragon* in Abhandlungen der Preuss. Akademie der Wissenschaften, Berlin, 1926.

contemporaries: they were not great castle builders; they had no rule of primogeniture, which in the North maintained the integrity of political units and worked for the amalgamation of great lordships. They preserved an easy-going aristocratic life, in which conservatism was tempered with a certain colonial largeness and freedom. Each generation brought a sub-division of the family estate among the male descendants of Wifred; but this territorial disintegration was to some extent compensated by the mingling of secular and ecclesiastical offices, and the concentration of both in the hands of the ruling family. The family divided among its members, as it thought best, all the offices, profits and responsibilities of government, both temporal and spiritual, throughout their possessions. The division was a matter which concerned themselves alone: they admitted no rival within their territories. Nevertheless they were deeply attached to the Papacy, and they preserved a sentimental regard for the King of France, which was the easier to maintain because they were never troubled by his authority. They valued this link with the French world, of which they rightly felt themselves to be a part. Towards the Papacy the sentiment of affection was more lively and more practical: there was no part of Europe with which the Popes of the early eleventh century had closer connexions. The Counts relied on Papal assistance in their ecclesiastical plans and in their family affairs: they knew the Popes personally and as friends.

Let us see how these various strands in the family tradition worked out in practice.

We shall concern ourselves only with a younger branch of the family which held the land in the North, stretching across the Pyrenees. In the year 1000 it consisted of four brothers, who were the sons of Oliba Cabréta, Count of Cerdaña and Besalú. The Count, their father, had gone to Italy towards the end of his life, and had died as a monk of Monte Cassino, leaving his children under the protection of the Pope. He died in 990 and when his sons appear in history they had made a thorough division of the family estate. Two of them had taken the temporal estate: one (Wifred) appears as Count of Cerdaña, and the other (Bernard) as Count of Besalú. The two others shared the most important ecclesiastical offices: one became Bishop of Elna and died young; the other (Oliba) was both Bishop of Vich and abbot of Ripoll and Cuxá. We know something about all of them, but most about Wifred and Oliba.

THE FAMILY OF THE COUNTS OF BARCELONA

WIFRED THE HAIRY

C. of Barcelona, Gerona, Ausona, Urgel, Cerdaña and Besalú[1]
d. 898

Wifred Borrell I
C. of Barcelona,
Gerona and Ausona
d. 912

Sunyer
C. of Urgel, and (later)
Barcelona, Gerona
and Ausona, d. 954

Borrell II
C. of Barcelona, etc.
d. 992

Miro
C. of Cerdaña and
Besalú
d. c. 927

Ralph
monk of Ripoll
and Bp. of Urgel

Wifred
C. of Besalú
d. 957

Sunifred
C. of Cerdaña
and (later) Besalú
d. 967

Oliba Cabréta
C. of Cerdaña 967
and Besalú, 984
d. 990

Miro
Bp. of Gerona
and (967),
C. of Besalú
d. 984

Ermengol
C. of Urgel
d. 1010

descended in the
male line till 1209

Ramon Borrell
C. of Barcelona
Gerona and Ausona
d. 1018

Berenger Ramon I
C. of Barcelona etc.
d. 1035

Bernard,
C. of Besalú
d. 1020

Wifred
C. of Cerdaña
d. 1050

Oliba
Abbot of Ripoll
and Cuxá and Bp.
of Ausona (Vich)
d. 1047

Berenguer
Bp. of Elna
d. 1003

Ramon Berenguer I
C. of Barcelona, etc.
d. 1076[3]

William I
C. of Besalú
d. 1052

Wifred
Bp. of Besalú

Garsinda = Berengar
Viscount of
Narbonne[3]

Wifred
Archbishop
of Narbonne
d. 1079

William
Bp. of Urgel
d. 1075

Berenguer
Bp. of Gerona
d. 1093

? Berenger
Bp. of Elna
d. 1053-4

Ramon Berenguer II
d. 1082

Berenguer Ramon II
d. 1096

Ramon
C. of Cerdaña
d. 1068

Persons mentioned in the text are shown in capital letters.

[1] These are all small countries between Barcelona and the Pyrenees.

[2] The attempt of Ramon Berenguer I to leave his undivided lands jointly to both his sons led to the discords mentioned in the letter of Gregory VII (see p. 123) and eventually to the murder of Ramon Berenguer II by his brother in 1082.

[3] This is the Berengar who made the complaint described on p. 122.

120

Oliba was a man of real note. As abbot of Ripoll he was in charge of the great family monastery, a monument at once to their pride and piety; it was the family mausoleum and it was constantly being added to and rebuilt. Oliba made it worthy of them.[1] Under him it was a centre of solid learning, with an active school of writers on music, chronology and arithmetic; it had a splendid library which existed almost intact until 1835, and there are still several volumes in existence which must date from the period of Oliba's rule. Oliba corresponded with scholars at Fleury on the Loire; he visited Rome, and brought back a Papal privilege authorizing some additions to the monastic services. There is no sign that he was himself a scholar, but he was a patron of scholars, a grand seigneur moving easily in the world, yet firmly attached to the traditions of his family. His uncle, who had been both Count of Besalú and Bishop of Gerona, was just such a man: he had been a man of splendid habits, a correspondent of the great scholar Gerbert, and at his death he distributed with careless liberality a fine assortment of rings, seals, vessels of gold and (the words are his own) "anything you can find in the way of books" (*quantum invenire potueritis de generis librorum*).

Oliba's brother Wifred, Count of Cerdaña, has already been met with in this book: it was on his behalf that the monks of his monastery at Canigou sent far and wide soliciting prayers after his death. The monastery of Canigou was his own foundation and the monks wrote a touching tribute to him: "It is impossible to say how good he was to us while he was in the world; he was our defender in adversity, our helper to the extent of his power in good endeavours, a staff to those of us who were old, a father to the young. . . . But since no one is made clear of sin except by God's help, especially one who has been great in the world, we pray unceasingly and with all our strength that the merciful God and just Judge will cleanse our most dear, memorable and venerated Wifred from all that he has done amiss."[2] To a later generation, there was indeed much that Wifred had done amiss, as we shall see.

Wifred left five sons: one of these became Count of Cerdaña,

[1] There is an account of the considerable literary resources of the great monastery of St. Mary at Ripoll (which seems to have remained almost intact until the destructive fire of 1835) and of the part played in the development of the monastery by Oliba, Abbot of the monastery from 1008 to 1046, in R. Beer, *Die Handschriften des Klosters Santa Maria de Ripoll* (Sitzungsberichte der Konigl. Akademie in Wien, 1907, vol. 155, and 1908, vol. 158.)

[2] Delisle, *Rouleaux des Morts*, p. 51.

and the others Bishops of Urgel, Gerona and Elna, and Archbishop of Narbonne respectively. This was an eminently satisfactory arrangement and quite in the family tradition—but the archbishopric was perhaps a venture; great prize though it was, it lay outside the ordinary family orbit. It became the cause of endless trouble, and of a breach in the good relations between the family and the Papacy.

The trouble started with a family bicker. The archbishop was evidently an ambitious man, very active in extending his rights over the country round Narbonne. This brought him into conflict with Berengar, the viscount of Narbonne, who came before a church council in Toulouse with a tale of the wrongs he had suffered. By way of introduction Berengar told the following story:

My uncle was archbishop of Narbonne, and, when he died, Wifred of Cerdaña came to my parents and offered to buy the archbishopric. They held back, but my wife was Wifred's niece, and I pressed them to accept the offer. So they agreed, and Wifred gave the archbishopric to his son, who was then a boy of ten. But it is not this that I want to complain about, but about his conduct since he became archbishop. . . .[1]

The Viscount's words, which I have paraphrased, show no uneasiness about the way in which the archbishopric was bought, but others were beginning to take a different view. We are now in the year 1056, and it was becoming dangerous to tell stories of this kind. A whole series of excommunications was let loose; at provincial councils, at general councils, by papal legates, by the Pope himself, the archbishop continued to be excommunicated for close on a quarter of a century. There is no evidence that he took any notice of these censures; when he died in 1079, the great Roman Council of that year had recently, among the odds-and-ends of its business, launched a fresh anathema against him, but Wifred's son held his own to the end.

It was his misfortune to live in a time when the old easy-going ways were coming under severe scrutiny. By the time of his death, the familiar intimacy between the descendants of Wifred the Hairy and the Popes had been broken, and had been replaced by new and

[1]Berengar's complaint is printed in Mansi, *Sacrorum Conciliorum nova et amplissima collectio*, XIX, 850, and in C. Devic and J. Vaissette, *Historie du Languedoc*, V. 496.

stricter ties. Gregory VII was at the height of his power and prestige, and in his eyes Spain was a Crusading country, directly subject to St. Peter. The new note of authority was sounded in a letter which Gregory wrote to Berenguer, Bishop of Gerona—brother of the recalcitrant archbishop of Narbonne—shortly before he excommunicated the archbishop for the last time:

We hear that strife has arisen between the sons of Ramon Berenguer (the late Count of Barcelona), and it grieves me greatly to hear it, both because I was a friend of their father, and because I foresee great danger thereby to the Christian people of those parts, who labour under the heavy threat of the impious Saracens. Wherefore I order you to take with you some neighbouring abbots and God-fearing clerks and laymen, and to strive to bring about peace between the brothers. If they refuse to hear you, show them this letter and order them on my authority to keep the peace until we can send legates thither *ex latere nostro*, who will give a just judgement in this dispute. And if they persist in their disobedience and remain at variance, we shall exclude the offender from the protection of St. Peter and cut him off from the Christian community, so that he shall enjoy no victory in battle and no prosperity in this world. But to him who obeys our commands, we shall lend the inexpugnable aid of our apostolic favour and help him as a son of the holy Roman church, by all the means in our power, to gain his inheritance; and we shall order all the Christians of those parts to do the same.[1]

One after another the counties and kingdoms of Spain submitted to—indeed sought—the Papal overlordship: the county of Besalú in 1077, the kingdom of Aragon in 1089, the county of Barcelona in 1090. The land of Catalonia had entered the "Liberty of the Roman Church". This is not the way in which the older generation had conceived the relationship. Popes and Counts had met on a ground of common feeling; they had not worried about hard words and difficult doctrines. After all, the Popes also were men with strong local connexions and aristocratic tempers, who understood well enough the feelings of other great men. The Counts

[1] *Gregorii VII Registrum*, VI, 16, ed. E. Caspar, p. 421-2. (M. G. H., Epistolae Selectae, II). The letter is dated 2 Jan. 1079. I have somewhat shortened the text in translating it.

addressed them in terms of high courtesy. Bernard, count of Besalú (brother of Wifred of Cerdaña) says in one of his charters that the Pope holds the sceptre of the world—the most extreme papalist could scarcely say more; but he adds "let no one, neither the Pope himself, nor a General Council, violate the conditions of this document."[1] This is the language of a man who felt that he could pay great deference without any loss of independence.

There is every reason to believe that this was the sentiment of all the great rulers of the first half of the eleventh century—of the Emperors from Otto III to Henry III, of King Canute and the Dukes of Normandy. The best of them were in no way behind the counts of the Spanish March either in devotion to Rome or in their sense of freedom. When all allowance has been made for differences in individual practice, the general attitude was the same everywhere: the filling of ecclesiastical offices was the responsibility (or the privilege, or the perquisite, according to the point of view) of the secular ruler. It was difficult to keep the matter of appointments free from family and monetary considerations—indeed, in general, they saw no necessity for trying to do so. No doubt it was wrong to give a church to an unworthy person for money: but it was foolish to give it to a stranger for nothing. We may remember the way in which so solid a churchman as Sir Thomas Bertram dealt with the living of Mansfield Park: it was to have been held for his second son, but the debts of the elder one "rendered a different disposal of the next presentation necessary"—it had to be sold to a stranger:

"I blush for you, Tom," said he, in his most dignified manner; "I blush for the expedient which I am driven on, and I trust I may pity your feelings as a brother on the occasion. You have robbed Edmund for ten, twenty, thirty years, perhaps for life, of more than half the income which ought to be his. It may hereafter be in my power, or in yours (I hope it will), to procure him better preferment; but it must not be forgotten, that no benefit of that sort would have been beyond his natural claims on us, and that nothing can, in fact, be an equivalent for the certain advantage which he is now obliged to forego through the urgency of your debts."

[1] *Marca Hispanica*, col. 1008. The date is 1017.

How many high-minded fathers must have addressed their eldest sons in this fashion in the eleventh century, as unconscious as Sir Thomas Bertram of any blame which they themselves might have incurred. They knew of course that there was such a thing as simony, but they would have denied that they were selling holy things—they were dealing only with the temporalities attached to holy things. But (in the eleventh, as in the nineteenth century) a conscience was stirring which set these dealings in a new and painful light. Bishops would appear in Rome to confess their simony and to lay down their office—such a one for instance as Reginald, Bishop of Liége, who had bought his bishopric from the Emperor Conrad II. He repented and went to Rome, laid his pastoral staff on the altar of St. Peter, and fell down at the Pope's feet confessing his fault. Since the Pope, Benedict IX, had probably bought the Papacy, and later certainly sold it, he must have found such conduct highly puzzling, but acts like this were a portent of greater things to come.

Only five years after Benedict IX sold the papacy, in the year before Count Wifred of Cerdaña died leaving his sons so firmly entrenched in the episcopacy, an event took place at the other end of Europe which struck a great blow at the manner in which he had provided for his family. In 1049 Pope Leo IX made a tour through his native land, along the Rhine and up the Moselle. The final stage of his journey brought him to the city of Rheims, where he was engaged to consecrate the newly built church of the monastery of St. Remigius, and to transfer to the high altar the bones of its patron saint. Here the Pope had summoned a large concourse of bishops and abbots to meet him. The response to the Pope's summons had been disappointing. There were no more than twenty bishops present —one from England, five from Normandy, but only a handful from the great provinces of Rheims and Sens, which should have provided most. From these unpropitious beginnings, however, there developed an awe-inspiring scene, and we are fortunate in having from a contemporary a day-to-day account of a Council which men later remembered as a landmark in the history of the Church.[1]

The Feast of St. Remigius, 1 October, had been fixed for the ceremony of translation, ·and the Pope arrived in Rheims on

[1]The account which follows is based on the *Historia Dedicationis ecclesiae Sancti Remigii*, by Anselm, a monk of that house. (P. L., vol. 142, 1417–40.)

29 September. The King of France had refused to be present, and he was largely responsible for the poor attendance of bishops. But the vast concourse of people who filled the town formed a striking and instructive contrast to the sparse gathering of notabilities. The 30 September was spent in rest; then, on the appointed day, amid scenes of immense popular enthusiasm and excitement, the bones of St. Remigius were carried round the town. The time had now arrived for the Pope to place them in their new resting place, but instead of doing so, he had them laid on the high altar of the church in which the Council was to be opened on the following day. The awful presence of the apostle of the Franks appeared from that moment to dominate the meeting. When the Council opened, the Pope—through the mouth of his chancellor, the cardinal deacon Peter, who was in charge of the business—made an unusual demand: before proceeding to the business of the meeting, each bishop and abbot was enjoined to rise and declare whether he had paid any money to obtain his office. The proposal caused considerable consternation. The Archbishop of Rheims asked for a personal interview with the Pope; the Bishops of Langres, Nevers, Coutances and Nantes remained silent. Of the abbots, only a few seem to have made the necessary declaration: the silence of the remainder expressed their embarrassment or guilt. Apparently the case against the abbots was allowed to drop; but during the remaining two days of the Council, in the intervals of the humdrum business of ecclesiastical disputes, the Papal Chancellor relentlessly pressed the bishops who had not dared to make the required declaration. The position of the Archbishop of Rheims, who was the host, was delicate: he was spared to the extent of being ordered to appear at Rome in the following year to make his explanation at the Council to be held in the middle of April. The full weight of the Chancellor's attack fell on the Bishop of Langres, a somewhat learned man, who, we notice, had just written a pamphlet against the heresy of Berengar of Tours. He asked for counsel: two archbishops undertook his defence, but one of them (the archbishop of Besançon) found some difficulty in speaking when his turn came, and the other (the archbishop of Lyons) made a partial admission of guilt on behalf of his client. The matter was adjourned, and came to a climax on the following day. The Bishop of Langres was found to have disappeared in the night. He was excommunicated;

and his counsel, the archbishop of Besançon, revealed that he himself had been struck dumb on the previous day when he attempted a defence of his guilty colleague. The assembly felt the influence of the awful presence on the altar, and a wave of excitement ran through the church. The Pope rose with the name of St. Remigius on his lips, and the business was interrupted while they all sang the antiphon *Sancte Remigi*. After these excitements, the case against the other bishops was quickly disposed of. The Bishop of Nevers confessed that his parents had paid a high price for his bishopric, but declared that he was ignorant of this at the time. He laid down his pastoral staff at the Pope's feet, and the Pope restored him to office, giving him (the symbolism is significant) another staff. The Bishop of Coutances then said that his bishopric had been bought for him by his brother without his knowledge; and that when, on discovering the transaction, he had tried to flee, he had been brought back and forcibly invested with the bishopric. He was declared innocent and he lived to be one of the builders of the Anglo-Norman state and one of the most magnificent prelates of his age. The Bishop of Nantes fared worse: he confessed that his father, who had been bishop before him, had obtained for him from the count the reversion of the bishopric, and that he himself had been obliged to pay a large sum to enter into his inheritance. He was deprived of his episcopal ring and staff, and allowed only to retain the status of a priest.

The business of the Council was now rapidly brought to an end. Various excommunications were pronounced against absent or contumacious bishops, decrees were promulgated which were long remembered for their disciplinary vigour, and a number of sentences and prohibitions were directed against laymen. On the day after the dissolution of the Council, the Pope raised the body of St. Remigius from the high altar and bore it on his own shoulders to its new resting place. He had been in Rheims just a week, and during this time, he had left a mark on the affairs of the Church which would not easily be effaced. The Pope had appeared in a more commanding position than at any time in living memory; out of the handful of bishops present at the Council, a quarter had confessed to simony, and had been judged as if they had committed a crime; an archbishop had been summoned to Rome. The promptings of conscience of men like Reginald of Liège were being stiffened by the sterner voice of authority.

We have been seeing, in the conduct of bishops and rulers, some examples of the persistent tendency to treat the organization of religion as a branch of secular life, and consequently to bring the property on which this organization was based under the same rules as secular property. This might have been unobjectionable if there had been any branch of secular law which dealt with corporations. But the legal conception of a corporation still lay in the future. The laws of property were concerned with the descent and division of property within a family, not with the rights of an undying corporation. Even in the eighteenth century it was difficult to prevent members of a corporate body from dealing with its property as if it belonged to themselves individually: in the eleventh century it scarcely seemed even curious to deal with it so. The only rival to the interest of the individual was the family: when the two were allied, they seemed impregnable.

The difficulty was not one which affected what we would now call the relations of 'Church and State' only at a high level of political responsibility, where the claims of rulers and their families were concerned. It was something which ran through the whole fibre of society and touched the parish priest and the canons of a cathedral church as much as great bishops and abbots. We happen to have a most vivid account of the cathedral church of Arezzo in Tuscany written at the end of the eleventh century by someone who could look back on the changes of the previous fifty years. The story he has to tell is an extraordinary one in the details which he supplies, but there is every reason to think that the general conditions which produced the state of affairs at Arezzo were by no means unusual. We may use his story to illustrate the pervasive influence of family interest as it affected the lower branches of the church in the century before Gregory VII.[1]

At the time of which we are speaking, the Cathedral church of Arezzo was the centre of an important pilgrimage, from which it received considerable revenues. The church was served by a small body of canons who performed the services; but alongside the canons there was another and larger body, whose usefulness was less apparent. The members of this second body were known as

[1]This account of the cathedral of Arezzo is taken from the *Historia Custodum Aretinorum*, a late eleventh century survey of the development of its constitution, printed in M. G. H. Scriptores, XXX, ii, 1471-82.

custodians. At the time when Gregory VII became Pope they were a miscellaneous lot, some clerks, some laymen, most of them married, numbering in all some twenty or thirty. For so large a body their duties were surprisingly light: they were responsible for cleaning the floor of the church, for keeping the lamps lit, for ringing the bell, for guarding the church and its treasures, and for studying. However all these tasks could be done by deputy, and (under pressure from the bishop) they clubbed together to pay a clerk to perform them. The arrangement did not work very well: one clerk was so bad that he failed to ring the bell at the proper times, another so good that he abandoned his duties in favour of a pilgrimage to Jerusalem. And there were other difficulties: the custodians sometimes failed to pay the stipend, and the bells were silent for days on end; the canons on their side were reluctant to let the clerk eat with them in case they were made responsible for his keep, and it was only with difficulty that an elaborate compromise was reached by which he had a loaf of bread and a cup of wine daily at the kitchen window. But whatever happened the custodians throve and multiplied. Their revenues were secure. They shared among themselves the profits of the various altars; they kept their agents always in the church to look after their interests and to work out the complicated arithmetic of division. Nothing escaped their vigilance: even the loaves which were offered at the altars during the Mass had to be divided among the various claimants—twelve to Gerard, twelve to John, three each to Ucellitus, Widolus, Pincus and Briccius, and so on.

How did this preposterous system ever come into existence? The rights of the custodians were of long standing. They can be traced back by lawful descent well into the tenth century. Half the profits, for instance, of the altar of St. Stephen's about 1078 were shared between twelve custodians in varying proportions—one took an eighth share, two took sixteenths, three took twenty-fourths, six (incredible though it may seem) forty-eighths. They derived their shares by inheritance from their great-great-grandfather, a priest of the church who was alive in the middle of the previous century. Before his time the history is obscure, but we can reconstruct what had happened. Some time between 835 and 843 the cathedral had been reformed, and a body of canons established. A hundred years later this body was still in existence, but it must have disintegrated very soon afterwards, for at the end of the century a new body of canons was formed. The new body however was not able to oust the descendants of their predecessors, and for a hundred years a curious double life continued: the new body of canons did the work, and the descendants of the old body took most of the profits. But in time the hereditary system died a natural death: in 1072 the system was in full vigour—the custodians dominated the church; by 1100 they had disappeared. It is remarkable that the change took place without violence, and without the exercise of external pressure. So far as we know there were no anathemas, no papal censure—the system simply collapsed voluntarily and ignominiously. Perhaps the much-divided profits were ceasing to be worth collecting; perhaps the custodians realized that their days were numbered. Whatever the reason, they began to get rid of their property. Most of them sold their rights to the canons, others bequeathed their shares, some became canons themselves. Within a few years the custodians had ceased to exist.

The case of Arezzo was not peculiar. Gregory VII's biographer tells us that he found a similar body of laymen—sixty and more—living on the profits of altars in St. Peter's itself, and that he rooted them out—with more violence, we can well believe, than those at Arezzo.[1] But whatever the local variations, the underlying theme was the same everywhere. It seemed impossible to preserve intact the property of the church, to keep it tied to the uses for which it was intended, or to relax the grip of a family into whose hands it had once fallen.

To many churchmen in the eleventh century, the root of all these evils seemed to lie in the mingling of sacred and secular things. The Church, so it seemed to them, was in danger of being swallowed by the world. In part, the effects of this mingling might seem innocuous, even beneficial to the church; the interest of lay rulers in ecclesiastical affairs had been the cause of most of the reforms and nearly all the good appointments to high places in the Church during the last two centuries. But it is useless in these matters to weigh the good and the bad points of a system as they may appear to our eyes. The deepest thinkers, the churchmen with most vigour and passion, and those with the most sustained sense of purpose, wanted something widely different from what they saw around them; and they thought they

[1]Bonizo, *Liber ad Amicum* (M. G. H., Libelli de Lite, i, 603.)

knew how to get it. It was not just that they wanted to sweep away the follies and confusions of a situation like that at Arezzo: these were cobwebs which the breath of ordinary life would clear away in time; and, in any case, the enforcement of clerical celibacy, on which the laity were just as keen as the high churchmen, was the best means of preventing situations like this arising. They wanted more than this. They wanted a church free from worldly entanglements, governed by its own laws, strengthened by a discipline which set it apart from the world, united in obedience to the successor of St. Peter. The older generation had thought of the church as a loose association of local units, comprising laymen and clerks on a more or less equal footing; it had been inclined to ascribe to lay rulers a spiritual authority not clearly distinguished from that conferred in Holy Orders; it had seen in a strong episcopate the best support of secular government. Very different was the picture which slowly made its way into men's minds in the second half of the eleventh century. In this view, the Church was a spiritual hierarchy culminating in the Pope; between clergy and laity there was a great gulf fixed; the lowest clerk in the hierarchy was superior to the greatest layman and this superiority had secular as well as spiritual consequences; he belonged to a privileged order, set apart by the conferring of spiritual gifts, judging laymen in his spiritual capacity but himself immune from secular judgement.

It was not only the persons of the clergy who belonged to this privileged order: the lands and possessions of churches were also set apart from the world. The Council of Clermont in 1095 pronounced that no bishop or priest should do homage to a king or other layman,[1] and the homage thus forbidden had no reference to spiritual office but only to the lands attached to the Church. In an age when the ceremony of homage was the chief symbol of the secular obligations attached to the holding of land, the cutting off of the Church from the lay world could scarcely be more trenchantly expressed; and, as if to emphasize the new relations between the Church and the world, the Council which promulgated this decree was the one at which Urban II called on lay rulers to

---

[1] The relevant section in the Council of Clermont (cap. 17) runs: *ne episcopus vel sacerdos regi vel alicui laico in manibus ligiam fidelitatem faciat.* (Mansi, *Concilia*, XX, 817.) There is an interesting discussion of the importance of this step in Z. N. Brooke, *Lay Investiture and its Relation to the Conflict of Empire and Papacy.* (British Academy, Raleigh Lecture, 1939.)

undertake the Crusade. In justice to Urban II, it must be said that it was probably not the secular obligations attached to church lands from which he wished to withdraw the Church (though there was plenty of room for argument on this head), so much as the contamination of the ceremony which preceded and justified these obligations. In 1099, an English monk in Rome heard Urban II repeat the censure of 1095, and he has left a vivid picture of the Pope's speech on that occasion:

> The Pope (he says) having excommunicated all laymen who gave investiture of churches, also bound by the same sentence of excommunication all who became the vassals of laymen for ecclesiastical estates, saying that it seemed a horrible thing that hands which had been honoured even above anything permitted to the angels, with power to create by their agency the God who is the Creator of all things and to offer Him to God the Father for the redemption and salvation of the whole world—that these hands should be degraded by the ignominy of being made subject to hands which were infected by filthy contagions day and night, stained with rapine and accustomed to the shedding of innocent blood. We were present at all this, we saw it, we heard these words acclaimed by all, "Fiat, Fiat," and thus the Council ended:[1]

Many practical consequences followed from this vision of a Church shaking itself free from the rough and tumble of secular life, asserting its divine origin, the privileges of its sacramental character, and its legal autonomy. Nothing, for instance was more offensive to the holders of these views than the way in which bishops were chosen by lay rulers, and received at the hands of the ruler their pastoral staff. It was a simple operation, and for long it had seemed a harmless one; judged by results, it is hard to say that any other system would have done so well. But on the new view, it was a proceeding which bristled with grounds of offence: it was against the ancient canons, which required an election by clergy and people; it was an invitation to needy rulers to practise simony; and, even if they resisted this temptation, it encouraged them to look on bishops as secular officials; it put into the hands of a layman the holy symbol of episcopal office—to be returned to the ruler on the bishop's death, like the arms of a thane. This last was the head and front of the

[1] Eadmer, *Historia Novorum*, ed. M. Rule, R. S., p. 114.

offence: it made the layman a dispenser of holy things. It was useless for the ruler to assert that he conferred nothing thereby but a title to certain temporalities and an authorization for the consecration of the newly elected bishop by his fellow bishops. Such a defence only aggravated the offence: it reduced the symbol of the shepherd's office to an instrument of secular policy; it made the consecration dependent on the ruler's will, and it laid the lands of the church at his mercy. Were these lands not also sacred, set apart for God? It was as if the wolf should claim to set up the shepherd, and guard the sheep-fold.

If the hand of a layman (wrote the successor of Urban II) delivers the staff which is the sign of the shepherd's office, and the ring which is the seal of faith, what are bishops doing in the Church at all? The honour of the Church is torn in pieces, the bonds of discipline are loosened and the Christian religion is dragged through the mud, if we allow the presumption of laymen to stretch out their hands to what we know to be the privilege of priests alone. It is not for laymen to betray the Church, nor for sons to stain their Mother with adultery.[1]

These are strong words, but they were written by the least violent of the Hildebrandine Popes, Paschal II. Nor are they to be treated as an emotional outburst: they occur in a business letter to the Archbishop of Canterbury, and they are a statement of a position which, by this time (1102), was almost ceasing to be controversial.

The many-sided 'Investiture' controversy, of which this question of the making of bishops was the centre, is the first major dispute in modern history. The discussion rolled and reverberated round Europe for half a century. It was in these years that the characteristic features of the medieval church began to be clear; and on the other side, arguments were heard, which were drowned in the rising tide of papalism and disappeared for nearly three hundred years— arguments in favour of a married clergy and an episcopate not subject to Rome; arguments supporting the rights of the lay ruler over the Church and asserting the superiority of the kingly over the episcopal office, which were to burst out with violent strength at the time of the Reformation. On both sides there was a great deal of crude and violent talk, and endless pillorying and misrepresentation

[1] *Historia Novorum*, p. 150.

of opponents; every consideration which could vex and complicate an issue was drawn in at some time or other. But in the main the victory—alike in consistency of thought, seriousness of purpose and practical success—lay with the adherents of the new views. The position of Rome as the legislative and administrative centre of the Church was established; the immunity of the clergy from secular jurisdiction and the special position of church lands were recognized, at least in part; the most offensive features in the election and investing of bishops disappeared. To this extent the ideal of a spiritual church became a practical reality. But the world, which was thrown out of the door, came in at the window. The experience of the hundred years after the end of the Investiture controversy falsified many of the hopes of the eleventh century idealists. The equilibrium between Church and World which was slowly established differed in many ways from that which had existed in the first half of our period; in detail it was much more intricate and it imposed many more restraints on the individual will. The Church, with its clear and authoritative system of law, its courts, its privileges and its formidable punishments was a great machine which had to be handled with care. The system commanded a fiercer allegiance, and excited a more ardent devotion than that which had existed in the tenth and early eleventh centuries. St. Thomas Becket was its martyr, and the men who overthrew the system in England in the sixteenth century recognized his symbolic importance: much more than Gregory VII he stood for the system, and the whole system, without compromise. But though the system had its heroes and its philosophers, it was also, as practical men knew, capable of being manipulated to give much the same results as had been obtained in a simpler and cruder age. The whole secret lay in knowing the ropes, and in sensing how far one could go.

II

ROME AND THE PAPACY

A. BEFORE GREGORY VII

All the changes which have just been mentioned are summed up in the changing position of Rome in the Christian world. The Rome of the early part of our period was a town sunk in deep material decay. Itself a vast area of noble ruins, it stood in a countryside littered with the fragments of an ancient civilization—useless monuments of a dead past except where ancient walls supported some modern stronghold. Sentimentally Rome was still the heart of Europe, but from an economic and administrative point of view it was a heart which had ceased to beat. The countryside in which the town lay had, through lack of drainage, lost much of its old fertility. The town was the centre of no large commerce. The greater part of the area of the Seven Hills was—as it long continued to be—a place of gardens, vineyards, ruins and emptiness. Within the walls, which had once housed over a million people, a small population was gathered in clusters in the lower town, along the banks, and on the Island between the banks, of the Tiber. It was a town of churches— over three hundred at the end of the twelfth century, and probably not much less two centuries earlier. They were ancient churches, most of them, treasure houses of the relics of saints and martyrs of the early church. These churches were of all sizes and degrees of importance, from small churches with a single priest—like the obscure church of St. Lawrence from which, by a pious fraud, the monks of St. Lawrence at Liège obtained relics of their patron saint during the absence of the priest—to the stately basilicas like S. Maria Maggiore, with its college of clergy presided over by a cardinal priest, and, greatest of all, St. Peter's in the Vatican. It was these churches which were the basis of Rome's life. The pilgrimage to Rome was the city's staple industry: everyone depended on it to some extent, from the clerical population which served the churches, and the lodging-house keepers, money-lenders, and middlemen of various kinds, to the small aristocracy who carved out impregnable fortresses for themselves in the ruins of ancient buildings. This last class drew its revenues and supported its dignity in part from country estates round Rome, but it aimed also at controlling the ecclesiastical, as well as the temporal, fortunes of the city. Its greatest prize was the Papacy.

How did men look on the Papacy in the early eleventh century? Leaving aside all speculation about what ought to have been, the Pope was (in the words of a great historian of the early church) "the high-Priest of the Roman pilgrimage, the dispenser of benedictions and of privileges and of anathemas".[1] The phrase admirably describes

[1] L. Duchesne, *The Beginnings of the Temporal Sovereignty of the Popes*, 1908, p. 271.

the practical position of the Pope—the place which he held in men's minds before they had been stirred by the challenge of the days of Gregory VII. Men came to Rome to pray at the tomb of St. Peter, to put their affairs under his patronage, to solicit his anathema on their enemies; and the successor of St. Peter, the ceremony of whose election had been completed by his being seated in the chair believed to be that of the chief Apostle himself, spoke in his name. Men went to Rome not as the centre of ecclesiastical government but as a source of spiritual power. The 'power' was St. Peter's; like St. Remigius at the council of 1049, he ruled from the tomb, but with a more world-wide view and a more compelling authority. This power brought many men to Rome who would have no thought of going there when Rome became the centre of the everyday government of the church. Several English kings, for example, made the pilgrimage to Rome before 1066: after 1066, not one. King Canute was the last English king to go to Rome to visit the tomb of the Apostle. "God has granted me," he wrote, "in my life-time the boon of visiting the blessed apostles Peter and Paul and every sanctuary within and without the city of Rome that I could hear of, to venerate and adore them in their very presence (praesentialiter). And I sought this blessing because I heard from wise men that St. Peter the apostle has received from the Lord a great power of binding and loosing, and bears the keys of the kingdom of Heaven; and therefore I deemed it useful in no ordinary degree to seek his patronage before God."[1] The pope of the day when these words were written (1027) is not generally reckoned one of the more distinguished or reputable occupants of the see, but he satisfied the requirements of the day. He presided with patriarchal dignity in a position where a legislator would have been frustrated and where an administrator would have found nothing to administer. Even a man like St. Odilo of Cluny seems to have expected nothing more. It was a simpler age than that which saw a stream of supplicants to the Papal court coming from every part of Europe.

Many men went to Rome in the twelfth century because they had to, but Rome was more loved in the days of the reprehensible Benedict VIII. Of Canute's successors, Richard I and Edward I both spent their energies and fortune on Crusade, but Richard I did not

[1]The text of Canute's letter is preserved in the early twelfth century Chronicle of Florence of Worcester, ed. B. Thorpe, i, 185-9.

turn aside to visit Rome, though he wintered in Sicily; and Edward I, though he went through Rome to visit the papal court at Orvieto, intent on the difficult business he had to discuss with the Pope, did not, so far as we know, visit the Roman shrines. They no longer had that overwhelming importance which Canute attached to them.

The noblest expression of the estimation in which Rome was held in these pre-Hildebrandine days is found in a poem, probably written in the tenth century, which begins with the words *O Roma nobilis*.[1] The short poem is so filled with the sense of the grandeur and dignity of the eternal city that for long it was considered a work of the late Roman Empire. The pride and confidence of its description of Rome as 'mistress of the world' consorted so ill with the ruin and impotence of the city in the tenth century that this date seemed to be ruled out. But, on a closer view, the material state of Rome is seen to be quite irrelevant in the poet's mind to the city's true dignity. The poem is written entirely in the spirit which animates the letter of Canute: Rome is the noble city, mistress of the world by virtue of the martyrs in whose blood she is dyed, and of the virgins with whose virtue she shines. Above all, the apostles Peter and Paul, the one the doorkeeper of Heaven, the other the seneschal of the household of God bearing the dishes of divine wisdom to those who seek to share the feast, ennobled and enriched the city by their presence. Classical grandeur and present squalor were equally trifling when compared with the rich deposit of Christian earth which formed the true wealth of Rome.

Rome of course never ceased to be venerated as a great repository of Christian relics, but it is doubtful whether they could ever again give Rome the kind of importance which they gave her in the tenth and eleventh centuries. When the machinery of government was simple or non-existent, these tangible agents of spiritual power had an importance in public life which they lost in a more complicated age. The deficiencies in human resources were supplied by the power of the saints. They were great power-houses in the fight against evil; they filled the gaps left in the structure of human justice. The most revealing map of Europe in these centuries would be a map, not of

[1]This poem is printed with a commentary by L. Traube in the *Abhandlungen der Bayerischen Akademie der Wissenschaften, Phil.-Hist. Klasse*, Munich, 1891, XIX, 299-309.

political or commercial capitals, but of the constellation of sanctuaries, the points of material contact with the unseen world. The resting places of the saints were the chief centres of ecclesiastical organization and of spiritual life. The saints were indeed very business-like; there was nothing mild or uncertain about the justice which they dispensed; they looked after their own. The monks of the monastery of Fleury on the Loire, for instance, had a precious treasure in the body of St. Benedict, and from the ninth to the early twelfth century they kept a record of what it did for them.[1] Whenever the rights or property of the monastery were endangered, St. Benedict was at hand to deal out vengeance with a mighty hand; and the monks sent portions of the relics to outlying properties as a means of defence in the midst of many dangers. It was all intensely local. But above the host of local saints rose the commanding figure of the chief of the Apostles, drawing men to Rome; a universal figure in a local world. Rulers like Canute went to Rome to visit St. Peter; they venerated his successors and treasured the great parchments in which he committed the despoilers of their favoured foundations to "the chains of everlasting damnation, to burn in the eternal fire with the Devil and his wicked angels and with Judas the betrayer of our Lord and Saviour Jesus Christ, where the worm dies not and the fire is not quenched". There was no material arm to enforce these censures—they belonged essentially to the world of the spirit. The Pope, speaking in the name of St. Peter, could command and he could threaten, but if men chose to ignore these commands and defy his threats their punishment was deferred until they appeared before the doorkeeper of Heaven.

Peter Damian protested to Pope Alexander II against the too lavish use of these ancient and unbridled anathemas which knew no distinction in crime or punishment.[2] They were too strong as heavenly, too weak as earthly instruments. They belonged to an age when government was in the hands of God, and men's hands were too weak or uncertain to guide or control. This age was coming to an end: the Papal documents with their new distinctions of form and their more refined adaptation of means to ends tell the same story as that told by the documents of secular

---

[1]This very interesting collection of miracles is printed by E. de Certain, *Les miracles de Saint Benoît*, Soc. de l'histoire de France, 1858.

[2]Ep. I, 12 (P. L. vol. 144, 214-5.)

rulers everywhere. Government was once more becoming active and directive. The bringing about of this change was the work of countless administrators, but the change had its prophets as well as its agents, and the greatest of these was Gregory VII.

B. GREGORY VII (1073-85)

Gregory VII was a man about whom many anecdotes circulated. Most of them were told by his enemies and are not to be trusted. Nevertheless they cast a vivid light on the passionate animosities which rent Rome in the days of his pontificate and divided Christendom on a theoretical question as it had never been divided since the days of the great heresies. All of them bear witness to the dramatic intensity of Gregory's character. The abbot Hugh of Cluny had more opportunity than most to observe the Pope with a detached but not unfriendly eye, and a special interest attaches to a small group of stories which were current in his circle. One of them tells of an incident in Gregory's life before he became Pope, when he was a papal legate. He and Abbot Hugh were riding together in a large company. The abbot had fallen behind and was reflecting on the character of the legate, and on the strange command which this small man of obscure origin exercised in the world; mentally, he wrote him down as proud, and accused him of seeking his own glory. Suddenly the legate turned on him and broke out with— "It's a lie; I seek not my own glory, but that of the Holy Apostles."[1] True or not—and there is no reason to doubt its substantial accuracy—the story reveals the man, explosive, filled with a dynamic power which brought on him accusations of dark practices, eaten up with the one burning passion to restore the glory of the Apostles.

The Apostles he was thinking of were St. Peter and St. Paul, under whose patronage he had lived since childhood. He was fond of recalling that he had been brought up from infancy under the shadow

[1]Casual stories about Gregory VII are preserved in several sources. The one quoted in the text comes from William of Malmesbury, *Gesta Regum*, ed. Stubbs, R. S., ii, 322-3, where it is given on the authority of someone who had it from the mouth of Abbot Hugh. It can be shown that the source of his information was a monk of Canterbury, probably Eadmer, who has left an account of the conversations, at which he was present, between Abbot Hugh and Archbishop Anselm, during the latter's exile from England. Among the anecdotes they exchanged there are several relating to Gregory VII of which this is one. For further details of these conversations, see below, p. 252.

of St. Peter's. How far he was Roman by birth is difficult to determine, but certainly in feeling, in background and in his social milieu
he was altogether Roman.[1] In this he differed from most other
members of the Reforming party: they were mostly foreigners from
Lorraine, Burgundy or Northern Italy. Indeed Rome was the despair
of the Reformers: however much they differed, they were all agreed
in denouncing the corruptions of Rome, and especially of its
aristocracy. All forward-looking policy for the last two hundred
years had come from outside Rome, particularly from Germany. But
Gregory had little use for all this. His eyes were fixed on a more
distant past before there were German Emperors. The first recorded
words of his we possess were a denunciation of the relaxation of the
rule for Canons authorized by the German Emperor, Louis the
Pious, in the ninth century—a ruler who, in the conditions of his
time, had done more than anyone else to restore the regular canonical
life. On another occasion, speaking of the practice of shortening
matins to three Psalms and three Lessons, Gregory writes of the
languor which has crept in "especially since the time when the
government of our church passed to the Germans. . . . But we,
having searched out the Roman Order and the ancient custom of
our church, imitating the old Fathers, have ordered things to be
restored as we have set out above."[2]

Gregory VII found his strength in Rome. He was allied to the
new urban families who were beginning to appear there, men who
were making a name and fortune for themselves as financiers and
men of business to the popes. Two of these families, the Pierleoni

[1]The family connexions of Gregory VII have been the subject of much discussion
among Italian scholars, most recently in *Studi Gregoriani*, 1947, ed. G. B. Borino, ii,
287-333. A notable contribution to the subject in English, which has not received
the attention it deserves, is the long paper by R. L. Poole, *Benedict IX and Gregory VI*
(reprinted in his *Studies in Chronology and History* (1934), from the *Proceedings of
the British Academy*, VIII, 1917). Whether or not (in a subject in which nearly everything is uncertain) Poole's conclusions can be accepted, his study throws a flood of
light on the state of Rome during the early years of the future Gregory VII.

[2]The speech by Hildebrand, then Archdeacon of Rome, attacking the relaxations,
which claimed the authority of Louis the Pious, was delivered on 20 April, 1059
at the Council held in Rome shortly after Easter. There is a contemporary account
of the speech printed in *Neues Archiv für ältere deutsche Geschichtskunde*, 1902, XXVII,
669-75. The text of Gregory's pronouncement on the shortening of matins is
preserved in the *Corpus Iuris Canonici*, ed. Friedberg, i, 1416 (where the most
illuminating phrases will be found in the footnotes). Another address of Gregory
(this time to the Lenten Council of 1078), attacking the new and unauthorized custom
which had disturbed the ancient practice of the Church with regard to Ember Days,
is printed in *Neues Archiv*, 1889, XIV, 620-2.

and Frangipani, were to have a great future in the history of the city
and the papacy. It was at Gregory's instigation that the first of the
Pierleoni used his wealth to support the fortunes of the reform party
in the critical days of Alexander II. Cencius Frangipane and Alberic
Pierleone were Gregory's intimates—"men" as he affectionately said,
"who have been brought up with us almost from adolescence in the
Roman court". When the Countess Matilda made her will in 1102
she recalled that they were at the Pope's side during the first moves
in that important transaction. Gregory was at home in Rome. He
was the first Pope since the unregenerate days of the Tuscular Popes
to make the city his normal place of residence. The constant perambulations of his immediate predecessors were discontinued; except
for his one journey north to Canossa and its neighbourhood, he was
rooted in Rome until he was driven out in the last months of his life.
His last words "I have *loved righteousness and hated iniquity*—therefore I die in exile"[1] show the bitterness for him of the loss of Rome.
Other Popes had been, and were to be, driven from the city without
experiencing any great diminution in their authority; but for
Gregory VII it meant the end.

This concentration gives Gregory his intensity. But he was only
the most intense to a group of men who had the same general
purpose. It is usual to call them the 'Reforming Party', but it would
be truer—and more suggestive of their revolutionary purpose—to
call them the 'Restoring Party'. They aimed at the restoration of
ancient discipline, or what they believed to be ancient discipline.
The names which they took when they became Popes show this
more clearly than many words: they abandoned names such as
John and Benedict, which had been common in the tenth and early
eleventh centuries, and took those by preference which had not been
used for many centuries—Clement, Damasus, Victor, and so on.
These names contained a challenge.

In thus associating themselves with the first centuries of Christian
history, they were going back to a past which in many ways seemed
clearer to them than it does to us. They had a series of documents,
stretching, as they believed, back to Clement I, the immediate
successor of St. Peter, which proclaimed the rights and authority of
the Roman see. Some of these, as we now know, were compositions

[1]Psalm 45, v. 8, with the last clause ('wherefore God, even thy God, hath anointed
thee with the oil of gladness above thy fellows.') altered.

of the eighth and ninth centuries; the most important of them was the Donation of Constantine, a document in which the first Christian Emperor purported to give extensive temporal rights over large parts of Italy and over all islands to the Pope Silvester I. This was a document to which Gregory VII and his successors attached great importance, and its authenticity was accepted (though its authority was not) by friends and foes alike. But the greatest treasury of documents which inspired the Reformers was of undoubted authenticity: it was the vast collection of letters of Gregory the Great. It was here that they found in its most practical form the lofty spirit of order and papal initiative in the affairs of all the churches of the West which they sought to renew. It was not an accident that Hildebrand (following his master Gregory VI) broke the sequence of popes who took names from the earliest centuries, and chose that of the greatest of his predecessors after St. Peter.

Gregory VII made no great innovations in the machinery of papal government, nor did he introduce into the papal service any body of new men to carry on his work. He took over the men who had been working with his predecessor, and the machinery which had been developed during the previous twenty years. But though he was not himself a great administrator, it is in his pontificate that the documents first become sufficiently abundant for us to see the papal administration at work. And though he almost broke the machine, he embodied more ardently and expressed more clearly than anybody else the impulses of the men who had built it. His pontificate was certainly not a success in any practical sense. Nothing that he did as Pope hastened the process of bringing business to Rome, or of giving the Pope a new place in the calculations of practical men. When he died he had been deserted by most of the cardinals on whom the work of government depended: for the timid he was too dangerous; too violent for moderate men; too autocratic for men of independence. Visionaries found him too much of a politician, and politicians found him too careless of consequences. For one reason or another the men fell away: the Councils of his later years (1080-4) are a shadow of the great manifestations of power which culminated in the Lateran Council of 1079; his staff deserted him and the secretarial work fell into arrears. Before the end of his life, his authority was denied or challenged over great parts of Europe. Everywhere there was bewilderment and confusion.[1] But his failures, however one judges them, were only temporary set-backs. The "zeal not for my own glory but for that of the Holy Apostles" was winning adherents all over Europe to the new ordering of Church government under Papal leadership; and pressing practical needs came in to reinforce the effects of this zeal. It is to this practical work that we must now turn, and to the men and machinery of government at Rome at the time when Gregory became Pope.

The men. The Pope's chief assistants were the cardinals who included at this time (1073) seven bishops, twenty-eight priests, eighteen deacons and possibly twenty-one subdeacons. It was a heterogeneous and rather unmanageable body. On the whole the bishops were probably the least important in the daily work of government. They had their sees outside Rome and the chief official duty which brought them into the city was that of taking their turn in the conduct of services in the Lateran church. They stood in relation to the Pope rather like the great barons of a kingdom to the king: they took no part in the routine of business, but at times their advice and their authority could be decisive. For example, although the whole body of cardinals had a voice in the election of a pope, it was only the bishops who could consecrate him, so that no election could be complete without the co-operation of some of their number. But it was among the cardinal-priests and deacons that the mainstay of papal government was found. Most of them in Gregory's day are mere names to us—some of them not even names. But they included some of the most vigorous and influential personalities in Rome, and among them two figures stand out, representatives of the men who conducted the two main types of papal business.[2]

The first of these is Hugh Candidus, Cardinal priest of S. Clemente. He must have been a brilliant figure in the papal circle,

[1]P. Kehr has shown that the area which at one time or another acknowledged the authority of Gregory's rival, the anti-Pope Clement III, is more extensive than has generally been supposed. Besides Germany and Northern Italy it included, for varying periods, Rome itself, Hungary, Serbia and Croatia, and possibly for a short time the England of William I and Lanfranc. (*Sitzungsberichte der Preussischen Akademie der Wissenschaften,* Berlin, 1921, 355-68).

[2]For the composition of the body of Cardinals in the eleventh century, see H. W. Klewitz, *Die Entstehung des Kardinalkollegiums* in Zeitschrift der Savigny Stiftung für Rechtsgeschichte (Kanonistische Abteilung, XXV), 1936, vol. 66. For a study of the career of Hugo Candidus, F Lerner, *Kardinal Hugo Candidus* (1931; Beiheft zur Historischen Zeitung, XXII.)

and in 1073 he stood at the height of his power and influence with a long record of devoted service in the papal cause. In many ways he was the antithesis of Gregory. His field of activity, like his origin, lay outside Rome.

He was one of the Rhinelanders who had been brought to Italy by Leo IX twenty years earlier, and he had done more than any man of his day to carry papal authority to new lands—to Aragon and Catalonia especially, where he had been outstandingly successful as papal legate. When Alexander II died, he had just returned from a legatine mission in Southern France, and it was he who took the leading part in Gregory's election. While the great concourse of priests and people was still busied with the burial of the late Pope, he rose in the pulpit and directed the energies of the turbulent gathering with the words: "Brethren, you know that from the days of Pope Leo (IX) it is Hildebrand who has exalted the Holy Roman Church and freed this city. Wherefore, since we cannot have anyone better fitted to be elected as Roman pontiff, we elect him now—a man ordained in our church, a man known to you all, and approved by all." One of the first acts of the new Pope, still exhausted by the tumultuous events of his election day, was to send Hugh on a new legatine mission—yet within a year Pope and cardinal were divided by a bitter hostility.

Hugh, the most active of papal legates, was the first cardinal to desert Gregory. Ten years later, one of the last of the cardinals to desert him was a man whose importance was of a quite different kind. This was the papal chancellor, Peter, Cardinal priest of S. Crisogono. His position was analogous to that of the head of the Civil Service. He was the most important of the officials whose place was constantly at the Pope's side. The Pope was ahead of most rulers of his day in the means at his disposal for making his will known by the written word. He not only had a small, expert staff engaged in the preparation and expediting of his correspondence, but he also kept (which no other ruler in the West did) a copy of the more important letters which he wrote. The chancellor Peter was in charge of this activity. We may think of him as a kind of secretary to the Pope, preparing drafts of his letters, correcting them before they were sent off, organizing the work of transcribing them, and filing copies for future reference. His personality remains quite obscure; he does not appear to have been a man of independent views like the Cardinal Hugh, but only an official who left Gregory in the end because he could not stay the course in adversity.

Between these two men, who typify the two kinds of agents on whom the conduct of papal business chiefly depended—the roving ambassadors or legates, often men of high spirit, determination and dangerous independence, and, on the other hand, the administrators with their clearly defined spheres of activity in the papal household—there were many cardinals whose position is not easy to determine. There was, for instance, Desiderius, abbot of Monte Cassino and Cardinal priest of the church of S. Cecilia, Gregory's successor as Pope. He was an important man in counsel, though it would seem of some feebleness of character. Then there was Beno, Cardinal priest of S. Martino, in later years the spokesman of the party of violent reaction against Gregory. He was probably a member of one of those Roman families which at first welcomed Gregory's election because of his Roman sympathies, but soon found that the Rome for which he stood was very different from their own. He is an interesting man, because he wrote two poisonous pamphlets which preserve the gossip and scandal of the day, and give us a glimpse of the narrow and truculent society which lived among the ruins of Rome.

Behind the cardinals, we can dimly perceive a host of miscellaneous assistants and followers: notaries who engrossed the papal letters; soldiers—whose importance Gregory did not underrate; adherents like Cencius Frangipane and Alberic Pierleone from the great city families; and the small band of faithful women, Beatrice and Matilda of Tuscany and the Empress Agnes. Except for the women none were to be depended upon without reserve—least of all the cardinals on whom the whole system of papal government depended.

The machinery of government. One common need at this time dominates the whole scene of human government, whether secular or spiritual: the need for justice. Justice was a word often on the lips of Gregory VII: some scholars have thought that he used the word to express a high ideal of righteousness; but more often he was simply concerned with the practical determination of disputes. In this he was like any other ruler of his day, and his problem was the same as theirs. The social arrangements of the eleventh and twelfth centuries were bedevilled by disputes about titles to lands and dignities, which were below the dignity of bloodshed—or at least offered no opportunity for a violent solution—but had the capacity to cause endless exasperation and confusion. As a consequence of this, the primary function of the medieval ruler was that of organizing justice and pronouncing judgement, either through his officials or in his own person. Men acquiesced in government because, whether themselves litigious or not—and most men were—they were involved in a web of conflicting claims and counter-claims which could have no end until they had been pressed as far as money and strength would allow. If this was true of secular government, it was also true of the government of the Church. At the time when Gregory VII became Pope we are entering an age of intense ecclesiastical litigation. Churchmen, forbidden to take the sword, exposed their bodies to dangers greater than those of battle in long and trying journeys in pursuit of justice, in the defence of the rights, dignities and prerogatives of their churches, in the vainglorious desire for prestige or the dour assertion of principle. It was this state of mind, far more than the actions of a small group of idealists, which was preparing for the Rome of the eleventh century a new position in the world.

The two essentials for giving judgement are a court and a judge, and the main problem of government was to bring court and judges to the scene of a dispute, while investing them with the authority of a distant superior; or, alternatively to bring litigants to a distant court, which would yet command the power to enforce its decisions in the provinces. Neither of these problems was easy, and the history of government during the next two hundred years is in large part the history of the attempts to solve them. But the Pope was better provided with the means for solving them than any other ruler. Most secular rulers had laboriously to create the means for conveying their authority to outlying courts; but the Popes had two ancient instruments which needed only a transforming touch to adapt them to new purposes.

The practice of holding councils, and of sending legates endowed with authority to settle particular cases in dispute went back into an impenetrable past. At the moment when Gregory VII became Pope, both practices were undergoing important developments which were to stamp a new form of papal authority on the church. On the one hand, papal legates, instead of going out at infrequent intervals for the discharge of some specific business were beginning to make lengthy perambulations over wide areas, taking up in their course whatever business came to hand. They held councils, heard disputes, pronounced judgement and remitted to Rome matters which could be brought to no conclusion on the spot. Among the earliest of these legates-at-large were the Cardinal priest Hugh Candidus, who as we have seen had lately returned from Spain at the time of Gregory's election, and the Cardinal bishop of Ostia, Gerald, who at this same time was moving through the chief cities of northern France, and showed no disposition to return to Rome in a hurry. These visits brought a considerable stir of ecclesiastical business in the provinces: the legates correspond to the later justices in eyre in England, who came with the authority of the king behind them, and on whose arrival the ordinary business of the local courts stood suspended. And just as these itinerating justices of English law fed the central courts with business, so Rome at an earlier date felt the effect of the legatine activities in the provinces. A crowd of unsatisfied litigants came to the city either at the bidding of the legate, or to appeal against his decisions. Such men required careful treatment: they were often important and nearly always sore. It would appear that their business generally waited until the Pope could have fuller counsel than was normally available to him. Hence there arose an important development in the holding of councils. This is the other side of the picture.

We do not know exactly when the practice grew up of the Pope holding a council in the first week of Lent each year for the dispatch of important business, but it was well established by the time of Gregory's election, and, within the next few years, the increase of business made a second annual council in November a meeting of almost equal importance. These meetings were naturally the occasion for papal pronouncements of general interest, and they were the scenes of important judgements which are milestones in the history of the church. But their routine business, which, as we can see from Gregory's letters, might continue for several weeks after most members of the council had dispersed, was concerned with the large number of local cases filtering through to Rome from the provinces. The analogy with the later English medieval Parliament is here very striking, but this only means that the problems of government were much the same for all rulers, whether secular or spiritual, and that the solution of these problems naturally followed somewhat similar lines.

The way in which legates and councils combined to give a new shape to the government of the church can best be illustrated by following a single case through its many stages. We select it not for its inherent interest—there must have been hundreds of similar cases—but because it is well documented, and it shows how the course of a vexatious local dispute was shaped by, and itself helped to shape, what was happening in Rome. It was one of the cases which came before the Cardinal bishop of Ostia in the course of his perambulation of France while Gregory was being elected Pope—but it was already old at this time, and was to be much older before it was finally buried.

On the border between Anjou and Brittany there is a village called Craon.[1] In the early eleventh century it was a centre of a small lordship, and its church evidently had substantial revenues. In about the year 1010 the lord of Craon gave the church to the monastery of St. Aubin at Angers, and the monks promised to make it a centre of monastic life. It is not clear that they ever kept this promise, though they seem to have tried to do so; but in the end they failed and their failure brought on them a suspicion of bad faith which told against them later.

In the course of time the whole lordship of Craon, like many others, fell into the hands of the Count of Anjou, Geoffrey Martel. Geoffrey and his wife Agnes (the mother of the Empress) were busy at this time with their new monastic foundation, far away on the east of their lands at Vendôme, and the church at Craon appeared a desirable addition to its possessions. On the pretext that the monks of Angers had failed to carry out their promise to establish monks at Craon, the Count transferred the church to his new foundation. This happened shortly before 1049 and it started a course of litigation between the monks of Angers and Vendôme which lasted close on fifty years.

The monks of Angers were hampered from the first by a very common misfortune, which was the cause of many law-suits: they had no title-deeds. The gift had been made to them without the intervention of a written document. Doubtless there had been some

[1]See the map on p. 84. The history of the case concerning the church of Craon can be traced through the documents printed in Ch. Métais, *Cartulaire de la Trinité de Vendôme* (4 vols., Paris, 1893-7).

symbolic ceremony before witnesses, but this had been nearly forty years earlier. Surprisingly enough, they do not seem to have attempted to supply the lack of a written document by the common expedient of manufacturing one after the event. They relied on the strength of testimony in their favour and brought their case before the Count of Anjou in his court. Not unnaturally they were repulsed. The next land-mark was in 1054 when Hildebrand came as a papal legate to Tours. The monks of Angers appeared with their complaint; the legate heard the case, but he left matters where they were. Then the Count died and the monks prepared to bring their case before his successor. But he, weary perhaps of a troublesome dispute, was persuaded that the case ought to go to Rome, and to Rome it went in 1060 or early in 1061. It came before Pope Nicholas II in his Lenten council, and the pope appointed a panel of bishops to hear the arguments, and to report to the Council. The bishops reported in favour of Vendôme, and papal letters announcing the decision were made out accordingly.

This might have seemed to put an end to the hopes of the monks of Angers, but when in 1067 a new legate appeared in France they presented their case once more—and once more without success. Then came the great legatine visit of the Bishop of Ostia in 1072. Once again the monks of Angers sought a judgement, and the Bishop heard the tangled case as he moved from Tours to Chartres, from Chartres to Paris and back again to Chartres. For a moment a more conciliatory spirit seemed to be at work: after two sessions in which nothing was accomplished, the legate, with the help of the Bishop of Chartres, brought the two abbots together, and they agreed that Vendôme should pay Angers £200 to be quit of any further disturbance. This reasonable compromise spoke much for the legate's patience, but it was unavailing. The word compromise is odious to the true litigant, and the monks of Angers now transferred their hostility to their own abbot for his rash, contemptible and wholly unacceptable sale of their rights. Words failed them to express their indignation, but, for the moment, they could only let their anger burn within them and wait for the death of their abbot.

It was possibly this event which roused the prior and monks of Angers to a last great effort in the years after the death of Gregory VII. They brought their case before Pope Urban II, who delegated it to his permanent legate in the south of France. Very reasonably the legate refused to upset the amicable settlement made between the two abbots in 1072, and once more the case of the monks of Angers seemed on the point of foundering. But this time they were determined to make an end. They sought out Urban II in Calabria in November 1092, and for three days he sat in Council to hear the case. Finally he judged that the monks of Vendôme should continue to hold Craon, but give up one of their other churches to Angers in exchange; in return, the monks of Angers at long last abandoned their suit.

So, with a typical compromise, this tiresome case, which had consumed so much of the time of Popes and legates, came to an end. At least four legates and three Popes had listened to the interminable arguments, which gained strength from the deficiency of written documents, and from the wilful obscuring and distorting of facts, which even good-will could scarcely have clarified. But, tedious though the case is, it reflects important movements in the life of the half century which it covers. We see the intimate connexion and interplay of legatine missions and papal councils and judgements, and we witness the beginnings of that regular flow of business to the papal court which is soon to swell into a torrent. We see how a case which began in a secular court and wandered indeterminately through many synods and assemblies, was gradually drawn into the orbit of Rome for a final solution. We learn too of the reluctance of judges to come to an irrevocable decision where rights were concerned, and of the pertinacity of litigants, which made any judgement less than that of the highest authority, pronouncing a decision in the most solemn manner, nothing more than a check in a game played without a time limit. We notice also how little jealousy secular rulers showed at this portentous growth of ecclesiastical jurisdiction: it was the Count of Anjou who first sent the case to Rome.

Looked at from the point of view of the litigants (and they after all were the people who made work for legates and councils) the 'reform of the papacy' was a practical question of adapting old machinery to new, or at least much extended, uses. The question of ideals was quite secondary. They wanted a judgement and everything—even the disposition of secular rulers—encouraged them to look for that judgement in Rome. The impulse which carried litigation to Rome was fostered and encouraged by the activity of men like Gerald, Bishop of Ostia, and Hugh Candidus: they smoothed the road, but unless men had been willing to take the road they prepared, their work would have been in vain. To this extent, the origins of the transformation of the papal position in the world during the eleventh and twelfth centuries are to be found not in Rome but in the provinces. It was a spontaneous movement growing from the needs of countless churches.

C. AFTER GREGORY VII

During the century and a quarter which followed Gregory's death, a vast amount of litigation found its way to Rome. In essence, most of the great cases were not much different from the dispute about the church of Craon: they had their origins in a time which had left either no documents or obscure ones ill-fitted to stand the scrutiny of a legalistic age; they had their continuance in a fanatical zeal for the rights of individual churches; and they had their end in the papal court. But besides the celebrated cases, there was a whole host of minor ones in which the details of church government were hammered out. The great contribution of this age in the sphere of practical life was the development of a system, or, rather, a number of interlocking systems, of law of a hitherto unknown complexity. Everywhere loose communal ties were drawn together in bonds of strict law; a vague sense of obligation was replaced by an exacting set of rules, and close definition was sought where general principles had formerly sufficed. By a kind of natural necessity these changes took place in every department of life, but nowhere with greater swiftness or with more general agreement than in the government of the Church. There was no need for Popes to seek for business—they were overwhelmed by it.

With the increase of papal business, the expedients which had been adventurous in the days of Gregory VII became antiquated. The bi-annual council and the itinerating legates, or even permanent legates, in the provinces could not cope with the business. Besides, men came increasingly to desire the highest judgement in the first instance without going through the tedious intermediate stages in local courts and provincial assemblies. Hence new mechanisms had to be devised to bridge the gap between Rome and the provinces: the business which flowed to Rome had somehow to be directed back to its point of origin with the imprint of papal authority. The most usual procedure in the later part of our period was for the Pope to remit the hearing of cases to small committees, generally of three local churchmen, who were invested with papal authority for the occasion. Committees of this kind were able to deal with far more business than could have been managed by earlier and less flexible methods; they were not only a great administrative convenience, but also a means whereby many men of only local importance had a share in the making of general law.

Almost without exception the Popes between Gregory VII and Innocent III were practical men, and most of them had already had long experience in papal business as legates or chancery officials before their election. To some extent this was no doubt due to the method of election, which finally (by 1179) put all power into the hands of the cardinals. It was natural that they should choose men from their own ranks whose abilities had been tested and on whose experience they could rely. Despite the long schisms with which the period was disfigured there was a continuity of ability and experience in the papal office, which is not found in the succession of any other rulers in Europe. Yet there was a price to be paid for this efficiency. There is no saint among the twelfth-century Popes. The position of Rome underwent a subtle change in men's minds. There are many poems on Rome written in the twelfth century, but none like *O Roma nobilis*. The prevalent mood was one of satire. Men became more conscious of the classical grandeur and present corruption, which to the author of *O Roma nobilis* seemed unworthy of remark beside the glory of the saints. The twelfth-century equivalent of *O Roma nobilis* is a poem of Hildebert, Archbishop of Tours, who died in 1133.[1] It breathes the new spirit of nostalgia and criticism: Rome is still great, but only with the ruins of her classical splendour; she is the supreme example of the decay of the works of human art, though even the ravages of time, fire and sword could not entirely obliterate the ancient comeliness; she is a noble ruin, defaced not only by decay but even more by the men who lived there, the representatives of a degenerate age. The men who lived in Rome in the twelfth century, from the Pope downwards, did not get much mercy from their contemporaries. They were the object of attacks which we should regard as both scurrilous and indecent. The picture in the *Gospel*

[1] P. L., vol. 171, 1409. The poem begins—
    Par tibi Roma nihil, cum sis prope tota ruina
        Quam magna fueris integra, fracta doces.
Some lines are printed in Bryce's *Holy Roman Empire*, Appendix D.

according to the Mark of silver,[1] of the Pope gathering his cardinals together and stimulating them in Biblical phrases to fleece the suitors at the Papal court—"For I have given you an example, that ye also should take gifts as I have taken them", and again, "Blessed are the rich, for they shall be filled; blessed are they that have, for they shall not go away empty; blessed are the wealthy, for theirs is the Court of Rome"—would seem today a crude piece of anti-religious propaganda; but it was a piece of twelfth-century writing of perfect respectability and orthodoxy.

It was at this time that the 'martyrs' Albinus and Rufinus—Pale Silver and Red Gold—began to take their place among the most widely celebrated of the Roman saints. These literary characters first appear during the pontificate of Gregory VII, and the most powerful piece of literature which they inspired—a burlesque account of the translation of some of their relics to Rome—represents Urban II as an ardent devotee of these 'saints'. The Archbishop of Toledo is depicted bringing to Rome the loins of Albinus, and some of the ribs, breast bone, arms and left shoulder of Rufinus, which the Pope placed "in the treasury of St. Cupidity beside the mercy seat of St. Avidity her sister, not far from the basilica of their mother St. Avarice. Here the Pope buried them in great magnificence with his own hands". In return for these pious gifts, the Archbishop obtained the legatine office, which was the object of his visit.[2]

It would be difficult to exceed the savagery of these satires, and though it would be wrong to over-rate their importance, they seem to reflect a fairly general mood, or at least a mood into which men easily relaxed. Even John of Salisbury, the friend of Archbishop Thomas Becket and the supporter of the high claims of ecclesiastical jurisdiction, allowed himself this relaxation.

I remember, he wrote, that I once visited Pope Adrian IV, to whom I was bound in the closest friendship, and stayed with him almost three months at Beneventum. One day, while we were talking as between friends, he asked me what men thought about him and the Roman Church. And I, making a mischievous use of my freedom, began to tell him what I had heard in various countries.

[1]Printed and discussed by P. Lehmann, *Die Parodie im Mittelalter*, 1922, 43–69, and *Parodistische Texte*, 1923, 7–10.
[2]M. G. H., *Libelli de Lite*, ii, 425–35.

They say, I said, that the Roman Church, which is the Mother of all Churches, behaves more like a stepmother than a mother; the Scribes and Pharisees sit there placing on men's shoulders burdens too heavy to be borne. They load themselves with fine clothes and their tables with precious plate; a poor man can seldom gain admittance, and then only that their glory may shine forth more brightly. They oppress the churches, stir up law suits, bring clergy and people into strife, have no pity for the oppressed, and look on gain as the whole duty of man. They sell justice, and what has been paid for today must be bought again tomorrow. Except for a few, who are pastors in fact as well as in name, they imitate the demons in this, that they think they do well when they cease to do evil. And the Pope himself, they say, is burdensome and oppressive to all: while the churches which our fathers built go to ruin, he builds palaces, and he goes about not only in purple but in gold.[1]

The satirical reaction to the building up of the Papal government of the Church is in some ways readily intelligible. Satire is an unwilling tribute to power; but it also implies the recognition of a certain inevitability in the thing satirized, a lack of any constructive alternative. The attitude to Rome in the twelfth century, the jokes and cynicism which it inspired, may be compared with current jibes at bureaucracy—they are a relief to the feelings rather than the symptoms of practical opposition. So far as the position of Rome was concerned, the question of principle had been settled in the generation of Gregory VII: it only remained to work out, perhaps to deplore, but not to upset, the consequences.

III

THE MONASTERIES

The religious life, throughout our period, meant pre-eminently the life of monastic discipline. But the monasteries were neither static institutions, nor were they remote from the lay world. Indeed, it was a cause of complaint that they were not remote enough, that the monks had their ears too close to the ground for news and

[1] John of Salisbury, *Policraticus*, ed. C. C. J. Webb, ii, 67-8.

rumours of wars, and that they could listen from their windows to the busy chattering of the world. And no amount of effort could really remedy this defect—if it was a defect. The monks were too much in the public eye to escape attention; they were moreover a costly institution, and it is scarcely putting it too strongly to say that their benefactors expected value for their money. Nor, even physically, was seclusion from the world easy to obtain; there was no Mount Athos in the Western Church dedicated to the religious life; the monks of the West were found in the greatest numbers where population and wealth accumulated. They were not town dwellers like the friars who were appearing at the end of our period, but they were seldom far from the centres of feudal government and social life.

This mingling of monastic and secular life did not please everyone, and it was certainly not foreseen in the Rule which St. Benedict had drawn up in the sixth century. But the intercourse was too engrained in the society of the tenth and eleventh centuries to be easily disturbed. We have already seen that there was, in the later eleventh century, a great reaction against the tendency to treat the Church as a branch of government under the control of the lay ruler; we shall see that the history of monasticism is deeply marked by a similar reaction against the type of monastery created by tenth and eleventh century rulers—but this reaction, though it caused much bitterness in monastic circles, did not affect the close relations between monasteries and their lay patrons. The monasteries were a force making for peace in a world which was rudely shaken by the controversies of the Hildebrandine age. The insistence that clerks were not to be treated as other folk came as a shock, and threatened to upset many well-established arrangements, especially in the field of law and government. But the parallel insistence that monks should be less concerned with the world had no troublesome secular reactions and threatened no man's rights. It was a point of view which found ready support among the laity.

Nevertheless this challenge threatened the peace of mind and questioned the vocation of many conscientious monks who had felt their lives safe in the routine of a well-ordered system. So far as the monastic life was concerned the century following the death of Gregory VII was an age of controversy, as the previous century had been one of steady conforming to a pattern admired by all. It was not one controversy but many—was the solitary life superior to the monastic life? Should monks exercise secular jurisdiction? How closely should they follow the Rule of St. Benedict? Should they introduce a greater simplicity into their church services? But all these controversies resolved themselves into the one all-important question—were the ideas which had guided the monastic reformers of the tenth and eleventh centuries to be thrown over or not? In the end, the work of these centuries proved extraordinarily solid, and it set the tone not only for the monastic life but also for much of the secular religion and private devotion of the whole Middle Ages. The corporate and institutional sense which formed Cluny was less logical and, in a sense, less spiritual than that which later formed Cîteaux or which, later still, informed the Franciscan way of life, but like the society itself which grew up in those hard times it was made to last.

In what follows we shall first say something about the relations between lay society and the monasteries, and secondly about the monastic ideal of the tenth and eleventh centuries, and the reasons why it came under criticism.

A. LAY SOCIETY AND THE MONASTERIES

The first contact between lay society and a monastic community was in the act of foundation. We have a great number of documents describing the foundation of monasteries in the period from the late tenth to the early twelfth century, and they show very clearly the sustained corporate effort which was needed to bring a monastery into being.[1] The initiative generally lay with a great baron who gave the site, provided an endowment of land and revenues, granted jurisdictional immunities, decided the affiliations of his monastery and regulated the future relations of his family to the community. But close on the heels of the baron came his vassals: they also contributed lands and rights, and claimed a share in the spiritual benefits of the monastery. The charters of foundation gave full weight to the part played by the vassals. More than any other documents of the age they symbolize the unity of a baron and his knights, and the social solidarity of the feudal unit. The religious foundations

---

[1]There is an important study of the background of monastic foundation charters in V. H. Galbraith, *Monastic Foundation Charters of the 11th and 12th Centuries*, Cambridge Historical Journal, 1934, IV, 205-22.

of the Carolingian age had rested on the precariously narrow basis of royal or semi-royal munificence; their large and compact estates proclaimed the generosity of a very few with very much indeed to give. But the strength of the later monasteries, like the strength of the new social order itself, lay in their widespread and intricate connexion with the countryside; their possessions were scattered, generally in small parcels, among the lands of the neighbouring aristocracy to whom they owed their origin. Like the society which produced them, these monasteries were intensely local in their interests and independent in their government. If they stand in strong contrast to the monasteries of a previous generation in the range of their social connexions, they are even more sharply divided from the religious orders of the thirteenth century in their localism and in the solidity of their economic foundations. The thirteenth-century houses of friars were merely the local offshoots of a great organization; starting from small beginnings and needing very little initial equipment, they were able to find lodgement in corners where no monastery could have supported itself. The eleventh-century monastery was a cumbrous and costly organism, but it was so well rooted in the soil that only Reformation or Revolution could uproot it.

The intimate association of lay benefactors with the monastery did not cease when the foundation was complete. The lay magnate who was also a connoisseur in matters of religious observance is a familiar figure at least from the time of Charlemagne till the seventeenth century. Charlemagne played the autocrat in church with as much confidence as in the council chamber, pointing, as one of his biographers tells us, with his finger or a stick to the person whom he wished to read the lessons, and peremptorily bringing the lesson to an end with a cough.[1] No one in a later age could compete with Charlemagne in the control of his clerks, but our period is rich in secular rulers of both sexes and all degrees of wealth, whose interest in the highly elaborate routine of religious observance

[1] The account of Charlemagne's behaviour in church is found in the *Gesta Karoli* by the Monk of St. Gall (M. G. H., Scriptores, ii, 734), who is admittedly not quite reliable. The most learned ruler of our period in matters of ecclesiastical observance was probably the Emperor Henry II. Rupert of Deutz (*Chronicon Sancti Laurentii Leodiensis*, in M. G. H. Scriptores, viii, 269) says that he was *non solum regalibus peritus institutis, sed in ecclesiasticis quoque perfectus disciplinis*, and he describes the Emperor's injunctions about processions and chants on Easter Day, Ascension Day and Whit-Sunday, and his regulations about the clergy wearing surplices on Sundays and Feast Days, and black copes in Advent and Lent.

in the monasteries was an important factor in the life of the time.

The Dukes of Normandy illustrate very well the persistent interest which men of different characters, in the midst of crushing practical difficulties, showed in the latest developments of monastic life wherever they might be found. We have already mentioned the periodic visits of the monks of Mount Sinai to Rouen, and the interest of the Dukes in fostering the pilgrimage to Jerusalem. But their first interest in religion lay in the ordering of the monastic life. The English Chronicler, who had reason to know of Duke William's fierce and primitive love of the red gold, noted that he was nevertheless mild to the good men who loved God—that is, to the monks; and men were astonished to see that the dreadful old man became gentle and affable in the presence of the Abbot of Bec. After William's funeral, when the company were sitting round the Great Hall at Caen, they remembered this trait in his character, and the talk turned on his admiration for St. Richard, the great Abbot of Verdun, who had been his father's friend. Someone told how William had maintained his father's generosity to this distant monastery, and how, after a period of silence, being anxious to continue his alms in a good cause, he had made enquiries about the community; but he received a poor account of the state of discipline, and kept his gifts to himself.[1]

Without a background of interest of this kind, the whole story of monastic foundations and reform during our period would be unintelligible. The laity not only watched the interior discipline of the monasteries with observant eyes, they also learnt from what they saw. We know little about the religious practices of the ordinary layman in the eleventh and twelfth centuries; but what is quite clear is that those who set themselves a standard higher than the ordinary looked to the monasteries for their examples. It was from the monasteries that the countryside learnt its religion. From their liturgical experiments and experiences there grew up a body of devotional practices which became part of the inheritance of every pious layman.

The influence of the monasteries on the lay religion of the later Middle Ages was deep and lasting, and in some ways surprising.

---

[1]The conversation at William the Conqueror's funeral was related by Hugh, Abbot of Holy Trinity, Rouen, to Hugh, Abbot of Flavigny, who put the story in his Chronicle (M. G. H. Scriptores, VIII, 407).

Few expressions of devotion could seem less nearly allied to the complex routine of a tenth or eleventh century monastery than those Books of Hours which became the main instrument of lay piety in the centuries before the Reformation. On the one hand we have the extreme elaboration of corporate services; on the other, a series of devotional forms which are short, simple, and full of emotional tenderness. Yet it has been amply demonstrated that the Books of Hours simply contain those additions to the monastic services which had been introduced into the monasteries in the period from the ninth to the eleventh century.[1] In their monastic context they were merely additions—at first private and later corporate—to an already heavy round of liturgical duties; in their later form they had an independent existence and met the needs of people whose lives were mostly occupied with secular affairs. The process of disentanglement was a long one, but it is surely a striking indication of the power of the monastic innovators to express the spiritual impulses of their own age and to form those of the future, that their novelties survived almost unaltered into times so different and among people so far removed from the life of monastic observance.

It argues a very sensitive relationship between the monasteries and the community that this transference of monastic usages to the world at large happened by a natural sympathy and without a struggle, despite a strong reaction within the monasteries themselves against the habits of mind which had produced the additional services in the first place. The channels of communication with the world which made this transference possible were almost infinite. Most obviously, there was the slow process of infiltration from the monasteries to the great collegiate and cathedral churches, and from them to the parish churches and the homes of the laity. More spasmodic but equally clear, there were individual laymen who, by an intense personal effort, adopted some part of the monastic routine in private life. Such a person was Queen Margaret of Scotland who died in 1093. Already, her biographer tells us, she had

[1] Edmund Bishop first made this clear in a great essay published in the Early English Text Society's edition of the *Prymer*, ed. H. Littlehales, 1897, vol. 109. (It has been reprinted in E. Bishop, *Liturgica Historica*, 1918). Besides this edition of a Book of Hours in English, a convenient Latin text with an account of the development of scholarship on the subject will be found in C. Wordsworth, *Horae Eboracenses* (Surtees Society, 1920, vol. 132).

seized on those additions to the monastic offices which made up the major part of the later Books of Hours, and she began her day by reciting the Offices of the Holy Trinity, the Holy Cross, and the Blessed Virgin, and the Office of the Dead.[1] Then there was a third channel by which monastic influence was communicated to the world, less clear-cut but perhaps no less powerful than these others: the channel of the ordinary lay magnate, illiterate himself and confined by this fact to a somewhat external view of monastic developments, who could nevertheless observe, admire and encourage with his wealth and protection. Such a man was King Malcolm, the husband of Queen Margaret, who (says her biographer) was unable to read, but turned over in his hands, kissed and fondled the books from which his wife prayed and—having found out which she admired most—had it bound in gold and precious stones. Such a man, in his own way, was William the Conqueror, with his far-flung yet judicious benefactions. Such, in varying degrees, were very many barons, who, having in solemn state been admitted to the fraternity of a monastic house, found there a centre of family interest: here they might end their days; here they would be buried with their fathers; and here, however little they knew of the liturgical innovations of the tenth century, they would know they could rely on the aid of the daily Office of the Dead.[2] Even those who are known in general history as despoilers of monasteries seem to have been glad to know that there was some monastery where they stood on this footing and might expect these benefits.

B. THE MONASTIC IDEAL OF THE TENTH AND ELEVENTH CENTURIES

What did men expect to find in a great monastery in the eleventh century?—what, for example, did William the Conqueror look for at Verdun and fail to find? Briefly, they expected to find a busy, efficient, orderly community, maintaining an elaborate sequence of church services, which called for a high degree of skill and expert knowledge. They did not expect to find a body of ascetics or

[1] Turgotus, *Vita S. Margaretae Scotorum Reginae*, printed in *Symeonis Dunelmensis Opera*, Surtees Soc., 1867, vol. 51, pp. 247-8.

[2] Ordericus Vitalis in his *Historia Ecclesiastica* (ed. Le Prévost and L. Delisle, 5 vols., 1838-55) has many examples of the intimate connexion between baronial families and the monasteries which they had helped to endow. See, for example, vol. ii, pp. 395-448, for the relation between his own monastery of St. Evroul and some of the great local families.

contemplatives, and they would have thought it a poor reward for their munificence if they had found marks of poverty in the buildings, dress or equipment of the monks. For them, monasticism was not a flight into desert places undertaken by individuals under the stress of a strong conviction; it was the expression of the corporate religious ideals and needs of a whole community.

This was a situation which could scarcely have been envisaged by the founder of the monastic rule in the sixth century. St. Benedict might have welcomed or deplored the circumstances in which new communities sprang up under the shelter of his Rule during the eleventh century, but clearly the Rule could not mean the same to his later followers as it did to his first companions. The Rule had assumed a more inward religion, a more sustained power of meditation, a greater self-discipline, than the reformers of the tenth and eleventh centuries could expect to find in their monks. It had *not* assumed the existence of highly developed social conventions and ideals, from which the monasteries were not a refuge, but of which they were rather an expression. The zeal of founders had made the monasteries less centres of private religious exercise, than centres of public intercession and prayer, performing a necessary service for the well-being of founders, benefactors and of society in general. The point of view of founders, made articulate by the churchmen who stood at their elbow, found expression in the communities which they established. Here is King Edgar founding his new monastery at Winchester in 966:

> Fearing lest I should incur eternal misery if I failed to do the will of Him who moves all things in Heaven and Earth, I have— acting as the vicar of Christ—driven out the crowds of vicious canons from various monasteries under my control, because their intercessions could avail me nothing . . . and I have substituted communities of monks, pleasing to God, who shall intercede for us without ceasing.[1]

For all we know, the secular clerks who were driven out were no worse than the clergy who in their turn took the place of the monks six centuries later: but for the purpose King Edgar had in mind, they

[1] *The Liber Vitae of New Minster and Hyde Abbey*, ed. W. de Gray Birch, (Hampshire Record Soc., 1892), p. 237.

were inefficient. He required not spontaneity, but a ceaseless penitential work, proceeding with tide-like regularity.

This ideal set a delicate problem to the spiritual guides and
leaders of the age. On the one hand the monasteries were too
numerous to be filled by voluntary recruitment—and they had no
desire to see them filled with men from the plough. It became a duty
to provide the men, as well as the means of support for the monasteries. Good birth lost none of its attraction by being in a monastery.
But how were sufficient men of good birth to be attracted? Partly
by providing a noble and colourful life. Partly also by bringing them
up in the monastic profession from childhood. To a naturally
community-minded age, there seemed nothing outrageous in
offering children to perform a necessary and dignified function for
the rest of their lives. There were abuses: "When they have got
their houses full of sons and daughters, if any of them is lame or
infirm, hard of hearing or short of sight, they offer them to a
monastery", wrote an eleventh-century Cluniac monk about the
nobility of his day.[1] But we may be more impressed by the number
of outstanding men who found their vocation by being offered as
children to a monastic house. This was not the only method of
recruitment—the number of those who came to the monastic life as
adults was never negligible; but it remains true that the proportion
of the monastic population of the eleventh century, which had
adopted the life by their own volition, was probably no greater than
the proportion of volunteers in a modern army.

The monasteries were filled with a conscript army. It was not an
unwilling or ineffective army on that account: the ideal of monastic
service was too widely shared for the conscription to be resented. But
the circumstance that many men and women in the monasteries
had no special aptitude for the life presented a further problem.
Communal effort, at the best of times, is easily dissipated, and readily
evaporates in a multitude of trivial channels. Sickness, absence, the
necessary offices of daily life call men away from the main task—the
'parade strength' is very different from the paper strength. This is a
problem of discipline, and this was something to which the monastic
leaders of the tenth and eleventh centuries devoted much of their
attention. The Rule of St. Benedict laid down a framework of daily
life, but it left many details unclear. If we attempt to regulate the

[1]Udalricus, *Consuetudines Cluniacenses*, P. L., vol. 149, 635-6.

activities of a community for each day in a year punctuated by frequent saints' days and revolving in methodical variety through the seasons of the church year we shall find that a great deal of regulation is necessary. Only so, in the circumstances of the time, could the ideal of a rich, varied and efficient service be fulfilled. So it came about that the eleventh century is the century of the fully articulated monastic customaries—books several times the length of the ancient rule, in which the activities of the community were set forth in minute detail. It was by means of these books, often informally circulating from one monastic house to another, that the standard of meticulous, highly organized and elaborate Benedictine life spread throughout western Europe. In the tenth century, such a life had been a wonder, confined to a few centres, to be sought out and learnt by painful steps: a century later, this life was—with infinite local variations, and differences of emphasis between one community and another—taken for granted in the family of Benedictine monasteries.

This phase of monastic development will always be associated with the name of Cluny. It was the active centre of Europe in the days before Gregory VII, when Rome with its great reserves of power was still quiescent. When men thought of religion, they thought of Cluny. They might doubt whether it was the place for them— St. Anselm for instance thought it would give him too little time for study—but it stood above all conflicts, and almost above criticism. In the noble surroundings of the Burgundian hills it offered, for those who could understand, all that the age knew to dignify and exalt the daily round of religious duties: the daily recital of large parts of the Bible in a regular sequence, obstinately maintained in the face of other claims which were beginning to make themselves felt; the leisurely absorption of the learning of the past; familiarity with works bringing memories of all ages of Christian history; the constant companionship of noble buildings, the solemnities of elaborate rites, the company of distinguished men, and that elevation and excitement of feeling which comes from the sense of being at once pioneers in the art of living, and yet firmly established in the esteem and respect of the world. It was a majestic life, incomparable perhaps in this respect to any form of the Christian life developed before or since. It is a far cry from the fastnesses of Subiaco where the Benedictine life was born, to the rich hills of Burgundy with Cluny in their midst;

but the monks of Cluny felt firmly rooted in the Rule which they were doing so much to interpret afresh.

Just as the small monastic foundations of obscure barons made for social unity in a disordered local society, so in the larger world of the eleventh century Cluny was a link between men all over Europe. Abbot Odilo, whose rule lasted from 994 to 1049 was the one man of his day of truly European stature.[1] Fulbert of Chartres called him the "archangel among monks", and the phrase had in it the recognition of a peculiar authority. Odilo was as much at home in Pavia as in Paris, at both of which he had the task of directing important monasteries. He was the friend of the 'unreformed' popes, Benedict VIII and John XIX, of the King of France and of three successive German Emperors. The kings of Hungary and Navarre, though they had never seen him, sent him letters and gifts, and solicited his prayers. More than any other man of his time he moved in a large world; yet at its centre was the ordered routine of Cluny. We have a picture of him, much occupied in the affairs of the world, hurrying back to the fellowship of the monastery for the great festivals. His biographer gives an account of him on one of these occasions. He was trying to get back to the monastery for Christmas, and his party was drenched and wearied after a long and hazardous journey. At length, late at night, they reached the monastery at Chalon where they were to lodge, and sat round the fire warming themselves and changing their clothes. The Abbot's heart was moved when he thought of all they had been through together and, to raise their spirits, he declaimed the lines,

> O quondam fortes per multa pericula fratres,
> Ne vestra vestris frangatis pectora rebus;
> Per varios casus, per tot discrimina rerum
> Tendimus ad regnum coeli sedesque beatas.
> Durate et haec olim meminisse juvabit.[2]

The words were an adaptation of some lines of Virgil in the first book of the Aeneid (lines 198-207) where Aeneas was encouraging

---

[1] The best contemporary source for the life of Odilo is the biography by his pupil Jotsaldus (P. L., vol. 142, 897-940 and *Neues Archiv*, 1889, XV, 117-26, where some additional passages are printed by E. Sackur.) There is also a life by Peter Damian which adds to Jotsaldus's account a single, but well authenticated story, which is mentioned below (p. 188.) This is printed in P. L., vol. 144, 925-44.

[2] P. L., 142, 921.

his storm-tossed followers as they lay exhausted and disheartened on the coast of Africa. The allusion was characteristic of Odilo's large and far-ranging mind. He used to say—looking round on the changes which had been wrought at Cluny in his day—that he had found it wood and left it marble, after the example of Augustus who found Rome brick and left it marble. He took pride in the comparison. Marble pillars, no doubt from ancient Roman ruins, were sought out and brought by water up the Rhône and Saône to decorate the new cloisters which he built towards the end of his life—and this was only the last work of a life-time's delight in making Cluny resplendent. In every way he was a big man, blending with singular harmony the traditions of a pagan and a Christian past, the corporate grandeur of the new monasticism and the simplicity of a monk. In outward things he helped to build up the massive structure of Cluniac greatness and splendour, but in private he felt forward to the new and intimate forms of devotion which captured the imagination of the succeeding generation.

This large and unfanatical spirit was the contribution of Cluny, and in their own degree of the many monasteries which embraced the same ideals of discipline, to a harsh and warlike age. The influence of Cluny had never seemed more secure than in the last quarter of the eleventh century; the expansion of its influence through the foundation of daughter houses was more remarkable than ever— they came to Spain in the wake of active and successful papal legates, and to England in the wake of the Norman conquerors. But there was an uneasiness in the air. Men who fifty years earlier would have found their peace in the established routine of monastic life, seemed bent on making some new experiment.

The most influential of these restless spirits of the late eleventh century was a runaway English monk whose name in his native tongue must have been something like Hearding, and in its Latin form was Hardingus.[1] He had been dedicated as a child to the monastic life in the monastery of Sherborne at about the time of the Norman Conquest, but when he came to manhood he cast aside the cowl, abandoned the religious life and set out on his

---

[1] The most remarkable contemporary account of Stephen Harding is in William of Malmesbury, *Gesta Regum*, ed. W. Stubbs (Rolls Series), ii, 380-5. There is also a lively, but less perceptive account of the debates which led to the foundation of Cîteaux in Ordericus Vitalis, *Historia Ecclesiastica*, ed. Le Prévost and L. Delisle, iii, 435-443.

travels. Any competent authority would have been bound to condemn his action in leaving the monastery to which he had been finally though involuntarily committed. The clue to his purposes at this time is entirely lost, but he was evidently not an ordinary rebel. After a good deal of wandering, he found his way (in the eighties or early nineties of the eleventh century) to a recently founded monastery at Molesme in Burgundy, which, under a remarkable abbot, Robert, was the scene of a vigorous controversy. On the one hand there were those who with their abbot were working towards a simpler and more rigorous life, in keeping, as they believed, with the primitive spirit of the Benedictine Rule; on the other there were those who stood firm for the innovations which had stamped the reforms of the last two centuries. The new arrival, who now, it seems, changed his name to Stephen, threw in his lot with the abbot and his supporters, and from this association there arose first the monastery (1098) and then the order of Cîteaux. Our earliest informant, the English historian William of Malmesbury, who from his nearby monastery knew Sherborne well and was evidently familiar with the Sherborne side of the story, says that it was Harding who began the controversy at Molesme. In this he may be mistaken, but it is certain that Stephen Harding, as he is known to later historians (though his contemporaries knew him only by one or other of these names according as they were French or English) had an extraordinary talent for giving legislative form to a spiritual ideal. He was the author of the two great documents of early Cistercian history, the *Carta Caritatis* and the *Exordium Cisterciensis Coenobii;* and it was during his abbacy (1110-33) that what had been an obscure experiment became the most stimulating source of religious life in Europe. The Cistercians challenged the accepted ideals of monastic life with peculiar force because they sprang from the older order—all the founders of Cîteaux, like Harding himself, had experienced the established monastic routine —and they confronted the immediate past with a past more ancient and more authoritative. Nor was Cîteaux simply a return to the past; it claimed also to be a revolt of reason and sound authority against the shackles of custom. It is striking that the earliest accounts of Cîteaux emphasize the atmosphere of debate in which it started; and the debate continued, though with dying force, for nearly a century. Just as Gregory VII and the circle of which he was the most eminent member focused the controversy about the ordering of the life of the Church as a whole, so the Cistercians became the centre of the controversy about the ordering of the monastic life. The Hildebrandine Reform of the Church has often been associated with the name of Cluny; but, considered as a principle—in its return to the ancient, Roman, pre-Germanic, past; in its appeal to reason and ancient authority against custom; and in its challenge, not simply to corruption, but to a recognized ideal—the kinship is rather with Cîteaux.

Just as the Hildebrandine Reform would not have succeeded unless it had been supported by widespread practical needs and spiritual enthusiasms, so the Cistercian controversy would have fallen on deaf ears unless it had reflected an uneasiness and expressed aspirations shared by many beyond the walls of the monastery. At the time when Harding was coming to his early manhood of discontent, there was in the Forest of Craon—that bone of contention between the monks of Angers and Vendôme—a group of hermits who were exploring in solitude the foundations of the monastic life.[1] These were men of local influence in the religious life of the Loire valley, but two hundred and fifty miles away, at Rheims, there were discussions which led to an experiment of wider interest. Three scholars of varied origin—Master Bruno of Cologne, Ralf Green (Radulfus Viridis), later Archbishop of Rheims, and Fulcoius of Beauvais—were sitting in the garden of Bruno's lodgings making plans to leave the "false lures and perishable riches of this world" and follow a monastic life. This must have been about the year 1080. Of the three men only one remained firm in his resolve: Ralf became an archbishop and Fulcoius an archdeacon, but Bruno became the founder of the Carthusian order, the most solitary of all the forms of organized religious life produced in this period, and the most withdrawn from the world. After twenty-five years of life at Chartreux, from his solitude in Calabria he wrote to remind Ralf of their discussion of long ago, and he sketched in a few words the circumstances of his own life:

I live the life of a hermit far from the haunts of men on the borders of Calabria, with my brethren in religion—some of them

[1]Some account of the hermits in the Forest of Craon and of their place in monastic history, will be found in G. Morin, *Rainaud l'ermite et Ives de Chartres: un épisode de la crise du cénobitisme au XIe-XIIe siècle* in the Revue Bénédictine, 1928, XL, 99-115.

learned men—who await the Lord's return in holy watching, that, when He knocketh, they may open to Him immediately. What words can describe the delights of this place—the mildness and wholesomeness of the air—the wide and fertile plain between the mountains, green with meadows and flowering pastures—the hills gently rising all around—the shady valleys with their grateful abundance of rivers, streams and fountains, or the well-watered gardens and useful growth of various trees? But why should I linger over these things? The delights of the thoughtful man are dearer and more profitable than these, for they are of God. Yet the weak spirit, which has been tired by the harder discipline of spiritual endeavour, is often refreshed and renewed by such things. For the bow which is kept at a stretch becomes slack and less apt for its work. But only they who have experienced the solitude and silence of a hermitage know what profit and holy joy it confers on those who love to dwell there.[1]

In varying degrees, all these men represented a movement back to simplicity and solitude. They sought to let light and air into an atmosphere heavy with the accumulation of customs, and to give freedom to men burdened with a multiplicity of duties. The intricate and dazzling solemnities, supported by every contrivance of art, and witnessing to a long period of communal growth, weighed heavily on the individual. There was—men came to feel—something lacking in all this: they wanted more time and room for privacy, for a more intense spiritual or intellectual effort, for the friendship of kindred spirits. Meditation and spiritual friendship: these things had never been lacking even in the most busily ordered monastic life, but they had existed in the interstices of scanty leisure; the system, at its most rigorous, had not provided for them. By the end of the twelfth century it is difficult to find any enthusiasm for that ornate and crowded life which a hundred and fifty years earlier had seemed like the doorway to Paradise. "What sweetness or devotion will you find among those whose mumbling and confused reiteration and long drawing-out of Psalms is repeated *ad nauseam*?"[2] This was the

[1]The letter of St. Bruno is printed in A. Wilmart, *Deux lettres concernant Raoul le Verd, l'ami de saint Bruno*, in Revue Bénédictine, 1939, LI, 257-74.

[2]This passage from a letter of Peter of Blois is the starting point of an intensely vivid meditation on the difference between Cluniacs and Cistercians by Edmund Bishop, printed posthumously in the *Downside Review*, 1934, lii, 48-70.

language of a scholar about 1185, and he was a man of moderation. Others spoke more harshly, and if any still regarded the monasteries as places of heroic struggle against the Devil, they kept the thought to themselves.

For better or worse, society had in the tenth and eleventh centuries espoused the cause of Benedictine monasticism. Whether it would have done so at the end of the twelfth century with equal fervour, it is useless to enquire. The monasteries were there; there was much criticism of them but no one proposed that they should be abolished. In a later chapter we shall be concerned with some aspects of the spiritual enthusiasm which refashioned the forms of religious devotion in the twelfth century; but the enthusiasms of an age have to work for the most part within institutions which were formed to meet quite different needs and as a result of quite different enthusiasms. It is very probable that there was more happiness, more largeness of life and recreation of spirit in a great Benedictine house in the year 1200 than there had been in 1050, but the fact did not seem worth recording. The monasteries were accepted as part of the order of things, as most people now accept the House of Lords or the Universities of Oxford and Cambridge, as objects of interest and even of pride and affection, but not as tremendous facts in their society.

CHAPTER IV

THE TRADITION OF THOUGHT

THE practice of the Christian religion—the ordered round of church services, the maintenance of discipline, the formulation of doctrine and the work of Church government—called for a large and varied body of learning, penetrating every field of enquiry. These activities were a source of continuous intellectual effort. If we wish to understand the thoughts of scholars during our period we must first know something of the place which intellectual pursuits had in the Christian life. This is a huge problem, to which contradictory answers can at all times be found; but even the contradictions will generally be found to have common foundations and to be guided by common limitations of knowledge and material, which bring to the historian a sense of unanimity and community of purpose. It is this community of purpose which we are to examine.

We may begin by distinguishing two influences of great importance in guiding the thought of our period. The first was the influence of the traditional syllabus of Christian studies which had come down from classical times. The second was the impulse to thought provided by the practical difficulties of organized life, whether in religious communities, or in the Church as a whole, or in secular society—chiefly in the first, but increasingly during the course of our period in the second and third. Without intellectual curiosity, these influences would have been quite sterile, but this curiosity is something we can take for granted as we watch it at work transforming the syllabus of studies and making the difficulties of practical life a starting point for the study of problems of universal significance.

I

THE SYLLABUS OF STUDIES

The most comprehensive syllabus of Christian studies which was available to scholars at the end of the tenth century was the plan sketched by St. Augustine in his treatise on Christian learning, the *De Doctrina Christiana*. This book was the expression of a great and challenging vision which had never been abandoned by the Western Church. It was inspired by the conviction that all the sciences known to the pagan world had their place in a strictly Christian curriculum. They were all essential ancillary sciences, and played their part, in ways which sometimes seem strange to us, in the task of interpreting the Bible. The uses of a knowledge of languages, of history, of grammar and even of logic, as aids to the study of the Bible, are obvious enough. But, in Augustine's view—and nobody in our period would have challenged him—these studies brought the enquirer only to the doorway of a rich country of spiritual truth invisible to the superficial observer. This truth was conveyed in allegory and imagery, the interpretation of which provided the true field of research for the Christian scholar. In the strictest sense, the work of interpretation was a scientific labour, not a matter of lucky inspiration. He who would search out the difficult mysteries of the Bible must be equipped with a knowledge of all sciences: he must know the nature of all animals and plants, and the strange lore about precious stones; he must recognize the symbolism of numbers, and understand the movements of the heavens and the harmonies of music. With these aids, he was equipped to comprehend the fullness of Biblical truth. In the light of a scientific investigation of the allegory, the simple injunction "Be ye wise as serpents" yielded a rich harvest of doctrine about the relation of the Christian to the Church, about his duties in this life and his hope in the next; and it yielded it in a way (so Augustine held) which surprised and enchanted the enquirer by its strange and mysterious beauty:

Why is there less pleasure in hearing that the Saints are men, by whose life and example the Church of Christ strips those who come to her of false doctrines, and receives into her body those who imitate their virtues; and that these faithful and true servants of God, laying aside the weight of secular affairs, come to the cleansing of baptism and arise thence informed by the Holy Spirit to bring forth the fruit of a two-fold charity towards God and their neighbour—why is this less pleasurable than to hear the exposition of that sentence in the Song of Songs where it is said of the Church as of a beautiful woman, *Thy teeth are like a flock of*

*sheep that are newly shorn, which come up from the washing, whereof
every one bear twins, and none is barren among them?* A man learns
nothing from this which he might not learn from the plainest
words spoken without the aid of allegory. Yet (I know not why) I
find it more sweet to think of the Saints as the teeth of the Church,
separating men from their errors and passing them as it were
softened and masticated into the body of the Church. And I find
an immense sweetness in thinking of the shorn sheep, laying aside
secular burdens—as it were their fleece—and coming from the
dip, which is baptism, each bringing forth two lambs—the double
law of charity—and none being sterile among them.[1]

Having, with the help of science and the arts, plumbed the depths
of Scriptural truth, it was necessary for the scholar to come to the
surface again, and reveal his discoveries to others. For this he needed
the queen of the arts, the art of rhetoric, to draw men's hearts to a
love of the knowledge he had found. The rhetoric of the Christian
scholar was a much chastened art, purged of the extravagances of
the law courts and the political platform, but it was still the art
taught by Cicero.

This was a programme of study at once simple and comprehensive, harnessed to the needs of the Christian religion and embracing
all the arts. How alive was this programme at the end of the tenth
century? Certainly its assumptions underlay much of the learning of
the time. But it was scarcely an active force in the discovery of new
truth. Men did not study music and astronomy in order to interpret
the Bible. They collected the results and steeped their minds in the
interpretations of previous enquirers; they were thoroughly imbued
with the mystical senses of Scripture; but the hope of discovering new
meanings gave no impetus to strictly scientific research. It was not
until the thirteenth century that there came a new urge to investigate
the nature of things in order to enlarge the understanding of the
Bible. This was one of the main impulses behind the scientific work
of Roger Bacon. But this scientific Biblical revival lies beyond the
limits of this book.

St. Augustine had seen the liberal arts and sciences as servants
in the interpretation of Scripture, but even those who agreed that
this was their proper function found it difficult to keep them within

[1] *De Doctrina Christiana*, ii, 6. (P.L. vol, 34, 38-9).

this orbit. This is illustrated by the fate of another popular handbook of Christian studies, of which the usefulness slowly declined in the eleventh century: the treatise on *Divine and Secular Learning* written by Cassiodorus in the middle of the sixth century. Cassiodorus adopted Augustine's view of the unity of the secular sciences in the service of Biblical interpretation, but the way in which he arranged his treatise made it easy to divide Biblical studies from scientific enquiry. He divided his survey into two parts; the first dealt with strictly Biblical knowledge, the second with the liberal arts which were necessary for its interpretation. But apart from general expressions of the unity of the whole plan of studies, the two parts are quite unconnected. It is very easy to read the second part simply as a treatise on the liberal arts, without realizing that it has any connexion at all with Biblical interpretation; and this is what many of his readers seem to have done. If they wanted a good handbook to the liberal arts—and from the sixth to the eleventh century, Cassiodorus (with some later additions which were made to his text) provided a fair summary of the state of knowledge—they copied Book II on Secular Learning. If, on the other hand, they wanted a summary of Biblical information, they copied Book I on Divine Learning. They seem seldom to have wanted both in the same context. Such at least would appear to be the lesson of the surviving manuscripts, for while there are many manuscripts of each separate book, there are only three which contain both books joined together according to the original intention.[1] In other words, secular studies had a life of their own, independent of any theory about their place in the general scheme of Christian knowledge.

It so happens that the divorce between Divine and Secular learning had become particularly marked at the beginning of our period. We shall find, in the two earliest of the scholars with whom we are concerned, that the secular sciences had no theological attachment, either in the old sense of furnishing the instruments of Biblical study or in the later sense of providing the weapons of theological speculation and dispute. They had, as we shall see, a connexion with the daily life of the Church, but that is a different matter.

But before examining the relationship between daily life and secular studies, we must say something about a third scholar of the

[1] There is a full account of the manuscript history of this work in the edition of R. A. B. Mynors (Oxford, 1937).

ancient world, whose works had a profound effect on the direction of learned enquiry during our period. Anicius Manlius Severinus Boethius (c. 480-524) left no programme of studies comparable to those of Augustine and Cassiodorus, but he left the materials for a secular curriculum different from that described by these authors. It was Boethius's ambition to present Greek learning to a Latin world which was rapidly being driven in on its own resources. The civilization of Rome had shown little aptitude for the systematic observation and analysis which had made possible the achievements of Greek science and philosophy; and the early Middle Ages inherited this deficiency in the Latin literature which was its sole link with the ancient world. But in this general picture, the works of Boethius formed a conspicuous exception. Perhaps no scholar has ever set himself a grander task, or, with so little original material, made so deep and original an impression on the future. He sat down among the ruins of Roman civilization at the end of the fifth century, not simply to make accessible to an uncertain future the fruits of Roman experience, but to hand on to the future that part of the intellectual heritage of Greece which Rome herself had never thoroughly absorbed. It was a great plan, left unfinished by a violent death; and it was a plan which could not, in the circumstances of the immediately succeeding centuries, bear rapid fruit. But, in time, Boethius's work did bear fruit, and never so abundantly as in the eleventh century. From a scholastic point of view, the eleventh was the century of Boethius, as the twelfth and thirteenth were the centuries of Aristotle. If Aristotle, in Dante's famous phrase was the "master of those who know", Boethius was the master of those who wanted to know. He was the schoolmaster of medieval Europe.

The most important part of Boethius's plan for presenting the essentials of Greek science in Latin, was a complete translation of the works of Plato and Aristotle. Only a small part of this aim was achieved, but by his translations, commentaries and summaries he succeeded in making available in Latin the main outlines of the Aristotelian system of logic. Now logic had a modest place in the plan of studies elaborated by St. Augustine and Cassiodorus; it could be useful, for instance, in elucidating the rapid and terse arguments of St. Paul's Epistles. But there was no place in the curriculum for the bulky and detailed translations and treatises of Boethius. Until the early eleventh century, the name of Boethius was kept alive by his books on Arithmetic and Music, and above all by his *Consolation of Philosophy* which brought many men, even those who, like King Alfred, were not professed scholars, into touch with a great philosophical tradition. But the logical works were neglected in favour of elementary outlines which preserved only a feeble reflection of the system on which they depended.

The bringing of these works into general circulation and making the thought contained in them part of the general stock of knowledge in the Latin world, are events of great importance in our history. Indeed the date (972) which has been given as the starting point for this book refers to a moment when a decisive step was taken in this direction. This is a point which requires some elaboration.

The first man in Western Europe, so far as we know, to lecture systematically on the whole range of Boethius's logical treatises, was the scholar Gerbert, who settled in Rheims in 972 in order to study logic under a certain Gerannus, archdeacon of the city. The pupil soon eclipsed the master, and during the next twenty-five years, in the midst of ever increasing political activity, he made a European reputation as a teacher. We are fortunate in having an account of Gerbert's teaching in the history of his time written by his pupil Richer.[1] It takes us into a scholar's workshop at a critical moment in the formation of Europe, and, short though it is, there is no comparable description of a master's teaching for many years to come. Gerbert expounded Porphyry's *Introduction* to logic, Aristotle's *Categories* and *De Interpretatione*, and Cicero's *Topics*—all of them with the Commentary, and several in the translation, by Boethius— as well as Boethius's own treatises on Syllogisms, Definitions and Logical Analysis. He put aside, it would seem, the superficial textbooks which had satisfied the scholars of the Carolingian age, and showed the way to a more intensive study and a higher level of proficiency in the science of logic than had been known in the West since the days of Boethius himself.

The sequence of logical teaching which Gerbert established

[1] In what follows, I am greatly indebted to a series of articles by A. van de Vyver: *Les etape du développement philosophique du haut moyen âge* (Revue belge de Philologie et d'histoire, 1929, VIII, 425-52); *L'évolution scientifique du haut moyen âge* (Archeion, 1937, XIX, 12-20); *Les premières Traductions latines de traités arabes sur l'Astrolabe* (Extrait du Ier Congrés International de Géographie Historique, 1931, Mémoires, vol. II.) The account of Gerbert's teaching at Rheims may be found in the Chronicle of Richer, ed. and transl. by R. Latouche in *Les classiques de l'histoire de France au Moyen Age*, Paris, 1930-7, ii, 54-6.

became the model for well over a century to come. Yet it is a striking thing that though this impulse to the study of logic was probably Gerbert's most important contribution to medieval learning, he did not allow it that pride of place among the arts which it later attained. Gerbert aimed at restoring the classical past, and nowhere was he more faithful to this aim than in the pre-eminence which he gave to the art of rhetoric. He had no room for the forward-reaching spirit of enquiry which animated the study of logic in the twelfth century. His energies were concentrated on the task of conservation, and on the worthy presentation of long-acquired, and sometimes long-lost, truths. Hence he was drawn to the art of rhetoric by a double chain: first because it was the chief literary science of the ancient world; secondly because it was congenial to his own spirit of conservatism. Rhetoric is static; logic dynamic. The one aims at making old truths palatable, the other at searching out new, even unpalatable truths—like the *invidiosi veri*, syllogized, in Dante's phrase, by Siger of Brabant.[1] Rhetoric is persuasive, logic compulsive. The former smooths away divisions, the latter brings them into the open. The one is a healing art, an art of government; the other is surgical, and challenges the foundations of conduct and belief. To persuade, to preserve, to heal the divisions between past and present—these were Gerbert's aims, and in this work rhetoric and statesmanship went hand in hand, with logic as their servant.

I have always (he wrote) studied both to live well, and to speak well. . . . For although the former is more important than the latter, and may suffice for someone in a private position, yet in public affairs both are necessary. To be able to speak appositely, to persuade and restrain with fair words the wills of lawless men, is useful in the highest degree. To this end I have laboured to collect a library, and I have spent great sums of money on scribes and copies of books.[2]

Hence for Gerbert rhetoric, not logic, was the queen of the arts. A century and a half after his death an ambitious student would pass rapidly through grammar and rhetoric, to arrive at the excitements of logic. The old-fashioned viewed this indecent haste and its

[1] *Paradiso*, x, 138.
[2] The passage occurs in a letter to the Abbot of Tours, written in 984 or 985. It is no. 44 in Julien Havet, *Lettres de Gerbert (983-997)*, in the *Collection de Textes pour servir à l'étude et à l'enseignement de l'histoire*, Paris, 1889, p. 42.

objective with concern, and Gerbert would have agreed with their strictures. According to Richer, he took his pupils forward from logic to rhetoric; from the treatises of Boethius to the works of Virgil, Statius, Terence, Juvenal, Persius, Horace and Lucan. Then, when his pupils were steeped in the diction of these authors, he handed them over to a sophist, to perfect them in the arts or tricks of debate. This exercise in debate was the crown of the rhetorician's training: even syllogisms and logical analysis were chiefly serviceable to this end—to detect the other man's tricks and to conceal one's own.

Gerbert's part in the intellectual formation of the Middle Ages was not exhausted by the impulse given to logical or literary studies. It extended also to arithmetic, musical theory and astronomy. He revived the practical study of the calculating device known as the abacus—an appliance known to the ancients but apparently neglected in western Europe until this time. In his teaching of musical theory he impressed Richer by his practical demonstrations on the mono-chord—a simple instrument for demonstrating the mathematical basis of musical intervals. "He made," says Richer with pardonable exaggeration, "the theory of music, which had long been unknown in Gaul, as clear as daylight." In these fields he still had Boethius as a guide, and fragments of his exposition of Boethius's treatises on arithmetic and music still exist. In astronomy he had no aid from Boethius, but Richer discourses at length on his labours in construct-ing models of the planetary system of a surprising intricacy. Gerbert's genius was a practical one. He lacked some of the scientific aids which were available even to his immediate successors. Despite his keen astronomical interest, he had, for instance, no instrument for measuring the elevation of the stars, and, compared with the resources of the twelfth and thirteenth centuries, he had a mere fragment of the works of Aristotle. But the practical vigour and order which Gerbert brought to his teaching made a deep impression on his successors. He put new life into the decrepit body of ancient learning, and the influence of his plan of studies can be traced in the schools of Northern Europe throughout the eleventh century. How far we are here from the plan of Augustine or Cassiodorus! There is only one point where he and St. Augustine meet in their scholastic curriculum, and that is in the typically Roman belief in the supremacy of rhetoric among the arts. But, in Gerbert, rhetoric is referred once more to its ancient position as an instrument of government, for the guiding and bending of men's wills; it is not the culmination of a programme of Christian learning.

Gerbert was a conscientious churchman and he became a notable Pope, but his thoughts, so far as they have come down to us, dwelt on a past which was older than Christianity. He was filled with a mournful vision of the glories of the Roman Empire, and of the vices and weaknesses of his own time. The revival of ancient learning was for him intimately bound up with the attempt to revive the ancient polity of Rome. As scholar and statesman alike he worked to gather up the threads of an ancient order, and in his most intimate words he seems to display the firm virtue and untroubled conscience of the ideal Roman, filled with the consciousness of his own rectitude and the purity of his motives. His political visions, however, faded away with his death; he had not that touch with the present needed to bridge the gulf between ideal and actuality. It might have seemed that the studies on which he nourished his political faith were in danger of disintegrating as well, leaving the ground finally cleared of the inheritance from the Roman Empire. But there was more life in the little books of logic and in the painful arithmetical calculations than in all the wisdom of the statesman. Men who had no sympathy with Gerbert's political designs, inherited and developed his scholastic tradition.

Behind Gerbert stands the figure of Boethius. For him Boethius symbolized both the might and the learning of Rome, and the eclipse of Boethius's influence during the preceding centuries was in his eyes a measure of the degradation of the Empire. In the palace of Otto III there was a picture of Boethius and beside it these verses which were ascribed to Gerbert:

> When mighty Rome held all the world in fee,
> She found her father and her light in thee.
> But cities and Empires fall at God's command,
> And Rome lies stricken by the Goth's foul hand.
> Freedom and learning felt the tyrant's hate,
> And thou with them didst meet a martyr's fate.
> Now Otto comes, the power of Rome to raise.
> And to Boethius' name renews the praise.
> Thy picture in the Emperor's hall is hung.
> For ever now be thy high merit sung.[1]

[1]For the Latin text of these verses, see A. Olleris, *Oeuvres de Gerbert*, 1867, p. 294–5.

The political vision passed, but Boethius remained. He introduced the scholars of the eleventh century to the exciting and unexplored world of thought which lay in the works of Aristotle. Until the first quarter of the twelfth century, when knowledge of Aristotle began to pour into Western Europe from the Arab world, Boethius was the transmitter and interpreter through whom scholars made their first acquaintance with Aristotle. It was indeed only a small fragment of Aristotle which became known in this way, but it was enough to provoke thought, and to let loose a stream of commentary and discussion; it gave men a familiarity with the method and outline of Aristotle's logic, and whetted their appetite for more.

It is appropriate at this point to ask what it was that the study of logic, which the influence of Boethius did so much to foster, contributed to the intellectual formation of the Middle Ages, and why it was that, from the time of Gerbert, this study assumed an importance which it had never previously attained in the Latin world. The works of Boethius are immensely difficult to understand and repellent to read. Why should the subject have taken such a hold on the imaginations of scholars, so that they pursued it with unflagging zeal through all the obscurities of translation, heedless of the advice of many cautious men of learning?

The cause of the fascination is perhaps easier to understand today, when somewhat similar causes have produced among philosophers a renewed interest in the grisly forms of logical analysis, than it was a hundred years ago when the philosopher Prantl wrote his history of medieval logic. Logic was an instrument of order in a chaotic world. The works of Boethius gave the eleventh century a glimpse of what was by far the most impressive body of systematic teaching about the world, which was accessible to men of those generations. The world of nature was chaotic—a playground of supernatural forces, demoniac and otherwise, over which the mind had no control. The world of politics was similarly disordered, intractable to thought. Only the dimmest outlines remained of any systematic teaching about law. On the intellectual plane, the art of rhetoric could perhaps claim to be as highly developed and systematized as the sister art of dialectic. But in the conditions of the tenth and eleventh centuries there was something unreal and futile about the exercise of an essentially practical art which had no roots in the practical life of the time: the pompous and pointless declamations of the practitioners of the art which have come down to us emphasize the point with tiresome conclusiveness.[1]

But logic, however obscurely at first, opened a window on to an orderly and systematic view of the world and of man's mind. The greater the decline of other sciences, the more pre-eminent appeared the orderliness of Aristotle's comprehensive picture of the workings of the human mind. The student began with Porphyry's *Introduction* to Aristotle, translated with a twofold commentary by Boethius, and learnt there the art of classifying the objects external to the mind. He learnt to play with the terms *genus* and *species, differentia, property* and *accident*, and to apply these conceptions in argument and discussion. He proceeded then to Aristotle's *Categories*, and learnt to classify the remarks which can be made about any object whatsoever —as that the pen with which I write is long and thin, that it is black, that it is mine, that it is resting on the point of its nib, on this piece of paper, at 9 p.m., that it is filled with ink, that it makes a blue mark, and that it is being held by my hand. These are examples of the nine Categories of Quantity, Quality, Relation, Position, Place, Time, State, Action and Affection, which were thought to exhaust the various ways in which any particular object can be regarded. This simplification of a vast wilderness of thought exercised an extraordinary fascination in the tenth and eleventh centuries. Not only did manuscripts of the *Categories* increase in numbers after a long period of neglect, but there even appeared a new translation made by some unknown hand, which drove Boethius's translation (though not his Commentary) from the field.[2] From this point the student progressed to Boethius's translation and commentaries on Aristotle's *De Interpretatione*. Once more he met the same miraculous order and simplicity—this time in the classification of the kinds of statement which we can make on any subject.

This was as far as the eleventh-century student could go in his study of the authentic works of Aristotle. The more advanced works were not accessible until the middle of the twelfth century, but the gist of these books was preserved in a series of small outlines, again by the indispensable Boethius, which like the other books in this list,

[1]See, for example, the absurd tirades of the Italian rhetorician, Anselm the Peripatetic, in his *Rhetorimachia*, ed. E. Dümmler, *Anselm der Peripatetiker*, Halle, 1872.
[2]See L. Minio-Paluello, *The Genuine Text of Boethius' Translation of Aristotle's Categories*, in Medieval and Renaissance Studies, 1, 1943, pp. 165-6.

began to have a wide circulation at this period. In these outlines, the student passed to the analysis of our mental processes. He learnt to classify the types of valid argument, to detect the causes of error and to unmask the process of deception. Once more he found, that instead of the bewildering variety which met the casual enquirer, the types of valid argument are strictly limited in number and can be classified on a simple principle.

The whole process of simplification and arrangement was a revelation both of the powers of the mind, and of the orderliness which lay behind a bewildering complexity of apparently unrelated facts. The world of learning and the world of experience were for the most part fragmentary and disjointed. Even in those subjects where the heritage of the past was richest and most fully mastered—in the field of faith and dogma—there was a great lack of system. The Fathers of the Church had written as the occasion required, but a close study revealed many gaps, uncertainties and contradictions. The experience of the completeness and order of the Aristotelian logic sharpened the perception of these weaknesses and at the same time provided, or seemed to provide, a method by which they could be overcome. Men who had learnt that there were only fourteen (or was it nineteen?) kinds of valid argument and only nine (or was it ten?) categories of experience, and that every possible statement could be classified on a simple system whose rules even a school-boy could learn to apply, were ready to extend the same process of analysis to the deadly sins, the cardinal virtues, the gifts of the Holy Spirit, the Sacraments, and even to the Persons of the Trinity, to the substance and accidents of the Eucharist, and the Humanity and Divinity of Christ.

The digestion of Aristotle's logic was the greatest intellectual task of the period from the end of the tenth to the end of the twelfth century. Men then debated about logic, as they do now about natural science, whether it was a curse or a blessing. But whichever it was, the process of absorption could not be stopped. Under its influence, the method of theological discussion and the form of the presentation of theological speculation underwent a profound change. It was in theology that the change was felt most keenly and fought most fiercely, but every department of thought was similarly affected. The methods of logical arrangement and analysis, and, still more, the habits of thought associated with the study of logic, penetrated the studies of law, politics, grammar and rhetoric, to mention only a few of the fields which were affected. Dante's *De Monarchia* for instance is arranged as a chain of syllogisms: as, for example,

1. *Human affairs are best ordered when man is most free*
2. *but it is under a monarch that man is most free*
3. *therefore the human race is best disposed when under a monarchy,*

and so on through a chain of arguments similarly disposed. No doubt the thing could have been done otherwise, but the parade of logical consistency was the best guarantee which Dante could find of the irrefutability of his arguments. Or, to take a more trifling case, we notice that when a cultivated man like the chronicler Matthew Paris wanted to clinch his objection to a habit which had grown up in the royal chancery of disregarding general phrases in charters unless accompanied by a distinct enumeration of the items included in such phrases, he said that it was against reason and justice, "and even against the rules of logic, the infallible guide to truth". It was as if one would say "All men are free", but deny that the phrase applied to Jones or Brown unless they were specifically mentioned.[1] There was no more to say: logic was the touchstone of truth, and to argue 'by figure and by mode' the foundation of all discussion.

There would be no more illuminating illustration of the continuance and decline of medieval influence in the modern world than a history of logic—not of logical doctrines but of the place of logic in education, the attitude of educated men to the subject, and the general confidence in the formal processes of reasoning. We should have to start with the revival of logical studies in the tenth century and note the process which made logic the subject of first choice for the majority of intellectually ambitious students in the first half of the twelfth century. We should then pass to the stabilizing of the University curricula in Paris and Oxford during the thirteenth century, which made Aristotelian logic—the listening to commentaries, the attendance at disputations, and the exercise in logical argument—the main feature of undergraduate studies. We should

[1]Matthew Paris, *Chronica Majora* ed. H. R. Luard, Rolls Series, V, 210-11. For this passage see F. M. Powicke, *Henry III and the Lord Edward*, 1948, i. 326.

have to note the influence of these studies on our language, in the assimilation into common speech of such terms as 'substance', 'accident', 'property', 'equivocal', 'common-place'; and we should notice the extreme tenacity of these studies long after the original impulse which generated them had passed away. Then, with the end of the seventeenth century, we should come to the decline in prestige, to the appearance of a strain of criticism which, if not sufficient to displace logic from its place in the University curriculum, was sufficient to bring it into widespread contempt. By this time Aristotle's logic had ceased to be an adventure and had become a drill. Almost exactly seven hundred years after Gerbert's revivifying influence had been felt at Rheims, John Locke in his *Thoughts concerning Education* (1690) struck these blows at a system which had been born and come to maturity between the end of the tenth and the beginning of the thirteenth centuries:

> Rhetoric and logic being the arts that in the ordinary method usually follow immediately after grammar, it may perhaps be wondered that I have said so little of them. The reason is, because of the little advantage young people receive by them. Right reasoning is founded on something else than the predicaments and predicables, and does not consist in talking in mode and figure itself. . . . Is there any thing more inconsistent with civil conversation, and the end of all debate, than not to take an answer, though ever so full and satisfactory; but still to go on with the dispute, as long as equivocal sounds can furnish a "medius terminus", a term to wrangle with on the one side, or a distinction on the other? . . . For this, in short, is the way and perfection of logical disputes, that the opponent never takes any answer, nor the respondent ever yields to any argument.

From this date the decline in the popular respect for formal logic can be traced in many unexpected places in the literature of the eighteenth century, and by 1835, when Macaulay wrote the following words, he was speaking to a public in which all but the stiffest pedagogues had been converted:

> Give a boy Robinson Crusoe. That is worth all the grammars of rhetoric and logic in the world. . . . Who ever reasoned better

for having been taught the difference between a syllogism and an enthymeme? Who ever composed with greater spirit and elegance because he could define an oxymoron or an aposiopesis? I am not joking but writing quite seriously when I say that I would much rather order a hundred copies of Jack the Giant-Killer for our schools than a hundred copies of any grammar of rhetoric or logic that ever was written.[1]

These sentiments are so natural to us that it is hard to enter into the thoughts of men who took the opposite point of view equally for granted. The weaknesses of the medieval system, of which Locke spoke from experience, were very real ones. The litigious and acrimonious spirit, which made itself felt in every walk of life, the assurance in dealing with abstract notions divorced from experience, the acquiescence in formulas of merely verbal significance, these were the weaknesses fostered by a training in medieval logic. By the end of the seventeenth century, it was hard to see the other side of the picture—the wide agreement in principle which these acrimonious disputes presupposed; the hard intellectual discipline; the order and system which the study of logic had diffused throughout the whole body of thought and learning; the awakening of the intellect to the study of itself and the arrangement of its impressions of the outside world; the recognition of the autonomy of reason in the discussion of philosophical and theological problems. In the late tenth and early eleventh century all this lay in the future. Logic was still almost a plaything with a strange fascination. In the second half of the eleventh century it was just stepping out into the arena of serious controversy and providing Lanfranc with some of his best arguments against Berengar's views on the Eucharist.[2] Lanfranc's victory was the first result in theological debate of the renewed teaching of logic. The way was prepared for the triumph of logic in medieval teaching.

We, however, must turn back from this prospect to the simpler order of things and to the communities where medieval learning was born.

[1]*The Life and Letters of Lord Macaulay*, by G. O. Trevelyan, Popular Edition, 1893, p. 296.
[2]I have tried to bring out the place of logical studies in this debate in a paper in *Essays in Medieval History presented to F. M. Powicke* (1948).

II

LEARNING AND THE PROBLEMS OF DAILY LIFE

A. IN THE MONASTERIES

At the beginning of our period, the continuity of organized study with few exceptions (among which the most important was medicine, with its long tradition of study at Salerno) depended on the existence of monasteries and other collegiate bodies such as the cathedral churches. The Benedictine monasteries stand out among all these bodies as the inheritors of a mature and well-ordered tradition. Elsewhere there were perhaps greater possibilities of development, precisely because purposes were less clearly defined and habits less distinctly formed. But we must start with the monasteries.

Something has already been said about the complex round of church services which was developed in the monasteries during the tenth and eleventh centuries. The arrangement of these services raised many difficulties, which required a varying degree of learning for their solution. The time was long past when the ordering of the church year had been a matter which called for a high degree of technical skill and scientific knowledge: the main task of calculating in advance the occurrence of Easter had long been accomplished, and the results digested in the form of 'perpetual calendars', with which each church would be supplied. But, in detail, much remained to be done, especially as the number of saints' days observed by special forms of service grew rapidly, and the taste for elaboration in liturgical matters became more widely shared. Apart from the task of writing the necessary books for these elaborate services, itself a work of high skill and scholarship, there was a demand for original compositions—for saints' lives, hymns, antiphons, the arrangement of suitable lectionaries, and so on. And there was the equally important task of setting the words to music. In all this, there was great scope for local talent and learning. No two monasteries were alike, and even those which started more or less alike soon developed wide differences of practice. Hence, throughout Europe, sparsely in the tenth century, but in increasing numbers throughout the eleventh, there were in the monasteries men, perhaps of no more than local fame, whom the ever-increasing elaboration of Church services had made into historians, prose writers, poets and composers.

This was work which might well occupy the best talent in a monastery, and if the products of all this activity appear to us very much on a level of mediocrity, it appeared otherwise to contemporaries: they rated these compositions among the notable achievements of their time. Orderic Vitalis, for instance, found room in the midst of his great History to commemorate the artists and authors who were responsible for the service books which he and his fellow-monks of St. Evroul handled every day. Looking back to the time of Abbot Osbern (1061-6)—at least half a century before the time when he was writing—he records the names of five or six men whose products were part of his daily life. There was Witmund, a scholar and musician, who had written antiphons and responses to go with the Legend of St. Evroul. Then there was Arnulf, the author of the Legend or series of Lessons for the patronal Feast. He had been precentor of Chartres and a pupil of the famous Bishop Fulbert, and he had not only written the words but taught the manner of chanting them to two monks whom the abbot sent to Chartres for the purpose. There was also Rainald the Bald who had composed the response in praise of the Lord, which the monks used at Vespers, as well as seven antiphons which (says Orderic) you will find in the Antiphonar of St. Evroul; and there was Roger of Le Sap who was the author of several hymns in honour of the patron saint of the monastery. This passage in Orderic shows well the co-operative activity and the combination of literary, poetical and musical gifts which lay behind the rich solemnities of monastic life. These activities required a foundation of learning, and they encouraged the growth of centres where this learning could be had; they brought this rather obscure Norman monastery—like many others—in touch with the great school of Chartres which owed its fame to Bishop Fulbert.[1]

There were other tasks which kept the monastic communities constantly alive to the world of learning—even, for example, the humble task of seeing that the services began at about the right time. There were no clocks, the times of the services varied with the seasons, and in the early morning at least the sequence was so rapid

[1] For this passage, see Ordericus Vitalis, *Historia Ecclesiastica*, ed. Le Prévost and L. Delisle, ii, 95-6.

that any considerable miscalculation would cause a grave interruption of the monastic day. The problem required careful thought, and the following passage will show one way in which it was solved:

On Christmas Day, when you see the Twins lying, as it were, on the dormitory, and Orion over the chapel of All Saints, prepare to ring the bell. And on Jan. 1st, when the bright star in the knee of Artophilax (i.e. Arcturus in Boötes) is level with the space between the first and second window of the dormitory and lying as it were on the summit of the roof, then go and light the lamps.[1]

This comes from the instructions for the night-watchman at a monastery near Orleans in the eleventh century. The monastery must have had someone watching the stars in a more than casual way. He knew their names, their courses, the times of their rising and setting, he could distinguish between the planets and the fixed stars. He had the elements of a simple cosmology. All this required study and teaching. It was not much, but it was by such small things that contact was maintained with the stock of ancient learning, and a curiosity to know more was born.

Another science which made its way forward rapidly in the eleventh century under the pressure of daily needs—this time as much secular as religious—was the science (or practice, it would be perhaps more accurate to say) of arithmetic. The only numerals known in the West at the time when our story starts were Roman numerals, and the inconvenience of doing complicated sums in these numerals will be appreciated by anyone who tries to add £mcmlxxxvii xixs. ivd. to £mmcccxcix ivs. xid. Yet monasteries as well as kings had estates which brought in large revenues, and bailiffs who presented accounts not above suspicion. There was urgent need for the development of some device which would make calculation easy, and many heads in the eleventh century were occupied with the problem. Gerbert had made a start in reintroducing to the West the study of the ancient calculating board known as the abacus. He and his successors spent a great deal of energy in working out the complicated processes of multiplication and division with the aid of this board. It had the charm of a scientific toy as well as the

[1]These instructions are printed by R. Poole, *A Monastic Star timetable of the 11th Century*, in the Journal of Theological Studies, 1914, XVI, 98-104.

promise of usefulness. When abbot Odilo of Cluny lay dying in 1049, we are told that he turned to the monastery's expert on the abacus and asked him to calculate the number of masses he had celebrated during his long abbacy.[1] But the machine had sterner uses: by the early twelfth century in England it had given its name to that session of the king's court which became the first Department of State. The Exchequer, so-called from its abacus or chequer cloth, was the centre of the most relentless financial system in Europe.

It is sometimes difficult to realize how much effort was needed to reconstitute the bodies of knowledge such as those of astronomy and arithmetic as they had been known in the ancient world. It was not a question of going beyond the ancients—the impulse to 'research', in the sense of extending the boundaries of scientific knowledge, was only faintly stirring even in the twelfth century—but simply to learn what had been known, and what the world had since lost, was a stupendous task, demanding the labours of many scholars through the whole course of our period. The regaining of this ground in the eleventh century was not specially a task of monastic scholarship, though it was one in which Benedictine scholars played a large part. Partly the needs of their daily life, partly the urge to conserve and to restore, which lay behind so much of the Benedictine achievement throughout the centuries, made the monasteries centres for the accumulation of scientific information on which the work of later scholars could be based.

Besides the learned work required to maintain the elaborate and many-sided life of the community, the Benedictine rule imposed on all monks an obligation to study. In doing so, it also set severe practical limits to the amount and type of study which was possible within the routine of monastic life. Originally some four hours a day had been set aside for this purpose, and although the liturgical developments of the tenth century had curtailed this allowance, the obligation still remained. Every year at the beginning of Lent each monk took a book from the library to serve as his reading for the succeeding year. The Rule laid down how the reading was to be done: the monk was to read the whole book and read it straight through—there was to be no 'skipping', no laying of it aside and taking up something else, nothing light-hearted about it. It was part of a discipline, an exercise in a penitential life. The part of the Rule

[1] P. L. vol. 144, 928.

which regulates the monastic reading comes, significantly, in the chapter on manual labour: the reading envisaged by the Rule was a painful business—it was meant to be. We must imagine it as slow, laborious, and contemplative, carried out with much movement of the lips and a low muttering throughout the cloister.

It is always difficult to know what, or with what profit, people read when they do so for their own purposes, without a creative intention. But we are given some insight into the way in which this part of the Rule was interpreted at Cluny in its greatest period by a chance survival. About 1040 someone made a collection of documents to illustrate the customs of Cluny, and among them (since, it would seem, anything done at Cluny was of interest in the monastic world) he included a rough library list with the names of the monks and the books they had chosen at the beginning of Lent.[1] It is a list such as a busy and not very well educated library clerk might make, with many slips and grammatical mistakes, but it is quite invaluable as a picture of the monastic life taken without any pose. There were sixty-four monks in the monastery on the day the book distribution took place. Of these, twenty-two chose works of the Fathers—St. Augustine on the Psalms or on Christian Learning, St. Jerome on the Prophets, St. Gregory on Ezekiel, and so on; twelve chose commentaries on various parts of the Bible by scholars of the Carolingian age—Rabanus Maurus on Ecclesiasticus, Haimo on Genesis, Remigius on the Psalms, and similar works. Another group of eleven took books on monastic discipline, or Lives of the saints and martyrs, or the Fathers of the Desert. The remainder mostly took works on ecclesiastical history (Bede, Orosius, Eusebius); and a single monk—the unexpectedness of his choice among all these works of Christian piety and scholarship gives the document the stamp of life—chose Livy. Of course, to borrow a book is not the same thing as to read it, but this list inspires confidence in the seriousness with which the Rule was observed. It is very different from some of the later lists of the same kind, where

[1]This list of books occurs in the customs of the Italian monastery of Farfa (printed in B. Albers, *Consuetudines Monasticae*, 1900, vol. 1). These customs come from Cluny, and Dom A. Wilmart has shown that the list of books corresponds to books which were in the library at Cluny in the following century, and that several of the monks can be traced in the charters of Cluny. The proof that this is a real library list from Cluny could scarcely be more complete: Dom Wilmart dates it about 1042-3. (See his article, *Le couvent et la bibliothèque de Cluny vers le milieu du XIe siècle* in Revue Mabillon, 1921, XI, 89-124.)

there are too many law books, sometimes kept out year after year no doubt for business purposes, and only a handful of commentaries on the Bible. Our list is solid and fitting, and the Livy adds a note of not too stereotyped piety to its seriousness.

So far as it goes, this list is a help in appreciating the temper of eleventh-century monastic studies. But it would be absurd to imagine that the chief reading and study of the monasteries consisted of the digestion of a yearly book—just as it would be absurd to imagine that all monks succeeded in accomplishing even so much. The Rule did not tie men of quick and capacious minds to this common ration. Nevertheless, it stamped the works of Benedictine scholars with a character which they seldom lost. The growth of a scholastic theology in the monasteries would be unthinkable: the endless systemization and articulation of details could not have been carried out by men working in small communities, in the intervals of a full communal routine. The work of extraction and arrangement was the true medium of the monastic scholars. They liked to think of themselves as bees gathering nectar far and wide, and storing it in the secret cells of the mind. In so far as thought became urgent, all-absorbing and harassing, it was straying beyond the bounds of the Rule. There must often have been individual monks who passed these bounds, but the conditions of the corporate life limited their influence and drew them back from the excitements of the intellectual chase. We have a picture of a struggle of this kind in the life of St. Anselm. His biographer tells us that when he was searching for his proof of the existence of God,

his thoughts took away his appetite for food and drink, and—what distressed him more—disturbed the attention which he should have paid to the morning Office. When he noticed this, and still was unable to grasp what he sought to understand, he began to think that such thoughts must be a temptation of the devil and he tried to put them from him. But the more he tried, the more his thoughts besieged him, until at last one night during Vigils the grace of God shone in his heart, and the thing he sought became clear, and filled his whole being with the greatest joy and exaltation.[1]

[1]Eadmer, *De Vita et Conversatione Anselmi Archiepiscopi Cantuariensis*, ed. M. Rule, R. S., 1884, p. 333.

Personal dilemmas of this kind cannot have been uncommon, especially at times when new and challenging ideas were in the air, but they subjected the Benedictine Rule to a strain for which it was not adapted. This atmosphere of intellectual effort and strife was very general a hundred years after the death of St. Anselm: it was the very condition of life of the Dominicans whose constitutions laid down that the friars were to be intent on study, to read or meditate something, day and night, at home or abroad; to stay up at night if they wished to study, and to make their church services brief so that this aim should not be impeded.[1] This feverish spirit was quite foreign to the Benedictine monasteries where study was incidental to the duties of a long day.

The typical product of this private monastic study was the *florilegium*, the collection of extracts in which individual monks arranged the fruits of their own reading for their own use and satisfaction. Hundreds of such compilations exist in the manuscript collections of Europe. Very few of them would be worth printing, but sometimes in an introductory passage we see the quiet, industrious unambitious mind at work reducing years of reading to an orderly form. The form was generally not very elaborate and the reading mostly followed well-worn tracks, but the process of collection and arrangement gave an impulse to thought and to methods of enquiry which bore fruit in the schools and universities of the twelfth and thirteenth centuries. The scholastic method was a development of the *florilegium*. In its simplest form, it was an attempt to solve by infinitely patient criticism and subtlety of distinction the problems posed by the juxtaposition of related but often divergent passages in the works of the great Christian writers. It was, one might say, the attempt of the intellect to discover and articulate the whole range of truth discoverable in, or hinted at in, the seminal works of Christianity. The idea of an all-embracing system of established theological truth was only slowly fashioned in the twelfth century, as the range of the questions asked and the authorities appealed to was enlarged. Even at the end of our period, we stand only on the threshold of the giant efforts of the thirteenth century, and the full self-consciousness of the intellect as the instrument of Christian truth. All this takes us very far out of the range of Benedictine studies, but the monastic preparation

[1]P. Mandonnet, *Saint Dominique: l'idée, l'homme, et l'oeuvre* (ed. M. H. Vicaire and R. Ladner), 2 vols., 1938, i, 52.

—corresponding in quite a different sphere to the agrarian preparation for the expansion of Europe in the twelfth century—was an essential preliminary.

We have spoken so far of the works of scholarship called forth by the daily routine of monastic services—the writing of saints' lives, the composition of hymns and responses, the arrangement of lectionaries; and lastly of the products of the private reading of the monasteries. Somewhere between these, partaking partly of the official character of the first, and partly of the private character of the second, come the works in which the Benedictine monasteries made their most original contribution to literature: in the writing of histories. There is something in the writing of history which has called forth at all times the best resources of the Benedictine scholar: it opened a field for the laborious, exacting, patient work of compilation and arrangement which the spirit of the Rule required. At the same time, it was fostered by the very practical and human desire which members of a community feel to preserve and glorify their past, to justify their position in the world, and—more questionably— to defend their privileges and assert their independence. Here was a vast field of research in which practical expediency and literary ambition could both find their place, and where the work to be done ranged from the classification of the monastic archives, the defence of the genuineness of its holy relics, and the history of its landed properties, to the writing of annals, biographies and the major histories of the time. It is to this complex activity that we owe our best materials for understanding the history of our period, at least to the end of the eleventh century: thereafter, in historical work, as in other forms of intellectual activity, the monastic leadership is less marked, but it was not lost for a long time to come. In some fields it has never been lost.

These are limited achievements, but it was precisely because, in point of originality or intensity of thought, the monastic scholars did not aim high, that the ground which they won was won for good. A John Scotus Erigena in the ninth century, or a St. Anselm in the eleventh century could flash out ideas which never became part of the general stock of knowledge, but the elementary things—the command of the Latin tongue, the digesting of the great bulk of material left by the Fathers of the Church, the physical transmission of the literature of pagan and Christian Rome, the preservation of some record of their own time—this was the work which could be done without strain, and perhaps could only have been done, in the framework of a monastic community.

B. IN THE CATHEDRALS

A very different picture meets us when we come to consider the communities of secular clergy, and especially the cathedral churches, as centres of learned activity. At first sight, the difference seems to lie chiefly in the deficiencies of the secular bodies. The same impulses are at work, but they work more feebly. In the development of their services, they follow the monasteries, but at a distance. Their libraries were on the whole less extensive, the obligation to study less well defined or lacking, the routine of life less regular. The corporate spirit was alive, and it sometimes aroused passionate feelings, but there was less for it to feed on—less to defend in the way of privileges and ancient rights. The individual members of a chapter lived apart, drew their own revenues, farmed their own estates; it was only in moments of crisis that they drew together.[1] In such conditions, the solid achievements of monastic learning are scarcely to be looked for. Even at their best, without the scandals which marked the church at Arezzo, the cathedral bodies were—in the eyes of many reformers of the tenth and eleventh centuries—disorganized and disgraceful bodies. They were strongholds of married clergy; the canons were in the position of monks without monastic discipline; their attendance to their duties in church, for which after all they primarily existed, was difficult or impossible to enforce. There were many attempts to discipline them, as the monasteries were disciplined in the tenth century. Rules were drawn up to give them a common life modelled on the Rule of St. Benedict, and in England, where the alliance between ecclesiastical reformers and secular princes was peculiarly strong and invited strong measures, a considerable proportion of the cathedrals were turned into Benedictine monasteries outright and remained so till the Reformation. But, on the whole, the cathedral chapters proved obdurate. Marriage had to go—the tide against that was too strong. But the other features which made the secular cathedrals hateful to the stern school of reform remained.

[1] A good illustration of the spirit of a cathedral chapter in the early twelfth century is to be found in the history of the archbishops of York by Hugh, precentor of the Cathedral, printed in Raine, *Histories of the Church of York*, R. S., vol. 2. (see esp. pp. 107-8, 112-7.)

The great cathedral dignitaries preserved their free, unregulated way of life, mixing their private secular cares—and often high secular office—with their spiritual duties. Throughout the centuries, the cathedrals opposed an obstinate individualism, localism and worldliness to all currents of reform. They were very hard nuts to crack.

What place was there in bodies such as these for the pursuit of learning? It is true that in the ambitious educational projects of the Carolingian age—among which must be reckoned the far-reaching plans for lay education in England attributed to King Alfred—the cathedral churches were to have had an important part. Numerous councils of the eighth and ninth centuries emphasized the obligation laid on both monasteries and cathedral churches to provide free instruction to all comers. But, so far as the monasteries were concerned, the ideals of later reformers generally discouraged any development of this kind. And, so far as the cathedral churches were concerned, the councils grew weary of reiterating a demand which could not be enforced, and they were silent on this subject for over three centuries.[1] It was not until 1179 that the Third Lateran Council renewed the injunction that all cathedrals should provide a suitable benefice for a master to teach, free of charge, the clerks of the church and other poor scholars. Yet it was during these centuries of legislative silence that the cathedrals made their great contribution to learning. How did this come about?

In the first place, the long silence of legislators could not do away with the need for some form of instruction in the great collegiate churches. The church services had to be maintained and elaborated, following the fashion of the time. Hence there was a need for that same wide range of activities which we have already noticed in connexion with the monastic services. It was not without reason that the precentor, who was responsible for the arrangement and execution of the daily round of services, was in many cathedrals next in importance to the dean. Then there were letters to be written and business to be transacted on behalf of the chapter which required gifts of scholarship and a fine knowledge of law. The dignitary who was responsible for writing the chapter's letters and keeping its correspondence was also, in many cases, responsible for directing the

[1] cf. E. Lesne, *Histoire de la Propriété ecclésiastique en France*, vol. 5, *Les Écoles*, 1940, p. 24.

school. We may suspect that this often took second place to his other duties. Organically the school had only a small place in the cathedral organization, but it could scarcely be omitted altogether.

In all this, however, we are still far from anything that could give the cathedral schools a title to fame. The impulse which raised some of them to heights of scholarly repute came from a larger world than that of ecclesiastical routine. It came from the intellectual restlessness, the desire to know more than the needs of daily life required or than local schoolmasters provided, which seems to strike us as a new factor in the general life of Western Europe as we turn from the tenth to the eleventh century. Certainly in the eleventh century there was a more general interest in intellectual questions than there had been previously. No doubt this only means that an easing of the material conditions of life gave more people a chance for satisfying their intellectual curiosity; but the effect of this was to add a new quality of widespread discussion and dispute, which distinguishes the period from the eleventh century onwards sharply from the preceding age. We have only to notice the different atmosphere of the very technical Eucharistic dispute in the mid-eleventh century as compared with the theological disputes of the ninth century to see the different conditions of intellectual controversy. In the earlier century we find scholars disputing among themselves, often with passion and vindictiveness, but still rather remotely, in a court circle, under the eye of an Emperor, with leisured rotundity of phrase, slowly wielding the heavy bludgeon of authority. The eleventh-century disputants, on the other hand, come into the arena like matadors, armed with the sharp sword of logical distinctions—and, what is more, cheered on by a crowd of supporters, pupils and colleagues. The eleventh-century scholar in controversy felt himself the representative of a school or a party, he appealed to provincial loyalties; he might easily find himself an object of popular hostility if his views were known to be unorthodox. It is in the eleventh century that we have the beginnings of popular heresies, and the beginnings also of popular persecutions. The teaching of the Church was beginning to stir a lively response at all levels of society.

Another aspect of the change was the rapid growth in the floating population of students of all ages and conditions, prepared to go anywhere for the sake of learning. Such men had always existed, but they now became sufficiently numerous to form a class by themselves, to influence the growth of institutions, and to make it possible to see 'trends' in their movements. The most significant of these trends is one which is noticeable from the end of the tenth century in the form of a persistent trickle of able men from Italy to Northern France. So far as we can see they were simply responding to an intellectual pull, similar to that which has drawn artists to Paris during the last hundred years. They left a society, on the whole, more comfortable and more literate for one which was cruder and more aggressive, in search of a learning which was not to be found in Italy. It is a surprising spectacle, for Italy had much to give. It was the home of an active legal science which could trace a faint but sure descent from Roman law. It had schools of learned legists, and the art of rhetoric was cultivated to a high degree. It boasted of the literacy of its laity. But there were things to be learnt in Northern France which satisfied intellectual aspirations, far beyond the range of the legal sciences of Italian communal life or the requirements of monastic routine. It was the desire to learn logic which brought Gerbert from Rome to Rheims; it was a desire to turn from law to grammar and logic which later drew Lanfranc from Pavia to Tours. These were the subjects in which intellectual novelties and excitements were to be found.

The abundance of scholars created a demand for teachers. Teaching—it is hard to believe it, but it seems to be true—became a road to profit as well as fame. It was noted that Lanfranc, when he became a monk of Bec in about 1040, gave up a profitable career as a free-lance teacher to sink himself in an obscure monastic community. Still more, that prince of free-lance teachers, Abelard, could find audiences, and profitable ones, wherever he chose to teach. But the cathedrals provided a natural focus for the activities of such men. The very great might be able to stand alone in the world and draw the world to them; but the not-so-great would prefer the security of an established institution and a ready-made audience. Cathedrals had libraries; they had schools, however dim; they offered the chance of an assured position, and of advancement to positions of high dignity and emolument. They drew to themselves activities which they did not create, and which no amount of legislating could have created within them. By their stability, they could serve a purpose which no other institution of the time was capable of serving—that of organizing and giving continuity to the keen but wayward impulses which were sending men through many countries and many vicissitudes in search of learning. In doing this, the cathedrals were helped by the very circumstance which had appeared to work against them as serious centres of study—the slenderness of the connexion between the work of the schools and the life of the cathedral body. It was easy for the cathedral schools to start a life of their own which reflected the changing interests, and drew on the energies, of the outside world.

We may here pause to consider a figure who in a remarkable way drew out the resources inherent in the cathedral body as a centre of learning in the eleventh century. Fulbert, Chancellor and later (1006-28) Bishop of Chartres, is the patriarch among the masters of the great cathedral schools.[1] He was the first to form a school with a distinctive tradition which persisted long after his death. Without himself writing anything great, or starting any new line of thought, he was able, by his sensitivity to what was going on round him, by his encouragement, and his genius for drawing men to him, to make the school of Chartres the most vigorous in Europe. In range of interests and in influence his only immediate predecessor was Gerbert. But Gerbert, despite the powerful impetus he gave to learning, founded no school; except for the excellent Richer, men did not boast that they were his pupils. It is in the society which Fulbert gathered round him at Chartres that we catch our first glimpse of those intimate and affectionate relations between master and pupils, and of that bond of common loyalty uniting the pupils of an outstanding master, which were the peculiar strength of the great medieval schools. After Fulbert, many masters—St. Bruno, Anselm of Laon, Abelard, Gilbert de la Porrée, Peter Lombard and others—won this same kind of loyalty, which kept their memories and their doctrines alive; but more than any of them Fulbert lived in his pupils.

There are many testimonies to the fact that Fulbert's memory was kept alive by his pupils almost to the end of the century, but the most touching of them is the earliest. Fulbert had a pupil from Liége called Adelman, who became Bishop of Brescia towards the end of his life and died in 1057. Shortly after Fulbert's death, he wrote a poem to commemorate the master and eleven of his disciples

[1] The works of Fulbert are printed in P. L. vol. 141; they have been studied, with special reference to the collection of letters, by C. Pfister, *De Fulberti Carnotensis episcopi vita et operibus*, Paris, 1885. Fulbert's place in the history of the school of Chartres is described by A. Clerval, *Les écoles de Chartres au Moyen Age*, 1895.

who had all died within a few years. It is an awkward poem because it followed an old fashion of starting each verse with a different letter arranged in alphabetical order, but through all the uneasiness of diction it glows with a warm sincerity and sense of past glories. Of Fulbert himself, it says:

> With what dignity of spiritual interpretation, with what weight of literal sense, with what sweetness of speech, did he expound the deep secrets of philosophy. The studies of Gaul flourished while he taught. He cultivated both human and sacred sciences, and never allowed virtue to be oppressed by poverty. Like a spring dividing into many streams, or a fire throwing off many sparks, so he propagated himself through his pupils in many different sciences.[1]

Then the poet described Fulbert's pupils and their attainments: Hildegar, philosopher, physician and mathematician, who copied the master's habits of manner and speech; Ralph, more a friend of letters than a learned man himself, who had risen from obscurity to an eminent position at Orleans; Engelbert and Lambert, who coming from a poor nest taught for money at Paris and Orleans; Reginald of Tours, a distinguished grammarian; Gerard who went to Jerusalem and died at Verdun on his return; Walter, who scoured Europe for learning and died by violence at Besançon; Reginbald of Cologne, a man of powerful mind and wide fame, who taught Latin to the barbarians of the Rhine; Odulf, Alestan and Gerard, all of Liége, who had helped to maintain the scholastic fame of that city and died before their time.

These men, who died young, were not the most distinguished of Fulbert's pupils: that distinction belongs to Berengar of Tours. Like many of Fulbert's pupils he would have called himself a grammarian —that is to say, he was interested in the meanings and derivations of words, in the relation between language and reality, and in the rules of eloquence. Of his eloquence, which is well-attested, we have little evidence; but that he was a fanatical speculative grammarian, anxious to push the conclusions of his subject as far as possible and to apply them to the clarifying of dogma, there can be

---

[1]This poem has been printed several times since the seventeenth century but in a critical edition only by J. Havet in a volume of *Notices et Documents*, ed. by various scholars to commemorate the 50th anniversary of the *Société de l'Histoire de France*, 1884. It is reproduced with notes by Clerval, *op cit.*, pp. 58–93.

no doubt. In this, he broke away from the temper of Fulbert's school with its many-sided interests and its reticence on dogmatic questions, and embodied the more combative spirit of a later age. Fulbert had been dead for twenty years before the implications of Berengar's teaching on the doctrine of the Eucharist began to be widely discussed. At this time, the faithful Adelman was teaching at Speyer, and he heard only distant reports of Berengar's controversial statements. It was many years since he had written the poem in honour of Fulbert and his pupils, but he felt he was the guardian of a tradition, and he wrote to Berengar begging him, *per suavissimam memoriam Fulberti*, to preserve the peace of the Christian commonwealth. He recalled "that most sweet fraternity which they enjoyed under the venerable Socrates of the Academy at Chartres" and charged him to remember the intimate evening conversations in the little garden by the city chapel, in which Fulbert had begged them with tears to keep the royal road marked out by the Fathers before them. It was probably to accompany this letter, and to enforce this plea, that he revised the old poem—substituting a distinguished musician, Sigo, for the colourless and doubtless long forgotten Ralph "more a friend of letters than a learned man himself"—and sent it off to Berengar. Berengar was not quite insensible to Fulbert's claims, for he quoted his authority for his views, but he was a better poet than Adelman, a better grammarian than Fulbert, and too sure of himself for reproof. He labelled Adelman's painful effort a *ridiculus mus*, and made some ironical jest on the author's name, of which the sense is now lost.[1]

A proud man would be apt to treat an appeal to the memory of school-days in this way, and Berengar, with all his piety and liberality, was proud. He was more brilliant than Fulbert, and he had the power of setting men by the ears and starting them discussing an old question in a new way: as one contemporary wrote to the Pope, the question he started "so filled the world that not only clerks and monks, whose job it is to watch over such matters, but even the laity talked about it among themselves in the streets."[2] But

---

[1]For Adelman's letter, see P. L. vol. 143, 1289-96, where the text is incomplete. A complete text is printed by R. Heurtevent, *Durand de Troarn et les origines de l'hérésie bérengarienne*, 1912, pp. 287-303. Fragments of Berengar's reply to the letter are printed in Martène and Durand, *Thesaurus novus anecdotorum*, 1717, iv, 109-13.

[2]The passage occurs in a letter to Gregory VII printed in M. R. James, *Catalogue of Medieval MSS in the University Library, Aberdeen*, 1932, pp. 36-7.

he lacked the benevolent wisdom of Fulbert, which enabled him to form a school at Chartres faithful to his general temper of mind for over a hundred years. Fulbert had a way of saying things which were remembered. The cathedral chapter testified that he was accustomed to speak to them in their distresses *constanter et comfortatorie*; he gave the impression that everything was under control. In all things, except where justice was concerned, he was on the side of moderation. His advice to his favourite pupil Hildegar when he became Treasurer at Poitiers is typical of his whole teaching: Hildegar was to divide his time between reading, prayer and teaching, and to look after the health of his pupils as well as their minds; he was to remember to care for the orchards and vineyards; he was to allow the church to retain the additional psalms which (here, as elsewhere) had crept into the service, though in Fulbert's view they were superfluous; and the letter concludes with an exposition of the symbolic meaning of some ecclesiastical ornaments, the solution of a small point of Canon Law, some advice on the teaching of grammar, and some books which had been asked for—Cyprian, Porphyry and the Lives of the Fathers.

Fulbert gave a stronger impetus to the development of a school than anyone before the beginning of the twelfth century. He was only able to do this because he was at ease, not only with his Chapter, his pupils and the ideas of his time, but also with the society around him. One can scarcely help comparing him in this respect with Gerbert, who in all probability had been his master. Gerbert was at home only in the past—a limitation which gave strength to his scholarship. But Fulbert entered into the small world of local affairs and personal relationships with the ease of a man at home in the present. He entered into the spirit, and examined the theory, of feudal relationships with a care which Gerbert reserved for the theory of the Empire. His brief exposition of the duties of a vassal to his lord became a classic and was copied more often than any of his works, except those which found a place in the service books of the Church. The correspondence of both Gerbert and Fulbert has been preserved, and to pass from one to the other is to pass from scenes of high life and somewhat artificial political intrigue to the problems of a society of country gentlemen, rough and violent as they were. Men felt that Fulbert was one of themselves, while Gerbert, for all his influence as a scholar, was an alien. The contrast was seized on with customary violence in popular legend, which portrayed Gerbert as a magician who had sold his soul to the devil and penetrated unlawful secrets, while Fulbert came down in tradition as the man who had been cured in illness by the Virgin's milk.

It is worth insisting on Fulbert's easy familiarity with the world, because this was the quality which the cathedral schools were able to add to learning. They brought learned problems—as distinct from problems of religious observance—home to a wide circle of men living in the world. It is doubtful whether Fulbert added anything to the sum of knowledge, but he touched every side of learning, and everything that he touched he made familiar. The range is important. He was in touch with the latest developments in the sciences of logic, arithmetic and astronomy, which reached Chartres from Rheims in the North-West and from Moslem Spain, and he wrote poems to familiarize his pupils with the processes of calculation and the Arabic names of the stars just coming into fashion. It was a simple form of instruction he practised, suitable to the rudimentary state of the sciences. In early life he was famous as a physician, and it is in keeping with the rest of his work that his fame rested on a large assortment of medicines intelligently applied, rather than on an armoury of difficult words and abstruse theory. There seemed to be no end to his versatility. Like other scholars immersed in the routine of a great church, he composed many pieces for the adornment of the church services—hymns, sequences, and homilies, and (most famous of all) the lessons for the Nativity of the Virgin which were adopted universally throughout the western Church. But if his learning had one foot in the Church, it had the other in a world of new problems. The point may be illustrated by a single incident.

One of the most curious testimonies to the learned interests of the early eleventh century is a small collection of letters which passed between two learned men of the cathedral cities of Liége and Cologne, the former called Ralph, the latter Reginbald.[1] The letters are chiefly concerned with mathematical problems. The writers were not mathematicians in any specialized sense, but like Fulbert and other scholars of the day they took every field of knowledge for

[1]The correspondence between Ralph and Reginbald is printed with a commentary by P. Tannery, *Une Correspondance d'écolâtres du XIe Siècle*, in *Notices, et Extraits des MSS. de la Bibliothèque Nationale et autres Bibliothèques*, 1901, vol. XXXVI, ii, 487. Reginbald is the scholar of that name mentioned in the poem of Adelman.

their sphere. They had been reading some of the books of logic which were then becoming part of the school curriculum, and here they found remarks which baffled them. Boethius, in one of his Commentaries on Aristotle, had mentioned that the interior angles of a triangle are equal to two right angles. Everyone will recognize the familiar theorem, and it comes as rather a shock—a forcible reminder of the vast scientific ignorance with which the age was faced—that these scholars had no idea what was meant by the interior angles of a triangle. Reginbald had formed the view that they were the angles produced by a line dropped from one of the angles to the opposite side of the triangle, and he recalled that once when he had been passing through Chartres he had taken the problem to Fulbert. He claimed that, after many talks, he had finally convinced Fulbert by his arguments. Whether this was so or not, the story illustrates the scientific gropings of the time, the intercourse between scholars, and the authority of Fulbert in a field where he was as much at sea as his contemporaries. This is only one of the strange misconceptions revealed in these letters, but it is perhaps more important that they also contain the first mention in the West of one of the important scientific novelties of the day, the instrument which had been developed by the Arabs and now (under the name of the astrolabe) was beginning to be known in the Latin world. This also must have been known to Fulbert in his watch-tower at Chartres —it has even been suggested that it was at Chartres that Ralph and Reginbald became acquainted with the astrolabe. Of this we have no evidence, but we may see a distant working of Fulbert's influence in the fact that Chartres remained a centre for the diffusion of Arabic science in the West until well into the twelfth century—and not for diffusion only, but for the most successful absorption of this science into the body of Christian learning which was achieved at any time before the thirteenth century.[1]

A hundred years later a correspondence like that of Ralph and Reginbald would scarcely deserve mention. It is full of crudities, but it shows that problems were being discussed, and lines of enquiry reopened, which had been closed for nearly five hundred years. And though they were being reopened at a level of ignorance which would have confounded Boethius, the letters have the distant

[1] On this point, see T. Silverstein, *The Fabulous Cosmogony of Bernard Silvestris*, in Modern Philology, 46, 1948, 92-116.

promise of an advance beyond the formidable barrier of ancient learning: the astrolabe was an instrument which had not been known in classical times, and its possession made possible a new beginning in the art of astronomical measurement. It is a small sign, but an important one, opening up a vista of a range of learning not derived from the past.

It was in the school of Chartres that a successor of Fulbert, the great scholar Bernard (Chancellor of Chartres from about 1119 to 1126), coined a phrase which sums up the quality of the cathedral schools in the history of learning, and indeed characterizes the age which opened with Gerbert and Fulbert and closed in the first quarter of the twelfth century with Abelard. He said that the modern scholar, compared with the ancients, was as a dwarf standing on the shoulders of a giant.[1] This is not a great claim; neither, however, is it an example of abasement before the shrine of antiquity. It is a very shrewd and just remark, and the important and original point was that the dwarf *could* see a little farther than the giant. That this was possible was above all due to the cathedral schools, with their lack of a well-rooted tradition and their freedom from a clearly defined routine of study. One must not press the distinction between the learned traditions of cathedrals and monasteries too far—their influence on each other remained strong throughout the eleventh century; but if the image of the bee collecting nectar from many flowers happily expressed the aim of the Benedictine scholar, Bernard's phrase equally happily expressed the aim of a man viewing the world of learning from the greatest of all the cathedral schools.

C. ON THE EDGE OF THE UNIVERSITIES

Fulbert's influence, as a perceptible force in the world of learned men, lasted for just over a century. In the first thirty years of the twelfth century Orderic Vitalis and William of Malmesbury could still write of Bishop Fulbert as a founder of a familiar tradition; somewhat as an Oxford historian might now speak of Bishop Stubbs. When they were writing, they would have found Fulbert's tolerant and humane spirit still alive at Chartres, and in other cathedrals and monasteries they could have found copies of his literary works.

[1] The saying is reported by John of Salisbury in his *Metalogicon*, ed. C. C. J. Webb, p. 136 (P. L. vol. 199, 900). There is an interesting note on the origin of the phrase and its later history, by R. Klibansky in Isis, 26, 1936, pp. 147-9.

Fulbert, it would seem, had not attached much importance to these —he was a teacher not a writer—and he left his 'papers' in confusion when he died. They were collected by two devoted pupils and enjoyed a modest success in the schools of Northern France. But the time came when, except for those compositions which had found a home in the service books of the Church, they ceased to be copied. The learning which they represented, the problems with which they dealt, even the style in which they were written, belonged to a past age. With St. Bernard, Abelard and Hugh of St. Victor, new and commanding figures of more fertile genius than that of Fulbert had appeared; and even masters of smaller stature, like the brothers Anselm and Ralph at Laon, had advanced far beyond the limits of technical achievement which had been possible in the early eleventh century.

It is never possible to say without qualification that the learning of the past—especially of so distant a past as that of Greece and Rome—has been assimilated; but we come to a point where scholars begin to feel comfortable about their command of the achievement of the past. This is the point which we reach in the second generation of the twelfth century. The past still had many shocks in store for Western scholars, and in the last years of our period the intellectual scene was being troubled—more deeply troubled than ever before—by the appearance in Latin versions of the metaphysical and scientific works of Aristotle and his Arabic commentators. These last discoveries open up a new era in western thought and learning, with which we are not here concerned. Throughout the greater part of the twelfth century there was a confident sense that the steady mastery of the works of the past was reaching its natural end.

It became possible at this time to envisage the consolidation of great tracts of knowledge in systematic form. Out of the endless glossing of ancient books there was emerging a view of large subjects, long obscured by a multiplicity of details. The word which came to be used with increasing frequency from the early twelfth century onwards to express this ideal ordering of knowledge was the word *Summa*. The idea of an outline of knowledge is not one which excites many people today: perhaps Mr. H. G. Wells has come nearest to feeling the same sort of excitement about it that twelfth-century scholars felt. To them it was certainly of absorbing interest, and every subject came under the influence of this enthusiasm for system. Indeed the idea sprang naturally from the efforts of eleventh-century scholars, and it expressed the sense which men had of mastering their past. More than that (since from the shoulders of the giants they could see a little farther than their predecessors), the *Summa* was an instrument for the advancement of knowledge: from the beginning it was alive with discussion.

Throughout the century there appeared a succession of works in many fields of study which summed up the learning of the past and, in doing so, became the basis of new enquiries and disputes. In theology there were the *Four Books of Sentences* of Peter Lombard (c. 1150); in canon law the *Decretum* or, more exactly, the *Concordance of Discordant Canons* of Gratian (c. 1140); in Biblical studies the standard gloss or *Glossa Ordinaria* of the school of Anselm of Laon (c. 1120) and the *Historia Scholastica* of Petrus Comestor (c. 1170); in grammar the *Summa* of Petrus Helias (c. 1140); in rhetoric a number of *Summae* or *Summulae* from the schools of Bologna and the valley of the Loire. These works took their place alongside those of the ancients as the text-books of the medieval universities. They had, for their period, a kind of finality which, without the need for any official recognition, won them a lasting place in the curriculum of European studies. Compared with the school-books produced in the previous century, they had an extraordinarily long life, and the end of their undisputed usefulness in the seventeenth century marks the end of the Middle Ages more decisively than the Renaissance or Reformation.

The central books in this movement towards consolidation of the past were the works of Gratian in Canon Law and Peter Lombard in Theology.[1] Although produced by different authors and in different countries—the one in Bologna and the other in Paris—they must be looked on as the fruits of a single effort. Indeed the effort running through all these works of consolidation is, in a sense, one; but the unity, the similarity of the problems, and the community of thought about the means for solving them, are clearer in these two works than in any of the others. In its graphic way, the legendary tradition of the Middle Ages recognized this unity of effort by picturing

---

[1]For Peter Lombard and the whole movement of thought which culminated in his *Sentences*, see the profound study by J. de Ghellinck, *Le Mouvement Théologique du XIIe Siècle*, 2nd edition, 1948.

Gratian, Peter Lombard and Peter Comestor, the author of the *Historia Scholastica*, as sons of the same mother. The truth is not quite so simple as this but the legend expresses a truth.

Gratian and Peter Lombard were both teachers, and their great works were the by-products of a long teaching activity. They both ministered to practical needs, for in canon law the need for a general text-book to replace the many incomplete, inadequate or merely local text-books of the previous hundred and fifty years was urgent; and in theology, not only were the needs of students to be considered, but the needs also of Church at large, harried by new opinions and movements of doubtful tendency. The *Sentences* and the *Decretum* were books of the schools, but they looked out on to the world. In every way, their appearance was a work of conciliation: conciliation between the discordant testimonies of the past, conciliation between the accumulated riches of the past and the sharp questionings of the present, conciliation between the dialectical and authoritarian tendencies of their age.

Peter Lombard is the chief representative of this comprehensive and conciliatory spirit. He was the heir of the two chief traditions of scholarship in Europe—the legal learning of Northern Italy, and the dialectical and theological learning of Northern France. He was, as his name suggests, an Italian, and his early and middle years were spent in the schools of Northern Italy. Here he would be familiar with the latest developments in the study of Canon Law, and particularly with the work of Gratian. Perhaps when he left Italy about 1140 he brought with him one of the earliest copies of Gratian's book; and when he died he left a copy to the Cathedral library in Paris. It was St. Bernard who was responsible for introducing him to Paris[1]; and here also it was the Lombard's task to mediate between two worlds. In Bologna he would have felt the influence of Abelard, and he must have been conscious of it even more strongly in Paris. The *Sentences* are a fulfilment of a plan of study which Abelard had adumbrated in his *Sic et Non*; they draw largely on Abelard's work. Yet it was St. Bernard who set Peter Lombard on his way as a theologian: he was St. Bernard's positive contribution to the development of scholastic theology. Amid so much that must be deplored in the controversy between those great men, here at

[1] St. Bernard, Ep. 410 (P. L. vol. 182, 619). For an account of the career of Peter Lombard, see J. de Ghellinck in Rev. d'histoire ecclésiastique, 27, 1931, 792–830.

least is the suggestion of a way of peace and ultimate reconciliation.

The Lombard, on his side, entered with grave and sober understanding into the bewildering and often light-headed controversies of the time, and in his *Sentences* we see him steering his way from one question to another as the arguments of the day suggested: "At this point it is customary to enquire. . . . Another point which seems worthy of investigation. . . . Certain men have here been inclined to ask. . . ." With such phrases he makes his way through the maze of contemporary argument. His task was to provide material for discussion, not to stifle it. Under the placid exterior of a text-book, the *Sentences* are alive with the intense and questioning intellectual life of the time. In many ways it was not a very attractive intellectual life: little men with little dialectical gimlets were offering to open all the safes in the theological world. It was this which had alarmed St. Bernard; but Peter Lombard shows no trace of apprehension or indignation at the questions which were asked. "There is," he wrote, "perpetual war between the assertion of the truth and the defence of our own fancies. Therefore with much sweat and labour I have put together this volume of testimonies of eternal truth, to stop the mouths of those who are hateful to God, lest the poison of their wickedness should be poured out on others."[1] This sounds repressive, but in the middle of the twelfth century, the quoting of authorities was the opening of a debate, not the end of it, and almost every section of the Lombard's book invited debate.

The *Sentences* were a tract for the times; they ministered to the needs of the moment. But they were also a source-book arranged with brilliant clarity and perspicacity. In this respect they had a long descent from the innumerable books of excerpts which had occupied the studious leisure of monastic scholars for centuries. In the meticulous sub-division of the material, they bear the mark of a new age in scholarship, but they present material which for the most part had been chewed over for a very long time. Yet they were not, as the monastic *florilegia* were, a personal record of a life-time's reading: they were a collection made for the purposes of the teacher and the pupil, to fill (as we should say) a gap. The book was made "so that the enquirer in future will not need to turn over an immense quantity of books, since he will find here offered to him without his

[1] *Libri IV Sententiarum*, ed. Patres Collegii S. Bonaventurae, 1916, i, 3.

labour, briefly collected together, what he needs". Here indeed was mastery of the past.

Peter Lombard taught quietly in Paris for nearly twenty years. In 1159, he became Bishop of Paris; he died in 1160. By the time of his death the scholastic map of Europe was beginning to take on the outlines which it retained till the fourteenth century. From the point of view of a young man beginning his career in 1160, the great difference in the situation, as compared with the position at the beginning of our period, was that he knew where to go to get the instruction he required, and he knew that he would be able to make use of it when he had got it. Gerbert's career as a scholar had been one of chance encounters: a chance visit of a pilgrim to his monastery at Aurillac took him to the Spanish March where it was believed that learned men were to be found; a chance visit of the Count of Barcelona to Rome brought him to the notice of the Pope, who kept him in Italy to teach arithmetic and astronomy; the chance visit of a scholar from Rheims showed him where logic was to be learnt and brought him to Northern Europe; the chance which made him Abbot of Bobbio gave him the run of an ancient library; and he was always dependent on chance correspondents for his knowledge of new books. All this was different for a young man starting his career in the middle of the twelfth century. For those who had not the money to travel far, there were the cathedral schools. He would be an unlucky man who had to travel more than a hundred miles to find one of moderate proficiency, and in many there were teachers of distinction. But above these schools of temporary repute, a few great schools were emerging, whose reputation did not depend on that of a single master, or even on a continued succession of single masters. Among the provincial centres, Chartres, Tours and Orleans still maintained a gallant struggle for pre-eminence in literary studies; but it was not to them that well-to-do or hard-headed students, eager for the advancement which could come from learning, were most likely to turn. They went for preference to places where there was a wider choice of masters and where subjects could be studied which led more directly to places of eminence in royal or episcopal service. Paris and Bologna were the scholastic summits of Europe, and they drew a crowd of students from every nation in Europe. There were of course adventurous spirits, of an importance out of proportion to their numbers, who sought those dangerous founts of new scientific ideas at Toledo or at the medical centres of Salerno and Montpellier. But whether he were timid or bold, a practical man in search of instruction or a scholar in search of inspiration, the mid-twelfth-century student knew his way about.

He not only knew where to study, he also knew that his studies would have a market value. This is the second great contrast with his predecessor of Gerbert's day. Like most modern graduates, the great majority of students in the late twelfth century who made any name for themselves became men of affairs—they did not become country gentlemen or country parsons, and very few spent their lives as teachers; in one form or another they became occupied in administrative work. The importance to government of this marriage with learning has already been mentioned, and a word must now be said about the influence of government on learning. The masters in the schools pursued their task of systematization, elaboration of detail and popularization: on the whole, it was a task in which during the second half of the twelfth century there were few great discoveries or excitements. By the nature of their task, the scholars of the second half of the century seemed to lack the creative power of those in the first half. But on the fringe of the learned world, drawing their power from the learning of the schools and their problems and incidents from the world of affairs, there were some of the most interesting and varied groups of writers which the Middle Ages produced. England, with its rapidly developing government and intense preoccupation with administration from the king's court downwards, was a great place for such men. John of Salisbury, Peter of Blois, Walter Map, Giraldus Cambrensis, and the authors of the first books on the practice of secular government—the *Dialogue of the Exchequer* and the *Treatise on the Laws and Customs of England*—all, in different ways, brought the learning of the schools to bear on the business of the world. As writers, none of them reaches the very first rank; but their appearance marks the full domestication of learning in the West. As we see it now, the intellectual world of Gerbert and Fulbert had been a very small one. Scholars learned with difficulty the elements of sciences to a schoolboy level, and they stretched out painfully beyond the learned needs of small religious communities. Slowly the range of learning transmitted from the ancient world had been mastered. This was the first task, and at the end of the twelfth century only those in touch with the Greek and Moslem world knew how far they were from having completed even this task in the fields of the natural sciences and philosophy. Fortunately perhaps most scholars felt more comfortable about the past than they had any right to feel; and they knew that they lived in a large world of knowledge and achievement.

We may illustrate the new conditions of study and learning, the market for learned men and a scholar's reaction to the world, in the person of one of the writers who found a home in England during the last thirty years of the twelfth century.

Peter of Blois was the son of a minor nobleman of the Loire valley, with the wide family connexions which even minor aristocracy carried with it, but without any prospects in the world except those which he could make for himself.[1] His situation was one which required exertion if it were to be improved, and his quick and lively mind indicated that, for him, the path of promotion lay through the schools rather than along the road of military service. The chronology of his early life is quite uncertain, but at some time about 1160, when he must have been between fifteen and twenty years old, we find him studying at Tours. It was here that he probably first showed his high talent as a poet, and there is no doubt that if he had been content to knock about the world in a more or less disreputable way he would have made his reputation as a poet. He was known to connoisseurs, then as now, as one of the masters of the new poetic idiom, and he handled the complicated forms of the lyric with an easy and subtle grace. But he was too ambitious, and also—to do him justice—too serious, to be content with this success. None of his early poems have come down to us, or if they have they are cloaked in anonymity; he tells us that they were lascivious and it is very probable that they were. But he also tells us that he turned to higher things, and this meant, in the first place, the study of law at Bologna and then theology at Paris. At Bologna, the thing which delighted him most, coming from his literary studies in Tours, was the rhetoric

[1]There is a study of the life of Peter of Blois in J. A. Robinson, *Somerset Historical Essays*, 1921, 100-140. His works are printed in P. L. vol. 207. A good idea of the diffusion of his letters during the Middle Ages may be gained from E. S. Cohn, *The Manuscript Evidence for the Letters of Peter of Blois*, E. H. R., 1926, XLI 43-60. I have discussed some unprinted letters of Peter's later life in the same periodical, 1938, LIII, 412-24.

of the law with its amplitude and sonority of words; the technicalities of the law, whether Roman or Canon, seem to have had little attraction for him. Once more, however, he became dissatisfied, and he abandoned law for theology, Bologna for Paris. We do not know who his masters were in Paris, but he must have listened to a good deal of technical discussion, for very late in life—in the early years of the thirteenth century—he turned up his theological notes from Parisian days and thought sufficiently highly of them to reproduce their arguments in his letters.

But he had no intention of becoming a theologian, and by 1167 he was looking round for a job. This was a delicate business. Everything depended on making the right contacts, and he had many disappointments and vexations before he achieved an enviable security as archdeacon of Bath and a man of importance in the household of two successive archbishops of Canterbury. He had hoped for more; but, still, to be an archdeacon and to hold canonries in four or five cathedral churches was comfortable, if not glorious; and he owed the position entirely to his own abilities, in a strange land, with no family influence. Moreover he was among a very interesting set of people. His real work lay not in his archdeaconry, which must for years on end have been left to the care of a deputy, but in the circle of the archbishops of Canterbury, whom he served for twenty years. These were the years after the murder of archbishop Thomas Becket when the relations between the English Church and the Papacy, and between royal and episcopal jurisdiction, were being worked out in detail. There was need of men of talent and education, and they took themselves very seriously. Peter of Blois must have met every man of importance in the kingdom during his twenty years with the archbishops Richard and Baldwin. He wrote many of their letters, and conducted negotiations for them at the royal court or at Rome or with the troublesome monks of Canterbury. Not without reason, he thought himself too great a man to accept the small bishopric of Rochester.

Peter of Blois was one of the most distinguished of the learned men who devoted their learning and talents to the work of administration in the late twelfth century, and he was conscious of the dignity of government. But in moments of repentance he made no secret of the motives which had induced him to turn his energies in this direction:

I was led by the spirit of ambition and immersed myself entirely in the waves of the world. I put God, the Church and my Order behind me and set myself to gather what riches I could, rather than to take what God sent. Forgetting those things which were behind, I reached forth (but not as the Apostle did) to those things which were before. (Phil. iii, 13) . . . Ambition made me drunk, and the flattering promises of our Prince overthrew me.[1]

When he wrote this, he had just recovered from a dangerous illness and he was full of repentance. He was not always so; but he was never quite at ease in the busy and competitive life of a court. He could not forget that he was a scholar and seriously a Christian, and his illness made him determine to put aside his ambitions and to break off his connexions with the royal court:

In being scourged by the Lord, I received the grace of fatherly correction. I communed with my heart in the night season and searched out my spirit, and I decided to leave this way of life, as Joseph his garment, Matthew his receipt of custom, John his linen cloth, the woman of Samaria her water-pot of avarice. The Lord heard me, and the dew of the divine mercy quenched the flame of ambition, which rivers of silver and gold had formerly been unable to restrain. Stablish the thing, O God, that thou hast wrought in me; permit me not to return to my vomit, nor ever to rebuild the Jericho I have destroyed.[2]

Once recovered, Peter retracted some of the severe things which he had said about the administrative life, and, in words which contain a recollection of the letter of Hildebert quoted earlier in this book,[3] he painted the other side of the picture.

I do not condemn the life of civil servants, who even if they cannot have leisure for prayer and contemplation, are nevertheless occupied in the public good and often perform works of salvation.

[1]Ep. 14 (P. L. vol. 207, 43).
[2]For the Biblical reminiscences of this passage, see Ecclesiastes xxx, 1; Psalms lxxvii, 6; Genesis xxxix, 13; Matthew ix, 9; Mark xiv, 51; John iv, 28; Psalms lxviii, 28; Joshua vi, 26.
[3]See above p. 95. We know that Peter had been obliged to learn Hildebert's letters by heart, as models of style, when he was a boy. (Ep. 101, P. L. 207, 314).

All men cannot follow the narrower path—for the way of the Lord is a strait and arduous road, and it is good if those who cannot ascend the mountain can accompany Lot to be saved in the little city of Zoar. . . . I think it is not only laudable but glorious to assist the king, to hold office in the State, not to think of oneself, but to be all for all. But no one shall be involved, and none shall be extricated, from curial chains by me. For Joshua gave the children of Israel a choice, whether to serve the gods of Mesopotamia and the gods of the Amorites, or the Lord God; being willing that none should bear the yoke of service except by his own choice.[1]

He was indeed, as he recognized, not always consistent, and in his different moods he reflected many aspects of his time and the thoughts of many other men. He was sensitive and impulsive, and perhaps after his outburst he would have liked to make his way back on to the royal road to promotion, but he either could not or would not return to the main stream of secular and ecclesiastical business. For the last twenty years of his life, until his death in 1212, he was on the edge of public affairs; his interests became more theological and his friends more narrowly ecclesiastical; he fell under the influence of Cistercian writers and increasingly reflected their ways of thought, as he had reflected those of many others. He never became a peaceable man, and he made an appalling fuss about the slights and set-backs which happen to most men now and then. But his feet were set in more tranquil paths, and he fulfilled in part the promise he had made to the king's clerks:

I am now well stricken in years, and as Job said 'My wrinkles bear witness against me' and again 'When a few years are come, then shall I go the way whence I shall not return.' I shall think over the time I have lost, in the bitterness of my soul, and I shall offer up the residue of my years to my studies and to peace. Farewell my colleagues and my friends. . . . [2]

It was during this 'time he had lost' that he had made himself one of the most widely read authors of the twelfth century. Indeed his

[1]Ep. 150 (P. L. 207, 440-1) written shortly after Ep. 14. For the Biblical reminiscences, see Matthew vii, 14; Genesis xix, 19; Joshua xxiv, 15.
[2]Ep. 14. For this passage, see Luke i, 7; Job xvi, 8 and 22; Isaiah xxxviii, 5 and 10.

success as a writer is intimately connected with his position in the world, for it was this which gave him an audience and provided his subject matter. The world knew him as a letter writer, and it read his letters because they were learned without being dead. Without losing anything of the correctness of form demanded by the literary conventions of the day, he made his letters an instrument for conveying moral, legal and theological instruction, and for satire on men and institutions which was one of the passions of his highly sophisticated generation. In his letters he gave to small matters the flavour of the wide world of scholarship.

People like to learn in informal ways and letters are one of the most agreeable forms of instruction that has ever been devised. Letters solved the problem of conveying to a large public some of the results painfully arrived at in the schools. But besides this, they had a practical value. Everyone who wanted to be an administrator needed to know how to write letters. With their passion for reducing everything to a system, the twelfth-century scholars had evolved elaborate rules for letter-writing which were gaining precision when Peter began his career. In the end, this precision killed the art, and Peter of Blois was almost the last of the letter writers before the fourteenth century whose letters could be read for pleasure and instruction by cultivated readers. Their success was enormous, and gathered strength in the fourteenth and fifteenth centuries. The humanists of the Renaissance found something to criticize in their form, but they read them, copied them and indexed them. They were printed before the end of the fifteenth century and it was only in the seventeenth century that they ceased to be part of the living literature of Europe.

This lasting success for a work which was neither a text-book for the schools, nor a religious book, is something of great significance. It indicates the arrival of a new taste. The secret of Peter of Blois's success as an author was the same as the secret of Fulbert's success as a teacher. They both spoke to their own age in language, and about things, which it could understand. If Fulbert spoke to a handful of scholars and was almost forgotten a hundred years after his death, while Peter had a large public which lasted for four hundred years, the reason lies not in their intrinsic merits but in the difference between their two ages. The period occupied by Peter's lifetime was a time when it was at last possible to write really popular works. In part, as we have seen, this was due to that mastery of the past which produced such works as Gratian's *Decretum* or Peter Lombard's *Sentences*. On these foundations a new structure of learning could be built. But in the arts, and in literature, the second half of the twelfth century has a different importance. Here also the task of assimilation had gone on; here also men had encompassed, and now commanded their past. But in the process of absorption they had been overtaken by a creative spirit, which was not derived from the past, though it was nourished by a medley of influences both past and present.

Above all, Peter of Blois was valued as a master of language, and nothing distinguishes the taste of an age more clearly than the language which it admires. Fulbert too in his day had been looked on as the master of an easy and clear Latinity, but I think that no one in the late twelfth century would have read his letters for pleasure. They lacked eloquence; they were incapable of stirring the emotions or arresting the attention. Fulbert was one of the best of eleventh-century writers—he was clear, and that was a quality which was much needed. Ambitious writing in the eleventh century is nearly always obscure, full of heavy pedantries and strange words—the relics of the learning of a former age. Clarity was a quality achieved by the best writers of the eleventh century, but it was achieved with difficulty: we can appreciate the difficulties when we try to follow the arguments of so accomplished a writer as Berengar of Tours. He lacked the vocabulary for subtle argument and the writers who aimed at stirring the emotions lacked the art for doing so. Of course, limitations of language can themselves be a source of strength, and St. Anselm (alone among the writers of his century) was the master of a language equally capable of conveying profound and subtle argument as of expressing the outpouring of an intimate devotion. But his language could never form a model for others: it was a mirror of his own mind and sensibility, a finely polished language of carefully cultivated art. It was not a popular language.

St. Bernard was the first writer for several centuries to write Latin which was both distinctive and capable of influencing the taste and practice of his own and succeeding generations. He was the first to make Latin a capacious language for the thoughts of the twelfth century. There were two elements which contributed to this result: the influence of the French vernacular, and the influence of the

Bible. The first let in new words and new constructions which gave the old language a fresh fluency and vivacity; the second gave a new richness and suggestiveness to old words. The revivifying effect of the vernacular can, for an English reader, most easily be observed in the Chronicle of Jocelin of Brakeland, which has recently been edited and translated by Professor H. E. Butler: here is a Latin style which reproduces the effects of every-day speech and sets the reader at once in the freedom of a monastic common-room. The subtle richness introduced into language by the exploiting of Biblical imagery is more difficult to appreciate. The effect depends on a course of study and an attitude to the Biblical text which have passed almost beyond recall. In modern times, the hymns of Charles Wesley have caught some of the effects at which twelfth-century writers aimed: we have here an ardent and personal eloquence which is given a mysterious depth of meaning by the abundant use of Biblical allegory. And Sir Walter Scott, in a passage of brilliant insight, caught the tradition in one of its latest manifestations among those who in the seventeenth century clung to an old-fashioned Biblical learning as the foundation of their faith, and made it the animating force in their eloquence. The exhortation of Ephraim Macbriar delivered after the skirmish at Drumclog in *Old Mortality* gave Scott the opportunity for catching some of the characteristics of an ancient style of eloquence, of which St. Bernard was the father and Peter of Blois one of the earliest and most successful practitioners:

"Your garments are dyed—but not with the juice of the wine-press; your swords are filled with blood, but not with the blood of goats or lambs; the dust of the desert on which ye stand is made fat with gore, but not with the blood of bullocks, for the lord hath a sacrifice in Bozrah, and a great slaughter in the land of Idumea. These are not the firstlings of the flock, the small cattle of burnt offerings, whose bodies lie like dung on the ploughed field of the husbandmen . . . they are the carcases even of the mighty men of war that came against Jacob in the day of his deliverance, and the smoke is that of the devouring fires that have consumed them."[1]

[1] The main Biblical references here are to Isaiah lxiii, 1 and xxxiv, 6; for the rest it is a medley of half-remembered Old Testament phrases. It is interesting to compare the Biblical texture of this passage with that of the passages of Peter of Blois quoted above.

The imagery here is more confused than we should find in the writings of a twelfth-century master like Peter of Blois. But, like Ephraim Macbriar, he too aimed at making his words glow. He once described how he would like to see the liturgy of the church rewritten in a way that would set the heart on fire—he would have it written, he said, in burning words, *ignita verba*. This was the quality which St. Bernard had introduced into medieval eloquence. So far Ephraim Macbriar would have gone with the twelfth-century wielders of Biblical imagery: but he would have been shocked by the uses which they made of this powerful weapon. For, unlike him, they did not assume the manner only in their serious moments. It was their habitual means of expression to be used for serious and comic effects alike. The Biblical images constantly intruded themselves into the picture of contemporary events—sometimes illuminating and often distorting the judgement on the present; these images were engrained in their talk and in their thoughts; and they were conscious of no incongruity in using the language of Holy Scripture to describe their very secular loves and hates.

At first sight it may seem strange that the Bible should first make its way into every corner and turn of speech at the very moment when the amount of the Bible which was read in church was falling away rapidly. As we have seen, the eleventh-century monastic scholar wrote his works in the intervals between church services which were heavily laden with readings from the Bible. But in the twelfth century this sequence of Biblical lessons had everywhere, inside and outside the monasteries, been thoroughly disturbed by the interjection of special lessons for a large number of saints' days. The state of affairs which Cranmer deplored in the sixteenth century had already in the twelfth century become an established fact:

These many years passed, this godly and decent order of the ancient Fathers (by which the whole Bible, or the greatest part thereof, was read over once every year) hath been so altered, broken, and neglected, by planting in uncertain Stories, and Legends, with multitude of Responds, Verses, vain Repetitions, Commemorations, and Synodals; that commonly when any Book of the Bible was begun, after three or four Chapters were read out, all the rest were unread.

But if the twelfth-century scholar heard much less of the Bible in Church than his predecessors, he heard much more of it in lectures. Here once more we are brought back to the influence of the Schools on everyday things. It was in the Schools that the Biblical interpretations of the Fathers were collected together in a convenient form and attached to the relevant section of the text. The *Ordinary Gloss*, that earliest of all the twelfth-century works consolidating past learning, was one of the indispensable hand-books for study. Everywhere the Biblical text was commented on, and became the starting point for discussions of many kinds—grammatical, dialectical, theological and historical. The twelfth-century schools were not centres of research into the mystical senses of Scripture of the kind which St. Augustine had urged scholars to undertake. But they made the Biblical text in all its many meanings more familiar than ever before. Never before had writers demanded for their understanding—and written as if they had a right to expect—so wide a knowledge of recondite Biblical allusions; never before had so many jokes depended on a familiarity with the Biblical story and with the mystical senses of Scripture.

And so, while scholars moved further and further from the framework of studies and outlook of St. Augustine, they also bring us back to the point from which we started. They made the Bible, in the sense in which St. Augustine had understood it, part of the idiom of both secular and divine literature.

CHAPTER V

FROM EPIC TO ROMANCE

THE time has now come to try to draw together the scattered threads of this book, and to face more directly than hitherto some of the fundamental changes of attitude, or shifts of emphasis, which have met us in every sphere of life. These changes are hard to define and their connexion can more readily be felt than explained. Indeed, in a strict sense, these changes defy definition, and the connexion between them cannot be explained—it can only be exemplified in the lives of individuals. At the deepest levels of experience, in intimations of the nature of God and the economy of the universe, in new insights into the powers and powerlessness of man, the changing scene of history has its focus and its justification. We have seen in the preceding chapters many changes which seem to be primarily matters of external relations between men and groups of men: we must now try to see them, as far as may be, from within, in their effects on individuals. Necessarily we shall be concerned only with a few individuals, and those few will be men of a capacity to draw insight from the scattered experiences of their age. But these insights become in a measure the common property, sometimes the unwanted or unregarded property, of the succeeding age, and become themselves part of the material of history.

We may begin by reviewing very briefly the changes which stand out in the course we have so far pursued. We have seen the enlargement of the physical and intellectual boundaries of western Christendom, until, at the beginning of the thirteenth century, statesmen and scholars stand face to face with momentous problems seen at last in all their difficulty and grandeur. The haphazard activity of the Crusades has finally brought the West up against the stark problem of a Moslem world no longer seeming to be withering away, but active and immense. And it has brought the Western Church up against the solid loyalty of the Greek church, which no formal arrangements—capturing of Constantinople, setting up a Latin Patriarch, Latinizing the rites of a conquered country, and the like—can repress. Farther east still, the barrier of total darkness is lifting here and there to reveal glimpses of a New World of fabulous wealth and alarming dangers: in the early thirteenth century, Prester John and Gog and Magog aroused hopes and fears quite as measureless as those opened up by the prospects of an atomic age.

All these new views of the world raised problems for scholars as well as statesmen—questions, for instance, about the bounds of the habitable world, or about the right use of force against heretics, schismatics and unbelievers. But if, for the scholar, the problems of the habitable world were growing in size and complexity, he was facing even larger problems as he looked at the physical universe and speculated about its origin and constitution. Students in the Arts Faculty were now learning about the heavens from Ptolemy and his Arab commentators—the 'real stuff' at last, undebased by the tradition of the Latins—and they were beginning to be able to discuss, with all the confidence of new-found knowledge, whether there was a heaven beyond the sphere of the fixed stars, and whether the spheres were contiguous or not. The vision of the heavens which would later stir the imaginations of Dante and Milton had emerged into the clear light of day: the lessons of Gerbert and his pupils had borne an abundant fruit.

It was the same on all the frontiers of knowledge. Scholars were at last at grips with the main body of ancient science and metaphysics. And, as in the physical world hope was mingled with the fear of great and menacing dangers, so this new theoretical knowledge menaced the traditional harmonies of Christian thought. Against the Christian picture of a created world, of man's free-will, the soul's immortality and God's omnipotence, there were arising new, and as some thought inescapable, arguments for the world's eternity, the ineluctability of fate and the final merging of the individual in a universal soul. In the face of these formidable difficulties, confidence in the ability to absorb all that the learning of the past could offer, which is such a conspicuous feature of the thought of the twelfth century, showed signs of faltering, and our period ends on a note of alarm.[1]

[1]The alarm is very clearly apparent in the decree of a Provincial Council at Paris in 1210 forbidding the reading of, or lecturing about, Aristotle's books on Natural Science, under pain of excommunication, together with other somewhat panicky measures. (Denifle-Chatelain, *Chartularium Universitatis Parisiensis*, 1889, i, 70-1.)

The extension of the boundaries of knowledge was accompanied by, and indeed made possible by, the changing structure of society, by the enlarging of the field of vision beyond the confines of highly localized interests. The fruits of the social changes of the twelfth century are to be seen in the internationalism of the great schools, or universities as we must now begin to call them, of the early thirteenth century; in the perpetual passing back and forth of litigants on the roads leading to Rome—or, for that matter, along the roads leading to Westminster or to Paris from distant parts; in the community of knightly ideals which identified the aristocracy from one end of Latin Europe to the other; in the new orders of friars, which carried the obliteration of localism further than ever before. And the converse of this extension of the community and the enlarging of the bounds of organized effort was the emergence of the individual from his communal background. This impulse towards individual expression was at work in religious communities in the enlargement of the opportunities of privacy, in the renewed study of the theory of friendship, of conscience and of ethics. In the secular life, it found expression in the theory of love and the literature of the passions.

Lastly, we have noticed the fascination and authority of logic, which from small beginnings as a school discipline in the days of Gerbert had finally attained an undisputed eminence as an instrument for the discovery of truth. It is in the love of logic that we come nearest to finding a common factor in the manifold changes we have so far noticed. It expressed the striving towards universality: it knew nothing of differences of place or time; it submerged all local peculiarities. Logic was the universal instrument, the bond between all subjects and the solvent of all difficulties. Like the Pope in ecclesiastical causes, it was—in a phrase which became current in the thirteenth century—the "universal ordinary". And, in a curious way, the devotion to logic fitted the mood of emotional tenderness which runs through the literature of the twelfth century. Whatever stands above space and time is amenable to the processes of logic, and the logic of the will and the passions became familiar to all readers of Chrétien of Troyes.

The change of emphasis from localism to universality, the emergence of systematic thought, the rise of logic—to these we may add a change which in a certain sense comprehends them all: the change from Epic to Romance. The contrast is not merely a literary one, though it is in literature that it can be most clearly seen. It is a reflection of a more general change of attitude which found expression in many different ways. Briefly, we find less talk of life as an exercise in endurance, and of death in a hopeless cause; and we hear more of life as a seeking and a journeying. Men begin to order their experience more consciously in accordance with a plan: they think of themselves less as stationary objects of attack by spiritual foes, and more as pilgrims and seekers. Of course, the idea of pilgrimage had long held an important place in the Christian life, and some of the greatest exponents of the spiritual advantages of physical journeying were the English and Irish missionaries and travellers of the seventh and eighth centuries. But their spiritual ideal was not *movement*, so much as *exile*: a removal from friends and homeland, rather than a search for new experiences and adventures. It was not until the twelfth century that the imagery of journeying became a popular expression of a spiritual quest. Then indeed it meets us on all sides—in the Arthurian Romances, in allegories of love, in descriptions of the ascent of the soul towards God. The imagery of movement seemed at this time to lay hold on the imagination, and it invaded secular as well as religious literature. The theme had a natural appeal to the age which produced the Crusades, but it outlived the Crusades, and produced in *Pilgrim's Progress* a last great popular masterpiece.

It was in the monasteries that new experiences were most quickly recognized and made intelligible. The critical period of discovery was the century from about 1050 to 1150. This century is almost coterminous with the adult lives of two men of great significance in the recasting of medieval ways of thought: St. Anselm (1033-1109) and St. Bernard (1090-1153). They never met; the elder exercised no direct, and little indirect, influence on the younger; they differed greatly in temperament and genius, and in the details of the monastic routine in which they spent the greater part of their lives. Their points of likeness, which are striking, have nothing to do with personality: they can only be understood against the background of the Rule which they both followed, and in the light of the strivings which many shared, but to which they gave luminous expression. They were both followers of St. Benedict, and it is to his Rule that we must first turn in order to understand the mould in which their experience was cast.

It is not possible to summarize the Rule of St. Benedict, for it is concerned less with theory than with practice: it is a mass of details which require, I imagine, to be experienced in order to be fully understood. But one thing stands out clearly: the life it prescribes is a static one in more than one sense. In the first place: physically. It forbids movement from place to place. The individual was shut up with his fellows within the wide walls of the monastic enclosure, and there (according to the Rule) he stayed till death, as it were in a state of siege, resisting the powers of evil. And the life is static in another sense: it promised no excitements of mind or body. It was a laborious and penitential life:

> They do not live by their own free will,
>   or obey their own desires and pleasures,
>   but walk by another's judgement and command,
>   and, living in monasteries,
>   desire that an abbot should be over them.[1]

That was the essence of the Rule. The life it enjoined was a ceaseless discipline, an unvaried round from year to year, a communal life where the individual was lost in the crowd and stripped of those eccentricities which we call his personality. The times of his privacy, even of his private prayers, were curtailed within narrow bounds. St. Benedict developed no theory of the spiritual growth of the individual—that was something outside the range of the legislator. But at the centre of the monastic life, surrounded by all else that was static or merely circular in movement—like the round of the seasons with their appropriate mealtimes and fasting and psalmody —he placed an area of freedom, of movement and of growth. This passage in the Rule is so important for our purpose, that it must be quoted:

Wherefore brethren (he says) if we wish to attain the topmost height of humility and to come quickly to that heavenly excellence which in this present life we reach by humility, we must raise up—

[1] *Regula S. Benedicti*, cap. 5. I have taken the quotation from C. Butler, *Benedictine Monachism*, 2nd. edit., 1924, p. 50.

and by our acts we must ascend—that ladder which appeared to Jacob in his dream whereon he saw angels ascending and descending. This ascending and descending doubtless signify nothing else than an ascent by humility and a descent by pride. The ladder itself is our life on earth, raised up by God towards heaven for the humble in heart. The sides of the ladder we call our body and soul, and into these sides God has inserted steps of humility and discipline for our ascent.[1]

It would be hard to find anywhere outside the Bible so short a passage which has worked its way so powerfully into Christian thought as this one. Our commentary must be confined to one or two points:

(1) Although by way of contrast with what was to come, it is legitimate to speak of a heroic view of life predominating in Europe during the period from the sixth to the eleventh century, the monastic life—or for that matter the Christian life in any form—could never be merely 'heroic' in its quality. That fatal struggle of man against superior forces, that meaninglessness of fate, and the purely resigned, defensive and heroic attitude of man in the face of fate could not, on a Christian view, be the whole story. As Europe became Christianized the epic was bound to decline, for it left out the personal and secret tie between man and God. The Rule of St. Benedict, unromantic though it is in its main outline, already contains the small germ of that freedom and movement which developed in every branch of life during the eleventh and twelfth centuries.

(2) Nevertheless we must notice the limitations of this movement as conceived by St. Benedict. He speaks of ascending and descending the ladder of life *by our acts* and he proceeds to list those acts, mostly external ones, by which the summit of humility was to be reached. These acts are the twelve rungs in the ladder. Now, since he has spoken of them as rungs in a ladder, we would expect them to follow a logical sequence in an orderly process of growth and development. But this is what we do not find. The rungs really turn out to be varying manifestations of a fundamental attitude. Indeed the first rung in the ladder is this fundamental attitude—the sense of living in the presence of God; the second and third are two general precepts, self-abnegation and obedience; and the remainder

[1] *Regula S. Benedicti*, cap. 7.

are the external acts which, in the framework of the monastic life, issue from these precepts.

This inner movement at the centre of the monastic life is therefore somewhat different from that which the simile of the ladder would lead us to expect. The steps are rather so many indications of spiritual life than stages of spiritual growth. Indeed the word 'spiritual' itself is probably out of place in this connexion: soul and body are specifically associated in the movement. We are far from any doctrine of spiritual development, still farther from any idea of the ascent of the mind to God. The emphasis is on the will, on obedience—and in obedience there can, strictly speaking, be no gradation: one is either obedient or one is not, and there's an end of it. In obedience there is no journeying; there is only arrival. That is why St. Benedict, having stated the general principle could only illustrate its operation in external actions.

Now until the eleventh century the doctrine of the monastic life laid down by St. Benedict does not appear to have been either greatly added to or altered. The Rule formed part of the daily reading of the monastic body, and the teaching about humility and the acts of humility must have been familiar to every monk. This teaching was made the subject of commentaries but it did not receive the silent criticism of being transformed in the process of exposition. It is probable that the elaboration of the monastic routine, which was especially rapid in the tenth and eleventh centuries, placed a check on theoretical speculation and concentrated the minds of those in the best-ordered monasteries on the things outside themselves. In reading the fully developed custumals of the period, the mind is swamped by the bewildering complexity of directions for the details of church services and church adornment. No doubt much of this detail became habitual, but it can have left little room for introspection or for reflection on the principles of the monastic life.

Then, as we have already seen, in the second half of the eleventh century there appeared signs of an uneasiness within the monastic order and among those converts to a religious life from whom the Benedictine order had drawn leaders in the past. The life of solitude, the religious life divested of those corporate ties which had stamped the old monasticism, began to appear with a new attractiveness. Not only did hermits multiply, but new corporate organizations also appeared which sought to introduce a greater degree of solitariness, a greater intensity, and a more acute spiritual strife into the religious life. These aims had their echo within the Benedictine Order itself.

The greatest Benedictine figure of the eleventh century was St. Anselm. At the time of his conversion to the religious life, he too, like many others, hesitated between the life of a hermit and that of a monk.[1] But having once chosen the latter, he set his face against the dissatisfaction with the weight of ceremonies and customs which was beginning to stir among his contemporaries, and counselled a willing acceptance of the established routine. In this he stood in marked contrast to the most powerful personality in the monastic world in the next generation, St. Bernard. Yet, though in externals a traditionalist, in a deeper sense he broke out of, or at least extended, the traditional orbit of the Benedictine life. The Rule of St. Benedict aimed at the stabilizing of the will and the subjection of the body through a corporate discipline. St. Anselm taught a reaching forward to the knowledge of God by a rousing of the mind: *Excita mentem tuam*, he wrote, "stir up your torpid mind, dispel the shadows which sin has cast on it . . . chew over in thought, taste in understanding, swallow in longing and rejoicing".[2] It was in the innermost recesses of the conscious and awakened soul that God was to be found: "Flee awhile your occupations, hide yourself a little from your tumultuous thoughts, throw off your burdensome cares and postpone your laborious distractions; enter into the chamber of your mind and exclude all else but God and those things which help you in finding Him; close the door and seek Him".[3] We enter here into an inner world of movement and struggle, in which attack has taken the place of resistance as the predominant mood. The same attitude is apparent in St. Anselm's famous programme of enquiry: *Fides quaerens intellectum*, "Faith seeking understanding". The static act of acceptance was replaced by a movement from acquiescence to understanding, in which there was no resting place short of a final illumination.

Once more, the transforming power of a new energy meets us in Anselm's account of the stages of Humility: in his private teaching he recast entirely the twelve stages described in the Rule, turned the ladder into a mountain, the twelve rungs into seven steps, and gave

[1]Eadmer, *Vita S. Anselmi*, ed. M. Rule, R.S., p. 319
[2]*Meditatio XI* (P.L. vol. 158, 763; no. III in Schmitt, iii, 84.)
[3]*Proslogion*, cap. 1.

them a strictly logical order and a more internal character.[1] The element of corporateness which was so strongly marked in the twelve steps of St. Benedict—he was thinking all the time of the sinner as a member of a group—disappeared entirely in Anselm's sequence. It ran as follows: self-knowledge, grief, confession, persuasion of guilt, acquiescence in judgement, suffering of punishment, love of the punishment. Almost all these steps touch the individual alone in the intimacy of his own mind and will; they form an inner progression similar to that intellectual ascent which Anselm elsewhere sketched from apprehension to understanding and from understanding to wisdom. In both cases, there is a movement from knowledge sought within the soul itself to an embracing of that knowledge in all its aspects and consequences.

St. Anselm was a scrupulous observer of the monastic routine. There is no suggestion that he disregarded it in any part. Of course, no monk was ever entirely sunk in this routine—indeed at all times we know a great deal about the activities of monks in their leisure hours. But what we find in St. Anselm is a complete programme of spiritual life in solitude, in the company of a few chosen disciples, and in contact with like-minded men and women, lay and clerk, throughout Europe, a programme which had no obvious connexion with the monastic routine. No doubt the connexion was there, but it was silent and unseen.

The urge towards a greater measure of solitude, of introspection and self-knowledge which is exemplified by St. Anselm in the bosom of the Benedictine order in the eleventh century ran like fire through Europe in the generation after his death and produced an outburst of meditations and spiritual soliloquies. Anselm was the founder of this new type of ardent and effusive self-disclosure, but for the men of the later Middle Ages the patron of this kind of literature was pre-eminently St. Bernard. There was some justice in this literary distortion, for though these personal outpourings of devotion were not confined to any one religious order, it was the Cistercians who produced the greatest volume and, as it were, set the fashion in this type of literature. The Cistercians wrote under the dominating influence of St. Bernard who, though he himself composed none of

[1] *Similitudines*, cap. C-CIX (P.L. vol. 159, 665-9). The authenticity of this part of the *Similitudines* is guaranteed by its appearance in the *Dicta Anselmi*, Corpus Christi College, Cambridge, MS 457, pp. 5-13.

the *Meditations* which later went under his name, gave a theological background and a doctrinal stability and consistency to the devotional writings of his followers. The Cistercians occupy the central position in the spiritual life of the twelfth century: the productions of the monasteries of the older type had in general—despite the influence of St. Anselm on a little group of disciples—a character too staid and stolid to exercise a widespread influence; and, at the other extreme of the religious life, the Carthusians moved in a world too remote and severe to communicate their power and originality of vision to a large circle. It was the Cistercian writers above all who communicated to the spiritual literature of the century the warmth and intimacy and movement, which twelfth-century audiences looked for as well in their serious as in their lighter moods.

In some ways it seems a strange thing that, just at the moment when the Christianizing of Europe was reaching a stage of external completion, there should have arisen men like Anselm and Bernard who evoked in the ordered routine of a monastic life the tensions and conflicts of an age of conversion. The congruity of these seeming opposites can be admitted by the historian, but it was not equally clear to contemporaries who often felt that the influence of such men threatened to bring a great upheaval in safe and long established routines.

It is a similar paradox that just at the moment when a systematic and impersonal body of law and theological teaching was appearing in the schools and making its way forward in the world, there should appear side by side with it an emphasis on personal experience, an appeal to the individual conscience, a delving into the roots of the inner life. It seems as if legalism was most pervasive when law was most difficult to come by. When the great difficulty was to know the law, and afterwards to obtain the observance of the law, the gift of stating the legal points correctly or of amassing texts on a controversial point was valued as a necessary general attainment. St. Anselm had risen above the texts—whether legal or theological—and he drew a few after him in the same path. More powerfully still St. Bernard rose above the texts, and in the bonds of a common experience he drew a whole host after him. If a monk had strayed from the monastery, he quoted no Councils to call him back, he swept aside Papal dispensations. He cited texts only as they tumbled out in the flow of his eloquence: he displayed without reticence the deep injury of his feelings, he made his appeal to every personal and intimate tie, and finally to the naked convictions of the soul.[1] He took law for granted—almost one may say that, going beyond St. Anselm in this, he took reason for granted, and sought to lay bare the recesses of the soul. His enemies might say that he turned a question of law into one of personal loyalty, and placed his injured feelings above the decrees of the church. Men were not lacking who felt in St. Bernard's presence and influence the intolerable inruption of the personal into the orderly life of convention and law.[2] But in the general view, consecrated by the authority of Dante, his experiences were the farthest point which the modern age had yet reached in the knowledge of God.

I have said that St. Bernard sought to lay bare the recesses of the soul. This might be taken as a somewhat loose form of commendation, but it is meant quite strictly. For all their love of an ornate and flowery diction, the generation of St. Bernard and those which immediately followed had also a love of logic, and St. Bernard would not have gone far in popular esteem if either his speech or his thought had displayed simply an uncertain but tempestuous search for deep thoughts and profound emotions. The searching of the soul was a programme consciously and systematically undertaken, and transmitted to the whole school of Cistercian writers. This is the 'Cistercian programme', expressed in the words not of St. Bernard himself but of one of his followers: "that, when body and soul and spirit have each been ordered and disposed in their rightful place, each esteemed according to their merits and distinguished according to their qualities, a man may begin perfectly to know himself, and by progress in self-knowledge may ascend to the knowledge of God".[3] Body, soul and spirit were technical terms in the Cistercian vocabulary and denoted the stages in the ascent of the soul to God. The first stage was that of the Body: a self-love without knowledge, limited to the immediate objects of gratification. The second stage was that in which reason, whose seat was in the soul, took a part and prompted a limited and selfish love for the Creator and Bestower of

[1] cf. S. Bernard, Epist. 1 (P.L. vol. 182, 74) especially the passage beginning *Tuum, Domine Jesu, tribunal appello ; tuo me iudicio servo ; tibi committo causam meam.*

[2] See, for example, the adverse judgement on St. Bernard in Walter Map, *De Nugis Curialium*, ed. M. R. James, pp. 38-9.

[3] William of St. Thierry, *Epistola ad Fratres de Monte Dei*, ed. M. M. Davy, 1940, p. 153.

earthly blessings. The third stage was that of the spirit, in which the love of God was freed from its merely selfish and limited aims, and was enjoyed in all its own sweetness and limitless satisfaction.

There is no place here to speak at length of the spiritual doctrines of the Cistercians, and I mention these stages in the ascent to God only to point out three things: firstly, it is an ascent in which each step proceeds by an intelligible development from the one which has gone before; secondly it is an interior movement beginning with self-love and continuing through self-knowledge to union with God; and thirdly it was not simply the doctrine of one man but the starting point of a whole generation of spiritual writers.

We may return at this point to St. Benedict's own statement of the stages in the spiritual life: the ladder of Humility. We saw that the steps in his ladder were not strictly progressive: they were more like notes in a scale from which harmony is produced than steps in a ladder. St. Anselm, however, had felt his way towards a different conception of spiritual progress: he introduced a new set of steps of Humility and made them stages in a logical progression. His arrangement does not appear to have been influential, but the urge towards logical arrangement and a new doctrine of spiritual progress was not a peculiarity of St. Anselm—it was part of the equipment of the age for which he helped to prepare the way. One of St. Bernard's first literary works was a treatise on St. Benedict's twelve steps of humility.[1] If he had never written anything else, this treatise alone would show him as a most fertile and original writer. It abounds in new definitions of familiar words, new arrangements of old thoughts, and new insight into states of mind. Without formally upsetting the ancient structure, Bernard gives it an appearance of logical coherence which was quite foreign to the original. He traces an ascent from self-knowledge and self-contempt, through neigh-bourly compassion, to perfect contemplation of the truth. He traces a descent from contempt of the brethren, through contempt of the superior, to contempt of God; and he follows with remorseless logic, the process of spiritual decay from the first movements of idle curiosity to the last state of disintegration, in which, sucked into the vortex of his carnal desires, forgetful of his own rational being and of the love of God, the castaway becomes the Fool who says in his heart "There is no God".

[1] P.L. vol. 182, 941-72.

This power to rethink old thoughts is most impressive, and it was clearly something more than a desire for logical arrangement which drove these men to recast the familiar thoughts of the Benedictine Rule. Indeed they seem to arrange their thoughts logically by habit, and this logical habit gave them a formidable tool for investigating the internal movements of the soul. They are more interested in analysing states of mind and in distinguishing the motions of the will than any writers since St. Augustine. This psychological interest is especially strong in St. Bernard: when he writes of the stages of humility, he is not simply interested as St. Benedict had been in the means of arriving at the state of perfection, but in all the hindrances and distractions which drew men away from it—in *curiositas, levitas jactantia, singularitas*, and many other states of mind about which the Rule is silent.

St. Bernard owed his influence as a guide to the spiritual life largely to the fact that men's minds had been turning already in the direction along which he impelled them. We have seen that both he and St. Anselm began their reconstituted ladders of humility with self-knowledge; and this theme of self-knowledge was deeply rooted in the new monastic movements of this time. The first abbot of Cîteaux wrote of his followers as "those to whom grace has been given to know themselves." Guigo, the greatest of the early Carthusian writers, in his Meditations composed between 1110 and 1116, which have been justly compared to the Pensées of Pascal, expressed more luminously than any contemporary writer the mystery of the self: "See how ignorant you are of your own self; there is no land so distant or so unknown to you, nor one about which you will so easily believe falsehoods." And in a very different atmosphere and spirit, the same theme inspired the *Scito te ipsum* of Abelard.[1]

This power of St. Anselm and St. Bernard to give varied and coherent expression to the perceptions and aspirations which they shared with their contemporaries is most clearly seen in their treatment of the central theme of Christian thought: the life of Christ and the meaning of the Crucifixion.

[1] For the letter of Robert of Molesme, first Abbot of Cîteaux, see P.L. vol. 157, 1293; for Guigo's *Meditations*, A. Wilmart, *Le Recueil des Pensées du B. Guigue*, 1936 (esp. no. 303).

The theme of tenderness and compassion for the sufferings and helplessness of the Saviour of the world was one which had a new birth in the monasteries of the eleventh century, and every century since then has paid tribute to the monastic inspiration of this century by some new development of the theme. The homage to the Virgin for which new and more intense forms of expression were found from a period quite early in the eleventh century was one symptom of the concentration of the humanity of Christ. We have already seen St. Odilo of Cluny (d. 1049) offering himself, in an act of extreme self-abasement, as a serf to the Virgin; and his biographer was quick to see a symbolic meaning in the fact that both he and the other great monastic figure of the time, St. William of Volpiano (d. 1031), died on 1 January, the Feast of the Circumcision: it was, he said, a divine recognition of Odilo's "pious compassion for the tender wounds of the Lord's body" and of William's "similar quality of affection for the humanity of the Saviour".[1] In the same generation we have seen St. Richard of Verdun (d. 1046) provoking in himself a sense of bitter affliction in visiting the scenes of the Passion These feelings of pious compassion were widely shared in the middle of the eleventh century, at the time when Anselm was wandering through France before he found a resting place at Bec. He was deeply affected by them, and in his earliest writings he gave these feelings a more poignant expression than they had ever had before. He dwelt with passionate intensity on the details of Christ's sufferings:

Alas that I was not there to see the Lord of angels humbled to the companionship of men, that He might exalt men to the companionship of angels. . . . Why, O my soul, wert thou not present to be transfixed with the sword of sharpest grief at the unendurable sight of your Saviour pierced with the lance, and the hands and feet of your Maker broken with the nails?[2]

In the handful of prayers composed during the period when Anselm was prior of Bec (1063-78), he opened up a new world of ardent emotion and piety, but it was once more St. Bernard who guided most men into this world. St. Bernard gave a more robust

[1] P.L. vol. 142, 911.
[2] *Oratio XX* (P.L. vol. 158, 903; No. 2 in Schmitt, iii, 7).

and a more integrated expression to the feelings which stirred St. Anselm's delicate and cloistered sensibility. In Anselm, thought and feeling are like two sides of a coin: they are strictly related, but only one can be seen at a time. In Bernard thought and feeling are one; the remote speculations of Anselm meant nothing to him, but he invested feelings, which in Anselm can scarcely be cleared of a charge of sentimentality, with a vigour of thought and practical application which ensured their survival and gave them a deeper importance. The imaginative following of the details of the earthly life of Jesus, and especially of the sufferings of the Cross, became part of that programme of progress from carnal to spiritual love which we have called the Cistercian programme:

> This was (says St. Bernard) the principal cause why the invisible God wished to be seen in the flesh and to converse with men, that he might draw all the affections of carnal men, who were unable to love except after the flesh, to the saving love of His flesh, and so step by step lead them to spiritual love.[1]

In words like these, the emotions which stirred in the eleventh century and were first given lasting expression in the works of Anselm, became firmly grounded in the spiritual life of the Middle Ages. It was the glory of the Cistercian order that it not only provided the most solid and rational justification for these sentiments, but made them popular as no strain of piety had ever been popular before. It was the Cistercians who were the chief agents in turning the thin stream of compassion and tenderness which comes from the eleventh century into the flood which, in the later centuries of the Middle Ages, obliterated the traces of an older severity and reticence. In this expression of an ever-heightening emotion all countries in western Europe had a share, and at different periods led the way. In the twelfth century the leadership belonged to France, and probably, one should add, England. At least it seems probable that it is to an English Cistercian at the end of the century that we owe one of the most popular and successful expressions of this new piety in the long poem *Dulcis Jesu memoria* which has been made familiar in the translation of J. M. Neale:

[1] *In Cantica Sermo XX* (P.L. vol. 182, 870).

> Jesu! the very thought is sweet;
> In that dear Name all heart-joys meet:
> But oh, than honey sweeter far
> The glimpses of His presence are.[1]

This surge of pious devotion must not however be considered simply in terms of its emotional content. In St. Bernard it was part of a highly disciplined religious life; and Anselm, in a more abstract way, prepared a theoretical justification for the new feeling about the humanity of the Saviour. His words on this subject had a decisive importance and marked a break with an age-long tradition. A few sentences relegated a long-cherished doctrine to the limbo of discarded thoughts: their success shows in a remarkable way how accessible his generation was to new thoughts as well as new feelings. It was indeed one of the characteristics of our period that the connexion between thought and feeling, between emotional intensity and the formal structure of thought, was close: it was only in the later Middle Ages that the intellectual structure seems too weak for the feelings which produced the somewhat hectic piety of the fourteenth and fifteenth centuries.

In order to explain this point, a short theological digression is necessary.[2]

Until the end of the eleventh century a very consistent view was held by theologians about the process by which Man had been saved from the consequences of sin. They argued that, by sin—by disobedience to God and obedience to the will of the Devil—man had voluntarily withdrawn himself from the service of God and committed himself to the service of the Devil. It was rather like the act of *diffidatio* in feudal custom by which a man rejected the authority of his overlord and submitted himself to another. Of course, the overlord did not acquiesce in this state of affairs: it meant war—but still, the rules of *diffidatio* having been observed, the war must be fought according to the rules. So it was in the war between God and the Devil over the soul of Man. God could not

---

[1]This poem, transmitted in a very large number of manuscripts from the late twelfth century onwards, has been edited by A. Wilmart, *Le "Jubilus" dit de S. Bernard*, Rome, 1944.

[2]For what follows, see J. Rivière, *Le Dogme de la Rédemption au début du Moyen Âge*, 1934. I have examined the circumstances in which St. Anselm developed his new interpretation of the dogma and his relations with Gilbert Crispin, Abbot of Westminster, at this time, in *Medieval and Renaissance Studies*, 3, 1953.

fairly use His omnipotence to deprive the Devil of the rights he had acquired over Man by Man's consent: the rule of justice must be observed even in fighting the Devil. The command over Man which the Devil had acquired by a voluntary cession, could only be lost in one of two ways: either Man could go back on his choice and voluntarily turn again to God; or the Devil could himself forfeit his claim by abusing his power and breaking the rules by which he held mankind in fee. But Man's tragedy consisted precisely in the impossibility of a voluntary return. The only hope for Man therefore lay in some breach of the rules by the Devil himself.

It was this which God brought about by a great act of strategy: God became Man, and the Devil failed to realize it. He failed to see the Divinity beneath the human form. He claimed Him as his own and subjected Him to Death. But in doing this he committed that great act of lawlessness—that extension of his authority over One who had made no *diffidatio*, no surrender of Himself to the Devil— and this lost him his empire. Henceforth, the Devil could be smitten hip and thigh, and God could save whom He would.

This summary does not do justice to the spiritual content of a doctrine which held the field for quite five hundred years, but it brings out some of its more striking features. We have here a view of a struggle in which Man is assigned a very static rôle. Man was a helpless spectator in a cosmic struggle which determined his chances of salvation. The war was one between God and the Devil, and God won because he proved himself the master-strategist. That God should become Man was a great mystery, a majestic, awe-inspiring act, justly acclaimed in such a triumphant expression of victory as the *Te Deum*. But there was little or no place for tender compassion for the sufferings of Jesus. The earthly incidents of his life were swallowed up in a drama enacted between Heaven and Hell.

It was this whole view of the Devil's rights and of God's aim in becoming Man that Anselm rejected, and which, once rejected, disappeared for good. He did not of course reject it because it failed to satisfy the emotional needs of his generation. Nevertheless it is a striking thing that the intellectual short-comings of this picture of Man's salvation only became clear at the moment when the heroic view of human life being lived between the mighty opposites of external powers was dissolving before a new romanticism, and when an intense commiseration for the sufferings of the Son of

God was becoming a central fact in the religious experience of the time. Anselm's attack was based purely on rational grounds:

> As for that which we are accustomed to say—that by killing Him who was God and in whom no cause of death was to be found, the Devil justly lost the power which he had obtained over sinners; and that otherwise it would have been an unjust violence for God to make Man free, since Man had voluntarily and not through violence given himself over to the Devil: as for all this, I say, I cannot see what force it has.[1]

Once this view had been discarded, the story of man's Redemption could be set on another plane. Man had sinned, and Man must redeem. But what the existing race of man was powerless to perform could only be accomplished by a new Man—either by a new creation, or by an Angel become Man, or by God become Man. Anselm attempted to prove that the third of these courses was the one which was logically necessary. His explanation did not win the universal approval which seems to have been accorded to his rejection of the older view; but, whatever new position was adopted, the way was now open for a fresh appreciation of the human sufferings of the Redeemer. The figure on the Cross was seen with a new clarity to be that of a Man. The Devil slipped out of the drama and left God and Man face to face.

Although Anselm based his argument on rational grounds, the awakening sense of the human sufferings of the Saviour gave a new urgency to the question which he set himself to answer in his *Cur Deus Homo*. His treatise was an answer to criticisms of the Christian faith, which had recently sprung into new life. These criticisms, though old in substance, were given a sharper edge in being directed against just those incidents in the human history of Jesus which were increasingly the subject of Christian meditation.

> The unbelievers (wrote Anselm) deride our simplicity, saying that we injure and insult God in asserting that He entered a mother's womb, was born of a woman, nourished with her milk and other human food, and—not to mention many other things which seem inconsistent with God's nature—suffered weariness, hunger, thirst, blows, crucifixion and death among robbers.[2]

[1] *Cur Deus Homo,* I, 7.
[2] Ibid., I, 3.

Doubtless it was an old objection, but it came home with a new force to men whose piety was nourished on these very subjects, and it had been vigorously pressed home by a Jewish critic only a few years before Anselm wrote his treatise. The Jew was a learned man —one of the recent immigrants to England who had followed in the wake of the Conquest—and his arguments had been reported to Anselm by his friend the Abbot of Westminster. It is almost certain that he had them in his mind when he wrote the *Cur Deus Homo*.

Among these arguments there was one drawn from the representations of the Crucifixion in art. To a Jew, these must always have been offensive, but they became doubly so when the Saviour was depicted with an intensity of human feeling 'as a wretched man, nailed to the Cross, hideous even to behold'.[1] It was the expression of this feeling which the artists of the late eleventh century were beginning to achieve. Until this time, the most powerful representations of the Crucifixion in Western Europe had expressed the sense of that remote and majestic act of Divine power which had filled the minds of earlier generations. But a change had been slowly creeping in, which led in time to the realization of the extreme limits of human suffering: the dying figure was stripped of its garments, the arms sagged with the weight of the body, the head hung on one side, the eyes were closed, the blood ran down the Cross. The change did not happen all at once, nor was the new influence of humanity felt everywhere at the same time. In England, for example, in the late tenth century there were already artists who could express the sufferings of the Cross with moving realism. The frontispiece of this book represents the high point of this compassionate tenderness for the suffering Christ in pre-Conquest England.[2] The picture dates from the time when Anselm was becoming a monk at Bec, and before he had written any of the Prayers or Meditations which are so full of this compassion. The artist—working in a monastery far removed from any strong theological impetus and remote (it would seem) from the centres of devotional innovation—had reached the same position as St. Anselm was led to by his monastic experiences and theological speculations. Elsewhere the new impulses came more slowly and

[1] The phrase is used by the Jewish disputant in Gilbert Crispin's *Disputatio Judaei cum Christiano*, P.L. vol. 159, 1034.
[2] See F. Wormald, *The Survival of Anglo-Saxon Illumination after the Norman Conquest* (British Academy Annual Lecture on Aspects of Art), 1944, p. 4-5.

arrived with the flood of French influence in the twelfth century. In Denmark, for instance, where the heroic traditions were strong, the mid-eleventh century figures of Christ on the Cross gave a powerful local interpretation to the theme of the triumphant Prince. The Aaby wood carving of Plate II is in this tradition: the figure is that of a young warrior, crowned and clothed in royal robes, with head erect and eyes open, full of power. Then slowly in the next century this conception changed. Plate III shows a comparatively early stage in this development: the Head is still crowned, but the face is that of a man, resigned and suffering, the eyes shut, the head slightly inclined; the arms are bent as if taking some strain, the feet are pierced. From this point the Danish development follows the same path as we find elsewhere, until all the attitudes and marks of pain and desolation had been exploited by the artists of the fifteenth and sixteenth centuries.[1]

The transformation of the theme of the Virgin and Child was a natural corollary to the transformation of the theme of the Crucifixion. In the eleventh century, the West had long been familiar with the Child seated as if enthroned on his Mother's knee, holding up his right hand in benediction and, in his left, clasping a Book, the symbol of wisdom, or an orb, the symbol of dominion. This conception persisted and was never abandoned, but it was joined by many other forms which expressed the more intimate inclinations of later medieval piety, such as the laughing Child, the Child playing with an apple or a ball, the Child caressing its Mother, or the Child being fed from its Mother's breast. Some of these attitudes of the Holy Child had had a long history before they became, slowly in the course of the twelfth century, domesticated in western Europe. There was a long tradition of restraint to be overcome before these themes could win unreserved acceptance. The theme of the Mother feeding the Holy Child, for instance, can possibly be traced back to the art of the catacombs in the third century.[2] Then it seems to have established itself in the Coptic Church.[3] But in the West it was for centuries unknown, until after wandering through

[1]For an account of the figures referred to above, see P. Nörlund, *Gyldne Altre*, Copenhagen, 1926 (with English summary).

[2]F. Cabrol and H. Leclercque, *Dictionnaire d'Archéologie Chrétienne et de Liturgie*, X, 1895, fig. 7704 and Pl. 86.

[3]There are two ninth-century Coptic illustrations of the theme in the Pierpont Morgan Library, M.607 and 612, reproduced in the Exhibition catalogue of 1933-4 (Plates I and II). Dr. O. Pächt, to whom I am indebted for much help on the subject

we know not what devious paths it reached Europe in the early twelfth century in a distinctly Byzantine dress. Plate I shows what appears to be its earliest form in medieval Europe, and the Greek inscription, Theotokos, *Mother of God*, bears eloquent testimony to the proximity of the Byzantine model from which it was derived. The picture occurs in a Cistercian lectionary, which is one of a remarkable series of illustrated manuscripts made at Cîteaux under the inspiration of Stephen Harding during the first quarter of the twelfth century.[1] The Cistercian setting is significant. The picture is a compendium of the new devotion to the humanity of the Saviour and His earthly Mother. It introduces several themes which ministered to the devotion of later centuries: the Tree of Jesse, surrounded by four Old Testament types of the Virgin Birth (Daniel in the lions' den, the children unscathed in the furnace, Gideon's fleece, the Burning Bush), and the Virgin feeding her child. These themes were new in Western art when this picture was made.[2] Brought together, they represent an extraordinary concentration of subjects which only found their fullest development much later in the Middle Ages. Yet, rich though the artist is in suggestion, he has not learnt to express the pathos with which already the pupils of St. Anselm, and later those of St. Bernard, approached the subject of his illustration. Considered as human beings, his central figures are not quite at ease in their new attitudes: the Child about to feed still raises his hand in benediction and still clasps his Book; the Mother gazes on the world with a detached dignity, and the proffered breast causes no interruption in the folds of her dress. There is no attempt here to portray the emotions on which the followers of St. Anselm dwelt as they pondered this theme:

Lo, brethren, let us try to understand the affection of this good Mother . . . the tenderness with which she beholds the Infant in her arms, sees him hang on her breast, hears him cry as children

[1] For a study of these MSS, see C. Oursel, *La Miniature du XIIe Siècle à l'Abbaye de Cîteaux*, 1926.

[2] For the place of this picture in the representations of the Tree of Jesse, see A. Watson, *The Early Iconography of the Tree of Jesse*, 1934, pp. 90-1.

of this paragraph, has also called my attention to a Coptic example in J. E. Quitell, *Excavations at Saggara*, 1912, IV, pl. xxii (dated before ninth century). cf. C. R. Morey, *Medieval Art*, 1940, p. 58.

do at the little hurts of his little body, and hastens to forestall all evils which may happen to him. . . .[1]

These are phrases taken at random from a devotional rhapsody (one of the best and most widely circulated of its day and kind) composed by Anselm's biographer at Canterbury, almost at the same time as our artist was at work at Cîteaux. Sixty or seventy years later, it was just this maternal tenderness which the artist of the 'Madonna of Dom Rupert' (Plate IV) set out to portray. The Mother has lost her remoteness; the Child has laid down the symbols of his wisdom and authority. Only the inscription from Ezekiel round the border discloses the hidden divinity; all else is humanity, frailty and love.

St. Anselm and St. Bernard are the chief influences in our period in making intelligible the spiritual impulses of their contemporaries. But before leaving them, one name must be mentioned which represents the climax of the developments we have been discussing: the name of St. Francis. The period of his public career from 1209 to 1226 lies outside the scope of this book, but he is the embodiment of the spirit of Christian romance which we have watched in some aspects of its development from the time of St. Anselm. The inward quest of St. Anselm or St. Bernard—faith seeking understanding, or carnal love seeking its spiritual object—was given an external symbolism in the homeless, wandering, unsheltered life of the beggar. The most negative and drabbest of the monastic virtues—Poverty—was transformed Cinderella-like into a fairy princess, and invested with the fascinating qualities of a romantic heroine. Above all, the tender, passionate love of Jesus had its earthly consummation in the vision of the Crucified and the crisis of the stigmata on Monte Alverna in 1224. With St. Francis and his followers, the fruits of the experiences of St. Anselm and St. Bernard were brought to the market place, and became the common property of the lay and clerical world alike.

[1]Eadmer, *Liber de Excellentia B. Mariae* (P.L. 159, 557-80 and esp. 564-5). This work circulated in the Middle Ages under the supposed authorship of St. Anselm. The chief genuine work of St. Anselm bearing on the subject is his series of *Orationes ad Sanctam Mariam* (Or. 50-52, P.L. 158, 948-59; Schmitt nos. 5-7, iii, 13-25), and especially the last of these. See also Homily IX (P.L. 158, 644-9), attributed to St. Anselm but really the work of Ralph, his successor as Archbishop of Canterbury—another capital text for the Marian devotion of the school of Anselm.

PLATE I
Tree of Jesse (Cîteaux, 1110-20)

PLATE II

The Aaby Crucifix (Danish, c.1050-1100)

PLATE III
The Tirstrup Crucifix (*detail*; Danish, c.1150)

PLATE IV
"The Madonna of Dom Rupert" (Liège, late 12th Century)

It would be a mistake however to suppose that these new ways of thought and feeling had an existence only in connexion with the religious life. That they had their origin and their most disciplined expression in the cloister seems very likely, but they also pervaded secular society, or at least that part of secular society which has left any record of its thoughts and feelings. This is simply what we should expect. We have already seen how close were the relations between the monasteries and their lay patrons, and how readily developments within the monastic life were communicated to men and women who did not always aspire to a high degree of personal sanctity. These men and women felt the same needs as those who were making new experiments in the life of religion, and their response to these needs was not limited to the encouragement of religious enterprises and the imitation of religious practices; it also found expression in purely secular ways. In an earlier chapter, for instance, the contrast has been noticed between the social ideals of knighthood at the beginning and at the end of the twelfth century. This transformation of the knightly ideal is a many-sided social phenomenon, but spiritually it is related—in a secular instead of a religious context—to the change exemplified in St. Anselm and St. Bernard. The contrast can be seen at its sharpest in comparing the *Song of Roland* with the Romances of Chrétien of Troyes.[1]

The *Song of Roland* might have as its sub-title 'a tale of heroism and treachery on the borders of Christendom'. No doubt part of its enjoyment came from the fact that it was listened to as a piece of real history. It was history seen down a long perspective, but still it was a piece of real life. We shall never know what it was that turned the obscure disaster which befell the rearguard of Charlemagne's army on 15 August 778, when Roland Count of Brittany was killed, into one of the most memorable incidents in Christian epic. No doubt, like many other military disasters, it was relieved by some signal act of heroism of which 'history' has left no record. But the story lived. We can dimly see that the names of Roland and Oliver were already famous in the tenth century; we know that their

[1]The most convenient French edition of the *Song of Roland* is that of J. Bédier, 2 vols. (several editions), but the older edition of Léon Gautier is also useful. There is an excellent translation, preserving the rhythm of the original, by C. Scott-Moncrieff, 1919. There is a useful introduction to Chrétien's works in the edition of *Yvain* by T. B. W. Reid (Manchester, 1948); a prose translation of the Romances by W. W. Comfort is in the Everyman Library.

story cheered William the Conqueror's army into battle at Hastings; but it was not until the late eleventh or early twelfth century that the great poem took the shape which we now know. Yet there is little in it which is foreign to any period of the eleventh century. Some of the characters belong to the eighth century, and others (like Geoffrey Greymantle, Count of Anjou) to the tenth, but necessarily the society which the poet took as his model was that of his own day. It is the society of Northern France in the great days of the Duchy of Normandy and the County of Anjou

The poem reflects the ideas of men who have not been stirred either to enthusiasm or to opposition by the church.doctrines which were becoming widespread in the years following the death of Gregory VII. It was taken for granted that an archbishop would be in his place among the fighters and that his counsel and strength in battle would be as good as another's, or better. The wisdom of the clerk was not distinguished from the wisdom of the layman. And the wisdom of the layman was that of shrewd and practical men. They were men grounded in the externals of feudal custom, well versed in the niceties of the bond which tied them to their lord and to their fellow barons. This was the world which they knew, and about which they felt deeply. They quarrelled like schoolboys about the fine points of social obligation and feudal etiquette, for these were the things to which they attached importance. It was a masculine society, and its members were more conscious of the group to which they belonged and of their duty towards it than of their own hearts. They were unmoved by the romantic loyalties of the heart. The heroes of the poem speak of women only in the crude way of the camp, and in hours of crisis they think more of their lands than of their loves. The dying Roland had no thought to spare for his betrothed, though she straightway died on hearing of his death. And when the heroes think of their lands, they think also of the ancient holy places of France, and call upon St. Michael or St. Denis —never on the Virgin. These are old ways of piety; the piety of a localized society closely tied to the places men know

We are in a limited world, the boundaries of which are clearly marked. It is for the most part (leaving aside some memories of an older time) the France from Mont St. Michel to the Rhine and from Boulogne to the Loire, with the coast road to the Pyrenees well mapped. Beyond the Pyrenees lies an unknown Moslem world, a wonder-world of fantasy and evil—a kind of parody of the Christian world, where a strange trinity of Gods, Tervagan, Mahomet and Apollo, are worshipped in 'synagogues and mahumeries' filled with idols and images. But within the narrow limits of the well known, the impossible is not expected to happen; there is a great respect for the obvious and inescapable limits of Nature. The barons of Charlemagne are indeed men of great strength, but then their muscles are large; ánd even they, when they meet an overwhelming foe, die. They know that they are in the right, for "Pagans are wrong and Christians are right", but they also know that a strong Pagan will beat a weak Christian. They have confidence in their saints, but they also shrewdly remark that "men fight well when they know that no prisoners will be taken".

The barons of the *Song of Roland* would have been considered 'unimaginative' by a later age, and the limits within which the imagination worked were certainly narrow. It was circumscribed by the ties of lordship and vassalage, by the recollection of fiefs and honours and well-known shrines, by the sacred bond of comradeship. The bond between them was very precious, and Guanelon who betrayed this bond was even more vividly pictured as the enemy than the pagan whom they scarcely knew. But both enemies, the traitor Guanelon and the Moslem king Marsilie, were enemies of society, endangering the Christian commonwealth. They were both external enemies in the sense that they were outside the pale of society, and the opprobrious word 'felon' was applied indifferently to each.

Such was—it does not seem fanciful to believe—the 'thought world' of the men of the last age of the old Benedictine monasticism, of the men who founded the communities of which the physical remains at Jumièges, Fécamp or Shrewsbury bear witness to their solidity and corporate wealth. The heavy communal life of the monasteries extended also to the world around them, and fashioned the ideals of social conduct no less than those of monastic discipline.

With the work of Chrétien of Troyes, who was writing in the third quarter of the twelfth century, we enter a new world. His romances are the secular counterpart to the piety of Cîteaux. Of both, love is the theme. Love is an inward thing, and therefore a lonley thing united only to its unique object. So the knight of Chrétien's romances seeks solitude for the exercise of his essential virtue. It is true that his life is centred on a community—the community of King Arthur's court—and that his highest virtues have their root in the everyday ties of loyalty to his lord and companions. But though the court is a school of discipline, it is in a higher sense a place of relaxation where virtue will become rusty unless sharpened by periodic flights into the wilderness. The life of the court forms a picturesque background rather than the focal point of knightly virtue: its rules sit lightly on those who aim at high things. In the *Song of Roland* the highest virtue was that of the good companion and the good vassal, to whom the words *baron* and *prud'homme* could be applied; the lowest infamy was that of the *felon*, the traitor to his lord and companions. In Chrétien, these words have gone a long way to losing their distinctive meaning: *felon* for instance can be applied to all kinds of things like bad luck or bad looks. The two poles of conduct are represented by words denoting more intimate qualities: *courtois* and *vilain*, the gentleman and the lout. These qualities will come out in action, but they refer in the first place to something which a man is in himself, and to the surroundings in which he is at home, the court or the pig stye—for *vilain* is the word also indifferently used for a peasant.

In the knights of Arthur, as in those of Charlemagne, there is a great sense of a common objective, but it is a wholly ideal objective, at once quite universal and quite individual. It is unthinkable that the knights of the *Song of Roland* should fight each other without a breach of their fundamental code of conduct: their ties of loyalty and vassalage were too serious for that. They fight as members of a body. However much a Roland may stand above his fellows in prowess, he takes part in a common action against a common enemy. But in Chrétien the enemy is dispersed; he is everywhere and may be found everywhere. The knights of Chrétien seek the enemy in solitude and in the course of their search they may well find themselves striving against one of their fellow knights. There was nothing disconcerting in this, for action was only a means to a spiritual end.

The whole action of Chrétien takes place as it were on the confines of the physical world, where reason and passion do not come up against the brute facts of resistant nature. In the *Song of Roland* we stand on solid earth, though we have glimpses into the cauldron of unreason behind the curtain of Christendom; but in Chrétien we take a bird's eye view of earth from above, where all unevennesses are levelled out, and from where it seems that men can go anywhere without difficulty but may meet anything by the way. The eye ranges far and wide, but the unknown is close at hand. Danger may lurk under every tree and the nerves are strained in anticipation. There is no security, no friendly society round the camp fire. The world is a wide one and we move effortlessly from Winchester to Regensburg or Constantinople; but wide though it is in geographical extent, it is wider still in the variety and mystery of its contents.

The *Song of Roland* told the story of an action in which each man had a part to play, and played it well or ill. Chrétien's knights are engaged, not in an action, but in a quest, which each man must undertake alone. A quest for what? Ostensibly for knightly adventure, but really for adventures of the heart. Chrétien's stories are stories of the heart in search of love, and his most penetrating passages are those where he analyses the strange twists and contradictions of the passions. Since he is writing stories and not a treatise he does not aim at any systematic doctrine; yet a systematic treatise could be written from his stories. It would distinguish three stages in the quest. The first is the life of the court, where men and women entertain each other with agreeable attentions without any serious wounds being given or received. Then there is the stage of lonely peril, grief and exertion in which the heart feels the wounds of love without attaining the assured possession of its object. Beyond this there is the third stage, always in the future, in which the heart and its desired object are perfectly joined in an unbreakable union. It was with the second of these stages that Chrétien's stories were chiefly concerned: the stage of journeying, seeking and suffering.

A treatise such as this would have many points of contact with St. Bernard's three stages of carnal, rational and spiritual love. But Chrétien, as an author, was neither religious nor, in intention at least, anti-religious. Religion was part of the furniture of his stories—indeed an essential part, for religious observance was one of the elements of good breeding. But the Christianity of Chrétien is an affair of externals, providing plenty of bishops and clerks to add to the dazzling throng, and a rich pageantry of mitres and croziers at weddings. The real internal religion of the heart was untouched by Christianity. There is in Chrétien none of the melancholy, none of the sense of the sinfulness of the heart, which we sometimes find in Malory. Chrétien probes the heart, but it is the enamelled heart of the twelfth-century secular world, not yet made tender by the penetration of strong religious feeling. There is nothing in Chrétien like the passage of the *Morte d'Arthur* when Guinevere takes leave of Lancelot.

The religious and the romantic quests were born in the same world—Troyes is only about thirty miles from Clairvaux—and drew in part on the same sources of inspiration, but they were in the twelfth century kept rigidly apart. They were indeed the great alternatives opened out to the imagination in the mid-twelfth century.

These alternatives, even regarded as food for the imagination and not as spurs to action, were for the few. But the many also enjoyed some of the fruits of these new ways of thinking and feeling about the world. The twelfth century saw the creation of a new popular literature which carried far and wide the conceptions of love and devotion developed in their different ways by St. Bernard and Chrétien of Troyes. The views which reached the popular ear were less disciplined and exacting than those we have hitherto examined, but the community of feeling cannot be mistaken.

One of the most novel and influential forms of this popular literature were the collections of *Miracles of the Virgin*, which began to appear at the beginning of the twelfth century.[1] It is probable that the interest in these stories was first fostered in churches which owed a special veneration to the Virgin by reason of their dedication, but they appealed to too many people to be confined to a few scholars or a few churches, and in the course of the twelfth century they spread to every part of western Europe. These stories were of a kind which had not hitherto been common in the West.

Until this time nearly all miracle stories were associated with

[1] There is no edition of these collections of Miracles which brings out their historical development, but the earliest stage in their growth so far as the West is concerned is represented by the collection printed by E. F. Dexter, *Miracula Sanctae Virginis Mariae* (University of Wisconsin Studies in the Social Sciences and History, 1927, vol. 12). This is the collection I associate (see below p. 251) with the younger Anselm. Later stages in the growth of this literature may be studied in T. F. Crane, *Liber de Miraculis Sanctae Dei genetricis Mariae* (Ithaca, 1925), H. Kjellman, *La deuxième Collection Anglo-Normande des Miracles de la Sainte Vierge* (Paris and Uppsala, 1922), and E. F. Wilson, *The Stella Maris of John of Garland* (Mediaeval Academy of America, 1946). The last of these publications contains full bibliographical references to the earlier literature.

the physical remains of some saint: these remains were the channel through which the spiritual power of the saint was communicated to the physical world. We have already seen how powerful were the links with the unseen world provided by the relics of the saints—how the presence of St. Remigius acted on the Council of Rheims in 1049, and how the monks of St. Benedict at Fleury used the body of their patron saint to defend their property and to wreak vengeance on the disturbers of their rights. In all these miracles, a great importance is attached to the place and generally to the circumstances of the event. The normal place of operation was where the saint's body lay. Indeed in an earlier stage of development there was a strong feeling that the place should be where the saint had died: it was only the eagerness of the northern peoples in the eighth and ninth centuries for a share of the sacred remains, which broke down the prejudice against the uprooting of the saints from their original resting places and led to the scattering of their dismembered bodies throughout Europe. Between the ninth and eleventh century every great church amassed a large collection of relics, and a list of these treasures, like the one drawn up by the abbot of Abingdon in 1116 shows the eager acquisitiveness of the previous two centuries where relics were concerned.[1] This dispersal of the saints carried their power to every corner of Christendom, and the stories of their miracles form one of the main branches of literature in the centuries of the dispersal.

This literature never ceased to be added to; the power of healing and the repair of injustice or injury could never lose their interest. But in the *Miracles of the Virgin* a quite new interest appears. Until the twelfth century the Virgin had played a minor part in the miraculous interventions recorded by pious writers. She sometimes appeared as a coadjutor of the local saint, but according to the views which were generally prevalent the lack of relics of the Virgin (whose body had been carried straight to heaven) was an obstacle to an independent intervention in these miraculous happenings. In the Eastern Church there was less restraint, and one story of Greek origin had gained currency in the West in the ninth century—the story of a clerk Theophilus who sold his soul to the devil and was saved in the moment of death by the intervention of the Virgin. This was, it will easily be seen, a somewhat unsubstantial story, quite unlike the

[1]*Chronicon monasterii de Abingdon*, ed. J. Stevenson, R.S., ii. 155-9.

matter-of-fact tales of practical affairs which appealed to the needs and piety of the Latin church, at least until the eleventh century. But then quite suddenly towards the end of the eleventh century these restraints in the West began to break down. Large numbers of miracle stories of the Virgin began to appear.

These stories were drawn from many sources: a few were taken from ancient Latin sources such as the sixth-century book of miracles of Gregory of Tours; others had a Greek origin; others again were stories which had originally been connected with St. Peter or St. James, but which were now given the patronage of the Blessed Virgin. But the vast majority of the stories were new coin, expressions of a new piety and a new imagination. The world in which we move in these stories is one of unbounded, unbridled imagination. Time and place lose all significance, and we come under the sway of a universal power, uncramped by local ties, and exercised with an appearance of caprice for the protection of all who love the person from whom these benefits flow. Like the rain, this protective power of the Virgin falls on the just and the unjust alike—provided only that they have entered the circle of her allegiance. The power portrayed in these stories is not at all exercised, as that of other saints often was, to protect the possessions or privileges of this or that church; it is not even often used to cure the ailments of the flesh; it is concerned above all with the salvation of souls. It is this which makes this literature—despite all its shortcomings—more spiritual and more exciting than the other miracle literature with which our period is so full. The *Miracles of the Virgin* were not written to proclaim the glories, or to enhance the reputation of any church or corporate body: they appealed solely to individuals; and if they had a propaganda purpose—as they very often had—it was the encouragement of pious practices, which came in time to occupy a position at the very centre of medieval personal devotion. The briefest outline of a handful of these stories will make this clear:

The sacristan in a certain monastery was a man of impure life, but he loved the Virgin and said an 'Ave Maria' whenever he passed her altar. He was drowned while on the way to visit his mistress, but his soul was restored to his body on the intercession of the Virgin.

A certain clerk of Chartres was also a man of impure life, but showed a similar devotion to the Virgin. He died and was buried outside the churchyard as a notorious evil-liver, but the Virgin appeared to one of his colleagues asking why they had so ill-treated her 'chancellor', and ordering his reburial in the churchyard.

A 'certain clerk in a certain place' was devoted to the Virgin. He was in the habit of singing an antiphon in honour of the Five Joys of the Virgin and, on his death-bed, she appeared to him and promised him a heavenly reward.

A certain thief called Ebbo was devoted to the Virgin, and was in the habit of saluting her even on his marauding expeditions. He was caught and hanged, but the Virgin held him up for two days, and when his executioners tried to fix the rope more tightly, she put her hands to his throat and prevented them. Finally he was released.

A certain clerk, a canon of St. Cassian at Pisa, was devoted to the Virgin and each day recited the services in her honour known as the Hours of the Virgin—a practice which few people followed at that time. (This remark, we may notice in passing, takes us back to some time in the eleventh century: we are at the very beginning of a practice which spread far and wide and gave its name to the Books of Hours of the later Middle Ages.) The clerk's parents died and left him a large inheritance, whereupon his friends insisted on his marrying. Gradually he grew lax in the service of the Virgin, but on his wedding day he turned aside to pray in a church, and said all the Hours of the Virgin. The Virgin appeared to him, reproached him for deserting her, and ordered him not to marry another. The marriage took place, but that night he left wife and home and was never seen again.

These few stories may stand for all. Before the end of the thirteenth century they are numbered in hundreds, or even thousands, but these examples belong to the earliest of the collections which gained general circulation, and they show that the type of the 'Mary-story' was already fixed, and did not vary greatly as the collections grew in size. One sees already the comparative vagueness as to time and place and persons—points on which the older types of miracle stories were generally so precise; one notices the wide sweep which takes in Pisa and Chartres (and, in other stories, Germany, England and Spain) all within a few pages; one sees how disinterested the miracles are, how indifferent to ordinary morality, and how personal in their interest. In a word, they are popular, and speak to the common man wherever he might be. The circle of those devoted to the Virgin appears almost as a wonderful club, a supernatural order of chivalry, confined to no single class or country.

But, for all their popularity, these stories have a high lineage. We owe them to men who were in close touch with all that was most aspiring in the spiritual experience and intellectual effort of the late eleventh and early twelfth centuries. They have an important place in the diffusion of new modes of experience, and it is fortunate that we know a good deal about the men who stood at the head of this great torrent which passed with overwhelming force over the older forms of piety and devotion.

Our first pointer takes us to Italy in the middle of the eleventh century. Peter Damian (1007–1072) was one of the earliest collectors of stories which became common property in the following century. It is he who first tells the story of the foolish, frivolous and ignorant clerk who was deprived of his benefice by the bishop, but restored after the Virgin had angrily intervened on behalf of her 'chaplain' because he always said an 'Ave Maria' on passing her altar; he tells also of a pilgrim of impure life who died unconfessed, but was saved from damnation and restored to life by the Virgin because he had died in her service. Now Peter Damian had these stories, he lets us know, from the cardinal priest Stephen, who was one of the most important men in the small group of Papal legates in the late '50s and '60s of the eleventh century—a Burgundian by origin and a man who served as legate at Constantinople as well as in Germany and France.[1] These stories, then, and others like them (for Peter Damian tells several) were being exchanged by very great men in these years. But Peter Damian introduces these stories in the course of writing about other things; we have not yet reached the stage when they formed a separate and well-defined literature in their own right. To reach this point it is necessary to go on about thirty or forty years, and to consider once more the activities of St. Anselm and his circle of friends.

Anselm, it may be recalled, came to England in the autumn of 1092, became Archbishop of Canterbury in the following year, and was soon occupied with the problem of the meaning of the

[1] P.L. vol. 145, 562–4; and cf. col. 230.

Crucifixion, which resulted in his *Cur Deus Homo*. This treatise was still unfinished when he left England in November 1097 for an exile which lasted three years. It was the most fruitful of all exiles in our history. He finished the *Cur Deus Homo* in the hill village of Liberi not far from Capua, in the summer of 1098; later in the same year, at the Council of Bari, he developed the argument which became the core of his *De Processione Spiritus Sancti;* and in the two following years he wrote his work *De Conceptu Virginali et de Peccato Originali,* and the greatest of all his meditations, *On Human Redemption* These are works with which his name will always be associated, but we are here concerned with some slighter and more personal activities. On the journey into Italy in 1098 the archbishop and his two companions from Canterbury—the monks Eadmer and Baldwin—turned aside from the way to pass Good Friday and Easter at the monastery of St. Michael of Chiusa in the foothills of the Alps. The reason for the diversion is not mentioned by his biographer, but we can be sure that it was to meet his nephew, who was also called Anselm, a young monk of this place. This was the beginning of an association which ended only with the archbishop's death in 1109. The younger Anselm joined his uncle, probably at Lyons in 1099, returned with him to Canterbury and died in 1148 as Abbot of Bury St. Edmund's. He is known to historians as the devoted protagonist of the most advanced form of devotion to the Blessed Virgin then known in Europe—the celebration of the Feast of the conception of the Virgin. And I believe that it is to him that we must give the chief place in making the collection of the stories of the Virgin, which first set the fashion in this form of literature and formed the nucleus of nearly all the later collections during the next hundred years or so. It would take us too far afield to set out here the evidence for this statement, but we may notice that one of the miracles in this early collection is related of the younger Anselm himself when he was a boy or young man at Chiusa; that another is told on the authority of a monk of Chiusa; that the distribution of the stories (in particular the large number of Italian and English settings) fits well the itinerary of the younger Anselm; and that the strong English connexions of the earliest manuscripts tell in favour of this hypothesis.[1] But

[1] Since writing this, I have found that a similar view of the place of the younger Anselm in the formation of this literature was put forward by the Rev. H. Thurston, s.J., writing in *The Month* for 1904, pp. 1-16, to which reference may be made for further details.

whatever may be the exact place of the younger Anselm as an initiator of one of the most popular forms of medieval literature, we are once more moving among men of the highest importance in the formation of medieval ways of thought and feeling.

Some of the most remarkable stories which found a place among the *Miracles of the Virgin* were exchanged between St. Anselm and his friends in private conversation. One of them was a story which Anselm remembered from his boyhood about two brothers in Rome in the days of Pope Leo IX. Another was a story of a pilgrim to Compostella, told by Abbot Hugh of Cluny when the party of exiles from England visited him in 1100 or 1104. Both these tales were records of the supremely marvellous—stories of men who had died, had been saved from eternal punishment by the intervention of the saints, and had been restored to life with memories of Heaven and Hell. Stories of this kind were not quite unknown in the early Middle Ages especially among men with Irish contacts: there was a famous incident of this kind, which happened on the Scottish border, recorded by Bede, and there were a few of a later date.[1] But those in authority seem to have preserved a certain reticence with regard to them. We hear of a ninth-century bishop denouncing as an impostor someone who claimed to have had some such experience, and a tenth-century abbot quoted St. Paul against those who pretended to reveal things 'which it is not lawful for a man to utter'. This reticence was not shared by the best minds of the late eleventh century and the stock of such stories in general circulation multiplied rapidly. If St. Anselm and Abbot Hugh led the way, who would lag behind? There were many men in different parts of Europe on the look-out for accounts of marvels of the spiritual world, and stories which fell from the lips of an Anselm or an Abbot Hugh in their hours of ease flew about Europe with astonishing rapidity. The process can be followed in some detail, and it illustrates the eagerness with which these marvels were snapped up.

The substance of Anselm's conversations was recorded by one of his companions, and in an informal way his record must have circulated fairly widely.[2] While Anselm and his friends were staying

---

[1]Bede, *Historia Ecclesiastica*, ed. C. Plummer, i, 304-9, and ii, 294-5, where the examples of opposition to these revelations are quoted.

[2]These conversations are recorded in a treatise called the *Dicta Anselmi*, preserved in a number of MSS of which the most important is Corpus Christi College, Cambridge, MS 457.

at Lyons, which was their headquarters in exile, they met someone who was compiling a book of *Miracles of St. James* in honour of the shrine at Compostella. To him they communicated three of the stories of Abbot Hugh, including the account of the pilgrim who had been brought back to life.[1] It was in this way that the incident obtained a European fame as the central piece among the stories of St. James which were current throughout the Middle Ages. Then, back in England, they met William of Malmesbury, a historian with an eager eye for wonders of every kind. To him they communicated some stories of Gregory VII's remarkable spiritual powers which they had heard from Abbot Hugh, and these stories found a place in William's *History of the English Kings*.[2] Finally, the recorder of St. Anselm's conversations sent his material to the younger Anselm, who had by now become a great man in his own right, and the younger Anselm (as I surmise) extracted the two most wonderful stories in the collection for his *Miracles of the Virgin*.[3] In doing this he allowed himself a certain amount of liberty, because his uncle's story made no reference to the Blessed Virgin. But the story was just the kind of thing he was looking for, and the small adjustment he made to fit it into his collection probably appeared too natural to call for comment. The falling asleep of the critical faculty—or, more precisely, the displacement of historical criticism by considerations of theoretical propriety—is one of the most revealing characteristics of this whole literature. The makers of this literature were

[1] The Miracles of St. James form one section of a very famous manuscript known as the *Codex Calixtinus*, of which the only complete edition is by W. M. Whitehall (2 vols., Compostella, 1944). The contents of the manuscript have been often discussed—most recently by P. David, *Etudes sur le livre de S. Jacques attribué au Pape Calixte II* (4 vols., Lisbon, 1946-49) and A. Hamel, *Uberlieferung und Bedeutung des Liber Sancti Jacobi und des Ps. Turpin* (Sitzungsberichte der Bayerischen Akademie der Wissenschaften, 1950). The connexion between the *Dicta Anselmi* and chapters XVI-XVIII of the *Miracles*, which is of some importance in establishing the methods of the compiler of the *Miracles*, escaped the notice of these scholars.

[2] *Gesta Regum*, ed. Stubbs, R.S., ii, 322-4.

[3] These were the stories of the two brothers at Rome (told to the author of the *Dicta* by St. Anselm) and of the pilgrim to Compostella (told by Hugh of Cluny), which appear in almost all collections of *Miracles of the Virgin*. (cf. H. L. D. Ward, *Catalogue of Romances in the British Museum*, ii, pp. 666-7, nos. 14 and 16.)

bridge, MS 457. Besides their influence on the works mentioned in the text, the *Dicta Anselmi* became the main source of a work very widely read in the Middle Ages, called the *De Similitudinibus* (P. L. vol. 159, 650-708). Dom F. S. Schmitt and I are preparing an edition of the *Dicta* and various related treatises which throw light on the popular influence of St. Anselm in the Middle Ages.

victims, it may seem to us, of their own prepossessions; but their stories were not for them—as they had become for many before the end of the Middle Ages—mere pious 'romances', but incidents and experiences of real life, extending the range of human experience.

These stories were among the new things struggling into prominence in the second half of the eleventh century. We must not, however, exaggerate the importance of what is new, at the expense of the old. In the company of St. Anselm we are at the source of many experiences which had a transforming influence on the spiritual world of men of all degrees. But, after all, the main landmarks in this spiritual world were in the eleventh century already very old. At one time or another in this book we have spoken of some of these landmarks: the story of the Passion, the Rule of St. Benedict, the discipline and the services of the Church, the resting places of the Saints. For most people—and those not the least learned—it is very probable that the resting places and relics of the saints were the most conspicuous feature in this spiritual landscape. There are countless testimonies to this fact. Confidence in the power of the saints is the most permanent and uncontroversial feature of our whole period. The flow of relics into the churches of northern Europe—fed by the opening up of new sources of supply in the eastern church during the twelfth century, and culminating, as we have seen, in the despoiling of Constantinople in 1204—continued with unabated vigour to the end, and beyond the end, of our story. Mere repletion and exhaustion of supplies arrested the process in the end, but not before the wealth of relics had altered the appearance of our churches, and made a profound impression on the forms of both public and private devotion. There were sceptics, but their scepticism seems to be based on disappointment or despair, and not to be the result of any rational system of doubt: reason and system were on the side of faith. Most men expected miracles, and miracles spoke to them more clearly than any argument. The miracle was an argument from which there was no appeal.

This is strikingly exemplified in the case of St. Thomas Becket, almost at the end of our period. Thomas Becket was a man about whom opinions were sharply divided in his lifetime, and these controversies were not silenced by his death. We know that there were men who continued to look on him as a traitor, and we are told that the masters of Paris disputed the point, a certain master Roger asserting that he had been worthy of death, while the well-known master Peter Chanter maintained that he was a martyr for the liberty of the church. "But"—our informant adds—"Christ has solved the problem by the manifold and great signs with which He has glorified him." The whole of Christendom concurred in this judgement.[1]

The 'Miracles of St. Thomas Becket' are the greatest collection of miracle stories connected with any single shrine in our period—or indeed in the whole Middle Ages. They are the culmination of this type of literature, for the great collections of the next century are the work of scholars ranging over a wide field of history, rather than the compilations of men in the heat, as it were, of battle, relating what is taking place under their eyes. With the new literature of miracles of the Virgin they do not compete, for they belong to the matter-of-fact world of cures, of deliverances from danger or captivity, of the restoration of mutilated members, of the recovery of lost property. Even the many accounts of the dead being restored to life are related in the style of a medical record. In their careful everyday setting, and their concern with the physical world, these stories stand far apart from the imaginative world of the Miracles of the Virgin. Yet even in this most conservative branch of human experience, there are striking differences between the miracles of St. Thomas and those performed at famous shrines in the previous century. The area of vengeance and justice has contracted; the area of the cure of mental and physical disease has grown; and people seem less surprised at events which are supremely marvellous. We hear nothing of the practice which had been extremely common in the tenth and eleventh centuries—the carrying out of the relics of the saint against the invaders of the church's property. Here, as elsewhere, the individual and his needs seems to occupy more of the picture than before.

It was the Franciscans who first brought the fruits of the monastic experiences of the eleventh and twelfth centuries to ordinary people. Before they came, and before preaching became an important means of spreading new ways of thought and devotion, it is probable that miracles and miracle stories, shrines and pilgrimages were the most important force in disseminating the ideas and sentiments to which St. Anselm and St. Bernard had given in different ways so

[1] *Materials for the History of Thomas Becket*, R.S., ii, 291-2.

strong an impulse. But it is possible also, that the vigour and long-lived influence of the thoughts of these men owed something to the fact that they were entering into a popular mood which learned men with classical examples before their eyes had long repressed. Stories of the Virgin, such as those collected by the younger Anselm and many others after him, were probably told long before the eleventh century, but all except a very few—and those chiefly of Greek origin —were beneath the dignity of letters. It was the growth of new devotional practices, spreading out from the monasteries, which suddenly gave them significance and brought them into prominence; and the stories in their turn were a powerful agent in advancing the popularity of the practices to which they owed their status in the religious world. It is possible too that the pioneers of medieval spirituality in the eleventh century did not so much initiate, as give way to a prevailing sentiment of pity and tenderness, which they interpreted and expressed in art and letters. It is possible that long before theory caught up with practice the sufferings of Christ had excited the pity of unlettered men, who knew nothing of the theology of Redemption which made pity irrelevant. This is something which we shall perhaps never know, any more than we shall know from what springs of popular imagination the creators of the Arthurian legend drew; but the springs were there, and the rehabilitation of Celtic things in the twelfth century, after a long period of disfavour, is a symptom of a change of attitude towards the creations of popular imagination. Logic came here to assist romance, for it gave scholars a means by which they could comprehend in a single rational system a great deal which on the surface might appear fantastical or merely emotional.

This union of learning and high spirituality with popular forms and impulses is something which meets us everywhere in the eleventh and twelfth centuries. Those who suffered from it felt it most. There was nothing which Berengar resented so much in Lanfranc as the fact that he lent the weight of scholastic erudition to the 'ravings of the multitude'. Whatever the merits of his case, he was certainly right in discerning the power of the multitude to raise new issues and to affect the solution of old ones. The unlettered world was breaking out in many ways in his day. When Fulbert was an old man, and Berengar and Lanfranc were young, it broke out into the first popular heresies which had troubled the West since the days of Arianism. At the same time it broke out even more powerfully in the suppression of heresy; and the conjunction of mass violence, secular power and ecclesiastical authority for this purpose formed a formidable combination. It broke out, too, into an enthusiasm for the Papal cause, which sometimes (as at Rheims in 1049) contrasts strangely with the coldness of bishops and rulers. It broke out in the following century in violence against the Jews to which the new religious sentiment gave a specious justification. And there was a people's Crusade before that of the barons whose exploits occupied so much of the attention of contemporary chroniclers.

The manifestations of popular emotion leave uncertain records behind them. But, whether in the field of thought or of action, they are sufficient to disclose, though dimly, the resources on which the eleventh-century pioneers could draw in bringing into existence a civilization, so different from the painful reconstruction of the Carolingian age in its apparently effortless variety and spontaneity.

BIBLIOGRAPHY

THE greatest collection of printed material for understanding the life and thought of the period down to 1204 is Migne's *Patrologia Latina*. This formidable body of reprints of Christian Latin works down to the early thirteenth century, in 217 volumes, each containing some 1,500 columns of closely packed type, "can scarcely be approached without an effort". Yet, repellent though they are in appearance, these volumes have the great virtue of being accessible in most great libraries and many are still obtainable from the booksellers. The editions printed by Migne, the fruit of the great effort in historical scholarship during the seventeenth and eighteenth centuries of which the most distinguished centre was the abbey of St. Germain des Prés in Paris, have in many cases been superseded by later ones, but for most purposes they are still serviceable. The Chronicles must nearly always be consulted in later editions, but there are no later, or at least no better, editions of most of the works of Fulbert of Chartres, Lanfranc, Abelard (with the exception of his technical philosophical works edited by B. Geyer, 1919–33), Ivo of Chartres (except for the beginning of a new edition of his letters by J. Leclercq, vol. 1, 1949), St. Bernard, Peter of Blois and a host of other writers of the period. The works of St. Anselm, which Migne reprinted from the seventeenth century edition of Dom Gabriel Gerberon have recently been re-edited by Dom F. S. Schmitt, 5 vols., 1938–51 (Nelson, Edinburgh: one volume still to come). Among other editions by modern scholars, the following may be mentioned for the light which they throw on the period as a whole and for the meticulous scholarship of their editors: Gregory VII's Register ed. E. Caspar (M.G.H. Epistolae Selectae, 1920–3); John of Salisbury's *Policraticus* (1909) and *Metalogicon* (1929) ed. C. C. J. Webb, and his *Historia Pontificalis* (1927) ed. R. L. Poole; Peter Lombard's *Libri IV Sententiarum* ed. Patres Collegii S. Bonaventurae (Quaracchi, 1916); Ordericus Vitalis, *Historia Ecclesiastica*, ed. A. le Prévost and L. Delisle (Société de l'Histoire de France, 5 vols., 1838–55); William of Malmesbury's *Gesta Regum*, ed. W. Stubbs, R.S., 1887–9. The early editions from which Migne drew his material should not however be forgotten. In particular, for the period down to the end of the eleventh century, Mabillon's *Acta Sanctorum Ordinis Sancti Benedicti* (1668–1701) contains a series of biographies edited with calm and assured learning by the greatest of all scholars in the field of medieval studies. Most of this material is reproduced in Migne but its force and unity can scarcely be appreciated when scattered through a hundred volumes.

One of the best approaches to the literature of the period is through periodicals such as the *Revue Bénédictine* where studies of manuscripts and editions of short texts will be found by such masters as the late Dom A. Wilmart. The many references to his name and to the *Revue Bénédictine* in the notes will show how much I owe to these studies. The numbers (and especially the earlier numbers) of *Neues Archiv der Gesellschaft für ältere deutsche Geschichtskunde* are important also for editions of short texts by scholars whose main work appeared in the *Monumenta Germaniae Historica*. For the hagiographical literature, which contains the main biographies of the period, the best guides are the publications of the Bollandist Fathers of Brussels, especially the *Bibliotheca hagiographica latina antiquae et mediae aetatis*, 3 vols., 1898–1911, and the periodical *Analecta Bollandiana* with its excellent indexes. Among more general guides to the literature of the period, there may be mentioned M. Manitius, *Geschichte der Lateinischen Literatur des Mittelalters* (vols. 2 and 3, 1923 and 1931, cover the period *c.* 950–1215) and two works of J. de Ghellinck: *La Littérature latine au Moyen Age*, 2 vols., 1939 and *L'essor de la littérature latine au XIIe Siècle*, 2 vols., 1946, which contain (in comparison to Manitius) a more personal appreciation of the great writers of the period. K. Strecker's brief *Einführung in das Mittellatein* (2nd edit. 1929; French translation, 1946) is a useful introduction to the study of medieval Latin; it supplements rather than supersedes the brilliant sketch by L. Traube, *Einleitung in die Lateinische Philologie des Mittelalters*, ed. P. Lehmann (1911). For the theological and philosophical literature, see B. Geyer's edition of the second volume of F. Ueberweg, *Grundriss der Geschichte der Philosophie (Die Patristische und Scholastische Philosophie)*, 1928, and M. de Wulf, *Histoire de la Philosophie médiévale*, 6th edition, 3 vols., 1934–47, where the bibliographies in Ueberweg-Geyer are brought further up to date. The annual bulletin of the *Recherches de Théologie ancienne et médiévale* (Louvain, 1929–), contains brief reviews of most of the relevant literature.

A very useful general guide to the bibliography of the whole period is L. J. Paetow, *A Guide to the Study of Medieval History*, 1931. This has sections on the bibliographies and reference books devoted to separate countries and subjects. Among reference books which appeared too late to be included in Paetow, the new editions of W. Wattenbach, *Deutschlands Geschichtsquellen im Mittelalter, Deutsche Kaiserzeit*, ed. R. Holtzmann, 1942–3, and of Dahlmann-Waitz, *Quellenkunde der Deutschen Geschichte*, 9th edition by H. Haering, 1931, are of special interest for this period.

There are now many periodicals devoted exclusively or principally to medieval studies. The following list, arranged in the order of first appearance, will give some idea of the growth and distribution of new periodicals in recent years:

Speculum, 1926, the Journal of the Medieval Academy of America;
Archives d'Histoire doctrinale et littéraire du Moyen Age, 1926, Paris;
Recherches de Théologie ancienne et médiévale, 1929, Louvain;
Medium Aevum, 1932, Oxford;
Medieval Studies, 1939, Toronto;
Medieval and Renaissance Studies, 1941, Warburg Institute, London;
Traditio, 1943, New York;
Medievalia et Humanistica, 1943, Boulder, Colorado;
Revue du Moyen Age latin, 1945, Lyons and later Strasbourg.

The contents of most of these periodicals are weighted on the side of literary and doctrinal, philosophical and theological studies, and in this they reflect some of the main trends of medieval research. The older journals of general history have no doubt lost something by the concentration of these studies in newer periodicals, but they remain the strongholds of political and constitutional, administrative and economic history. The annual survey of periodical literature in the English Historical Review (July number) will show where studies on these subjects are to be found. The reviews in Speculum may also be mentioned for the range of Continental literature surveyed, a point in which English journals are somewhat deficient.

The following is a selection of books and articles on the subject-matter of each chapter, omitting however in general those which have already been mentioned above in the footnotes and which are briefly listed in the Index under their authors' names.

CHAPTER I

FOR the general political background of the period, see vols. 3–6 of the *Cambridge Medieval History*. On the Byzantine Empire and its relations with the West, see A. Vasiliev, *History of the Byzantine Empire*, latest edition 1952, and L. Bréhier, *Le Monde Byzantin*, 3 vols., 1947. Both have abundant bibliographies.

On the subject of Mediterranean trade, old books like W. Heyd, *Geschichte des Levantehandels im Mittelalter* (2 vols., 1879; French translation, 1885–5, reprinted, 1923) and A. Schaube, *Handelsgeschichte der Romanischen Völker des Mittelmeergebietes bis zum Ende der Kreuzzüge*, 1906, retain their importance on account of their abundance of detail and solid documentation. But the recently published second volume of the

Cambridge Economic History of Europe, 1952, (which unfortunately appeared too late for me to make use of it in this chapter) marks a considerable advance on previous attempts at interpretation. A stimulating treatment of the subject in a small compass is H. Pirenne's *Economic and Social History of Medieval Europe* (English translation, 1936). The provocative views of this great scholar on early medieval commercial history expressed in his *Mahomet et Charlemagne* (1937) must, as is now generally agreed, be treated with considerable reserve. (See, for example, the article of R. S. Lopez, *Mohammed and Charlemagne: a Revision* in Speculum, 18, 1943.)

For the Crusades, Steven Runciman's *History of the Crusades*, of which two out of three volumes have appeared (1951 and 1952) is a learned and stimulating survey, giving full weight to the point of view of the non-Christian world. In this, Mr. Runciman continues the tradition of R. Grousset's *Histoire des Croisades et du Royaume franc à Jérusalem*, 3 vols., 1934-6. On the difficult subject of the origins of the crusading ideal, see C. Erdmann, *Die Entstehung des Kreuzzugsgedankens* (1935), and more recently the articles of A. Gieysztor on *The Genesis of the Crusades: the Encyclical of Sergius IV (1009-12)* in Medievalia et Humanistica, V, 1948, and VI, 1950.

The study of the translations from Arabic and Greek during the eleventh and twelfth centuries has made considerable progress since C. H. Haskins published his important *Studies in the History of Medieval Science* in 1924. On various aspects of this subject, see besides the works mentioned above on p. 66 n., A. van der Vyver, *Les premières Traductions latines de traités arabes sur l'Astrolabe* (Extr. from the Mémoires du 1er Congrès International de Géographie Historique, Brussels, 1931, vol 2); Marshall Clagett, *Some General Aspects of Physics in the Middle Ages* in Isis, 39, 1948; R. de Vaux, O.P., *Notes et Textes sur l'avicennisme latin aux confins des XIIᵉ-XIIIᵉ Siècles* (Bibliothèque Thomiste, XX, 1934). The best survey of the subject is by A. Pelzer in M. de Wulf, *Histoire de la philosophie médiévale*, §§ 28-9, 204-7.

CHAPTER II

THE best general survey of the subjects dealt with in this chapter is Marc Bloch, *La Société Féodale:* vol. 1, *La Formation des liens de dépendance* (1939); vol. 2, *Les classes et le Gouvernement des Hommes* (1940), in the series *L'Evolution de l'Humanité*. With this should be studied the articles by the same scholar on related subjects, especially his *Liberté et Servitude personnelle au Moyen Age* in the Annuario de historia del derecho español, 1933, and *Les "Colliberti", étude sur la formation de la classe servile*, in the Revue Historique, CLVII, 1928, 1-48, 225-63. J. Boussard has criticized some of Bloch's conclusions in his *Serfs et Colliberti (XIᵉ-XIIᵉ) Siècles* in the Bibliothèque de l'Ecole des Chartes, CVII, 1947-8, 205-34, but his argument is not altogether convincing.

For studies of the liturgical aspects of kingship during the period see in addition to the works mentioned on pp. 92-3, E. H. Kantorowicz, *Laudes Regiae, a study in liturgical acclamations and medieval ruler worship* (Univ. of California publ. in history, 33, 1946). For medieval treatises on the duties and training of a ruler, see W. Kleineke, *Englische Fürstenspiegel vom Policraticus bis zum Basilikon Doron König Jakobs I* (Halle, 1937) and W. Berges, *Die Fürstenspiegel des hohen und späten Mittelalters* (Leipzig, 1938). Perhaps the best introduction to medieval teaching on law, liberty and serfdom is to read the relevant passages in the works of St. Thomas Aquinas. There is a useful selection of these passages, with text and translation in *Selected Political Writings of St. Thomas Aquinas*, ed. A. P. d'Entrèves, (1948).

<h3 style="text-align:center">CHAPTER III</h3>

THE books on Benedictine monasticism are countless and it will suffice to mention here two books, in which references to others will be found, and which are themselves outstanding contributions to the subject: D. Knowles, *The Monastic Order in England, 943-1216*, (1940) a work of wider scope than the geographical limitation would suggest, and C. Butler, *Benedictine Monachism* (2nd edit., 1924), a work of interpretation which is informed by great historical learning. The fundamental text is the *Rule* of St. Benedict of which a convenient and informative edition is that by C. Butler (3rd edit., Freiburg, 1935). For the elaborate customs of the Benedictine houses of this period, see B. Albers, *Consuetudines Monasticae*, 5 vols., 1900-12; an easily accessible text for the customs of a single house is *Lanfranc's Monastic Customs* (for Christ Church, Canterbury), ed. and transl. by D. Knowles in the series *Medieval Classics* (1951). The best edition of the Cistercian customs is P. Guignard, *Les Monuments primitifs de la Règle Cistercienne* (Dijon, 1878). L. H. Cottineau, *Répertoire topo-bibliographique des Abbayes et Prieurés*, 1935, is a useful guide to the literature on individual monasteries.

For the organization of Papal government, see R. L. Poole, *Lectures on the History of the Papal Chancery*, (1915). The main source is the series of Papal letters listed in P. Jaffé, *Regesta Pontificum Romanorum ad annum 1098* (2 vols., 2nd edit. by S. Loewenfeld, etc., 1885-88) and A. Potthast, *Regesta Pontificum Romanorum*, 1198-1304 (2 vols., 1874-75). These are supplemented by the great series of *Papsturkunden* for various countries published in the *Abhandlungen der Gesellschaft der Wissenschaften zu Göttingen* under the direction of P. Kehr: 2nd series, vols. XVIII (1926), XX (1927), XXII (1928), XXV (1930); 3rd series, vols. XII (1935), XIV

(1935), XV (1936), XXI (1937), XXIII (1940), XXVII (1942). The sole survivals of the Papal registers of the period are those of Gregory VII (in the edition of E. Caspar mentioned above) and Innocent III (in Migne, P.L. vols. 214-7). There is a vivid account of the conduct of a great case at the Roman Curia at the very end of our period in Giraldus Cambrensis, *De Jure et Statu Menevensis Ecclesiae* (*Opera*, R.S., vol. III).

For the history of Canon Law see P. Fournier and G. le Bras, *Histoire des Collections Canoniques en Occident depuis les fausses décrétales jusqu'au décret de Gratien* (2 vols., 1931-2) and, for the period after Gratian, S. Kuttner, *Repertorium der Kanonistik* (1140-1234), (Studi e Testi 71; Città del Vaticano, 1937). There is a pioneering and learned study of *Anglo-Norman Canonists of the Twelfth Century* by S. Kuttner and E. Rathbone in Traditio, vii, 1949-51, 279-358, which gives a good idea of the kind of work which was going on in one part of Europe during the half century after the appearance of Gratian's book. The best available text of Gratian is vol. 1 of the *Corpus Iuris Canonici*, ed. A. Friedberg (1879-81); but on the deficiencies of this edition see S. Kuttner in Speculum, 24 (1949), 495f.

CHAPTER IV

THE book to which I owe most as a starting-point for the discussions in this chapter is J. de Ghellinck, *Le Mouvement Théologique du XIIe Siècle* (1914; 2nd enlarged edit., 1948). On various aspects of the subject see—for Boethius, E. K. Rand, *Founders of the Middle Ages*, 1928, and P. Courcelle, *Les Lettres grecques en Occident de Macrobe à Cassiodore*, 1943; for the work of Biblical scholars, B. Smalley, *The Study of the Bible in the Middle Ages*, 2nd edit., 1952; for the schools and their methods of teaching, G. Paré, A. Brunet and P. Tremblay, *La Renaissance du XIIe Siècle: Les Ecoles et l'Enseignement*, 1933, and E. Lesne, *Histoire de la Propriété Ecclésiastique en France*: vol. 4, *Les Livres*, "Scriptoria" et Bibliothèques, (1938); vol. 5, *Les écoles de la fin du VIIIe Siècle à la fin du XIIe*, (1940), where there is a vast store of details on these subjects not readily available elsewhere.

For the impact of Continental learning on England in the late twelfth century, of which an example has been given in the text in the person of Peter of Blois, the two lectures of Bishop Stubbs on *Learning and Literature at the Court of Henry II* (printed in his *Seventeen Lectures on the Study of Medieval and Modern History*) are still indispensable, as also are the contributions to the subject by C. H. Haskins in all his books and especially in his *Studies in the History of Medieval Science*. For a more recent survey of the subject, see R. W. Hunt, *English Learning in the Late Twelfth*

Century, in the Transactions of the Royal Historical Society, Fourth Series, vol. XIX, 1936.

For a description of the long intellectual preparation and activity which culminated in the work of St. Thomas Aquinas, see M. D. Chenu, *Introduction à l'étude de Saint Thomas d'Aquin*, (1950). Sir Maurice Powicke's *Stephen Langton* is a penetrating study of one of the outstanding figures in Paris in the late twelfth century; and the edition of H. Rashdall's *Universities of Europe in the Middle Ages* by Sir Maurice Powicke and A. B. Emden, 3 vols., 1936, should be consulted for an account of the growth of the universities of Paris, Oxford and Bologna.

CHAPTER V

THE title of this chapter was suggested by the work of W. P. Ker, *Epic and Romance*, which appeared in 1896 and still retains all its freshness and value. It has been frequently reprinted. The sub-title, *Essays on Medieval Literature*, sufficiently indicates the scope of the book, but it should be added that Ker's sympathies were all with the Epic, and that he is less satisfying when he deals with Romance. A useful corrective to this point of view is C. S. Lewis, *The Allegory of Love; a Study in Medieval Tradition*, 1936.

Of the two central figures in this chapter, St. Anselm and St. Bernard, there is no large-scale study of the former which is really satisfying, though the biography of R. W. Church, which first appeared in 1870, has great charm and simplicity. The most illuminating studies of St. Anselm's literary activity and influence in detail are by Dom A. Wilmart reprinted in his *Auteurs Spirituels et Textes dévots du Moyen Age Latin*, 1932; see also his introduction to A. Castel, *Méditations et Prières de Saint Anselme* (a French translation of Anselm's Prayers: collection "Pax", 1923), and his essay on the homilies attributed to St. Anselm in the Archives d'histoire doctrinale et littéraire du Moyen Age, 2, 1927. There is a characteristically powerful interpretation of the greatest moment in St. Anselm's thought by Karl Barth, *Fides Quaerens Intellectum: Anselms Beweis der Existenz Gottes*, (1931). On St. Bernard, besides the well-known *Vie de St. Bernard* by E. Vacandard, 2 vols., 1894 and frequently ‑eprinted, see the study by E. Gilson. *La Théologie Mystique de Saint Bernard*, 1934.

INDEX